HILLSBOROUGH
VOICES

HILLSBOROUGH
VOICES

THE REAL STORY TOLD BY THE PEOPLE THEMSELVES

Compiled and edited by

KEVIN SAMPSON

in association with the

HILLSBOROUGH JUSTICE CAMPAIGN

EBURY
PRESS

1 3 5 7 9 10 8 6 4 2

Ebury Press, an imprint of Ebury Publishing
20 Vauxhall Bridge Road
London SW1V 2SA

Ebury Press is part of the Penguin Random House group of companies
whose addresses can be found at global.penguinrandomhouse.com

Penguin
Random House
UK

With thanks to Peter Marshall and the BBC for permission to reproduce BBC *Panorama*'s
interview with Anne Williams for 'Hillsborough – How They Buried the Truth' 2013

Photo credits: **p1** top Ross Kinnaird/EMPICS Sport, middle REX/TODAY, bottom
ACTION PLUS sports images/Corbis; **p2** top Mirrorpix, middle and bottom Bob Thomas/
Getty Images; **p3** top REX/John Sherbourne/ Daily Mail, middle Ian Stewart / The Times /
Newssyndication.com, bottom John Giles/PA Wire/Press Association Images; **p4** top REX,
bottom REX/Colorsport; **p5** top REX/Jim Hutchison / Associated Newspapers,
bottom left & right Mirrorpix; **p6** top Mirrorpix, middle Jamie McDonald/Staff,
bottom REX/Offside; **p7** top REX/Bruce Adams / Associated Newspapers,
bottom Mirrorpix; **p8** top Christopher Furlong/Staff, bottom Paul Ellis/Staff.

First published by Ebury Press in 2016
www.penguin.co.uk

A CIP catalogue record for this book is available from the British Library

HB ISBN 9780091955618
TPB ISBN 9780091958206

Printed and bound in Great Britain by Clays Ltd, St Ives PLC

Penguin Random House is committed to a sustainable future for our
business, our readers and our planet. This book is made from Forest
Stewardship Council® certified paper.

For the 96 who lost their lives at Hillsborough,
Anne Williams, and John and Joe Glover.

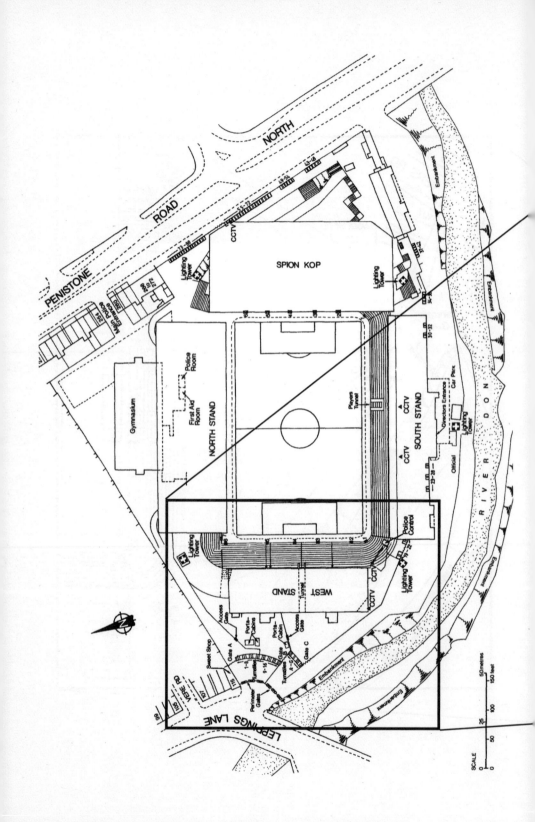

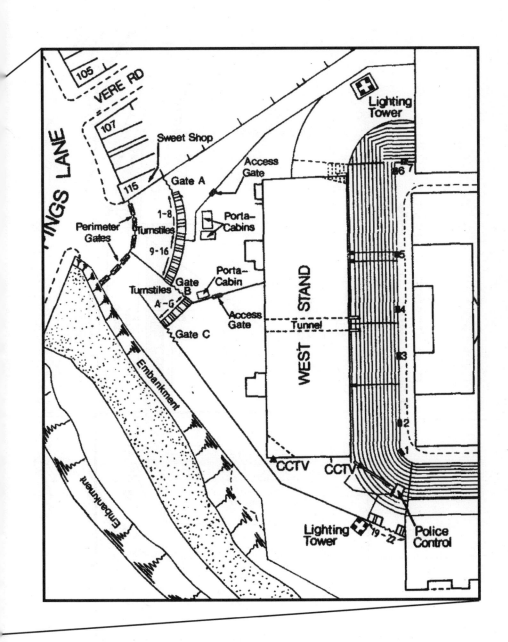

FOREWORD

BY ANDY BURNHAM, MP

For many people of my generation who grew up in the North West, Hillsborough will always be the definitive event of our lives. It didn't matter who you supported, we all said the same thing: 'It could so easily have been us.'

15 April 1989 was the day when all the injustices of 1980s Britain suddenly hit very close to home for its teenagers. The riots in Toxteth and Moss Side as well as the miner's strike had been on our doorstep, but involved people we did not know. By contrast, Hillsborough affected our family, our friends, our football clubs, our world. And it confirmed a feeling that had been building inside many of us during that divisive decade: we were indeed second-class citizens in our own country.

I was 19 at the time and can remember that fateful weekend as if it were yesterday.

The back room of the Cherry Tree in Culcheth was a long, long way away from the dreaming spires. But that's where I was on the evening of Friday 14 April 1989, home from university and glad to be back in a world where the only Blues that mattered were not of the Cambridge Varsity variety, but the ones who played at Goodison Park.

From the moment we walked in, the air was thick with talk of the semi-final weekend.

Culcheth back then was a Kopite stronghold – most likely the legacy of local hero Roger Hunt. The Burnham brothers, on the other hand, were known as the only match-going Evertonians, so we were well used to being on the receiving end. We were ready that night to be reminded several times of the results of the previous all-Merseyside Finals. But once the jokes had subsided, we did all agree on one thing: how on earth could the Football Association, for the second year running, have allocated the inadequate 'away' end at Hillsborough to Liverpool?

I remember telling my old school friend Stephen Turner, who had a ticket for the Leppings Lane the following day, about our experience in its dreaded central pens the year before.

Everton had drawn with Sheffield Wednesday away in the Third Round in 1988. I recounted how, in the second half, I hadn't watched anything happening on the pitch. I was so worried that my dad and younger brother John were in the same discomfort as me that I kept my eyes trained on the back of their heads, determined not to lose them in the crowd. In 40 years of going to matches, it remains the worst experience I have ever had.

Less than 24 hours after that conversation in the pub, I was in a car on the M6 with my dad and brothers, heading away from Everton's game at Villa Park and listening in stunned silence as the first reports of the horror at Hillsborough drifted in. On the radio, they were already blaming the fans. We knew different from our own experience: the ground was unsafe.

That Saturday night we returned to the Cherry Tree and waited for friends to return from Hillsborough. They arrived in dribs and drabs, in varying degrees of trauma. They were never the same again.

In the years after Hillsborough, throughout the 1990s, it would be a common experience to be out on a Friday night with friends who had been at the match and, after a few social drinks took effect, they would start talking distractedly about what they saw. They would ask endlessly why there had never been any real accountability for what happened. At the same time, the very same conversation was being played out in thousands of other homes and pubs and clubs across the country.

These were the real Hillsborough voices – the lost souls who went to a football match and ended up witnessing scenes akin to hell on earth; who drifted home from the scene of a disaster but got no professional help to cope, and who, just days after the tragedy, found themselves being blamed by police and press for what had happened.

For 20 years those haunted voices were shouting into a wilderness. Nothing came back. The country wasn't listening. 'Why can't these whingeing Scousers let it go?' was an infuriating comment in the South throughout the 1990s.

It took a strange twist of fate to change the course of events.

In early January 2008 I attended the opening night of Liverpool's year as European Capital of Culture. I was then Chief Secretary to the Treasury. The following week a call came through to my private office from Number 10: the Prime Minister wanted to speak to me urgently. Out of the blue, Peter Hain would have to resign. The Culture Secretary James Purnell would be moving to the Department of Work and Pensions to replace him. Would I like to take on the role of Culture Secretary?

My feet didn't touch the Treasury tiles. Within minutes I was floating up Whitehall towards Trafalgar Square and the Department of Culture, Media and Sport. When I arrived, a couple of cameras were waiting outside. Instead of doing what I probably should have done, and given a sober tribute to Peter Hain which regretted the circumstances that had brought about this move, I gave enthusiastic vent to my true feelings: genuine elation at being appointed Culture Secretary in this special year for the city of my birth. I served notice on the London cultural establishment. I wouldn't be doing what Culture Secretaries were expected to do – spending all of my time paying court to them – but would be in Liverpool instead.

And that's what I did. Barely a week went by without me attending an event there. And at every venue I visited, the then Lord Mayor of Liverpool, Steve Rotheram, would be there too. He was a Red but we got on famously from the off. We did everything together, including working on the repatriation of the body of a young Evertonian, Gary Dunne, who had died in Spain.

In early 2009 Steve and I were on the front row of the pews in Liverpool Anglican Cathedral for Gary's belated funeral. As we waited for the coffin to arrive, Steve whispered in my ear. What he said made my blood run cold.

I was about to get an invite to address the twentieth anniversary of the Hillsborough Disaster. He said that he thought it was crucial that I accepted.

And so began weeks of turmoil. I knew the truth about Hillsborough, and a big part of it was that my own party, Labour, had not done anywhere near enough to put right the terrible wrongs that had been done. Instead, we had become enmeshed with the Establishment that had gone to great lengths to cover it all up.

I spent hours agonising with my family over whether I should accept the invitation. How could the Government not be represented at a service to commemorate the victims of one of the largest peace-time tragedies this country had ever seen? But what did I have to say to people who had been so cruelly let down by the Establishment of which I was now a leading representative?

It was the dilemma to end all dilemmas. As ever, it was my younger brother John who cut through the fog. 'Go if you're going to do something for them. If not, stay away.'

My decision to attend was the best I have made or will ever make.

On the night of the twentieth anniversary, the long-lost Hills-borough voices that for years had been vanishing into the abyss rolled off the Kop and into every living-room in the land. It was the moment when the dam broke; when everything changed.

Looking back now, I shudder about how close we came to missing that moment. If things hadn't changed on the twentieth anniversary, would they ever have? Possibly not. But thank God they did. Because establishing the full truth about Hillsborough is not just vital for the people who suffered directly, it fills in missing pages of the social history of our country. Having a full and true record about what happened on the day and in the aftermath will be important for future generations. It tells us how we were governed and policed in the second half of the Twentieth Century.

Hillsborough is part of a jigsaw that includes other injustices like the trials of the Shrewsbury 24 in the 1970s, the Battle of Orgreave in the 1980s, the death of Stephen Lawrence in the 1990s and the hacking of phones in the early part of this century. A single thread ties them all together: a nexus of power created by a colluding elite of politicians, the press and the police, which served to protect each other and ride roughshod over ordinary people.

In the end, Hillsborough is a story of power and class. If we are ever to make this a more equal country, its full story must be known and understood. Because the battle for fairness goes on: even during the recent inquest on Hillsborough, almost unbelievably, police representatives have re-run their discredited slurs about the Liverpool supporters.

That is why this book is so important. Those authentic Hillsborough voices must be set down and allowed to echo through the decades and centuries to come.

I want my own great-grandchildren to be able to hear these haunted Hillsborough voices. I want them to ask themselves how it ever came to pass that, in the hours after one of the biggest man-made disasters in the history of this country, the Establishment turned on the dead, the bereaved, the injured and the traumatised – on an entire English city in its moment of grief.

And I want those future generations, fired up by the injustices of the past, to resolve to carry on the centuries-old fight to make all British citizens truly equal.

INTRODUCTION

Just like thousands of other Liverpool supporters, I set off for Sheffield on the morning of 15 April 1989 with that giddy mixture of excitement, anticipation and anxiety that accompanies an FA Cup semi-final. I'd been to four FA Cup finals by then, sampling two wins and two defeats. And I'd been there, too, when Liverpool were knocked out of the Cup at the semi-final stage in 1979, 1980 and 1985. If the Cup final defeats were hard to bear, it was tougher still falling at the penultimate hurdle. There's no pain quite like a semi-final knock-out blow – or so I thought.

There were four of us in the car. Hobo – Ian Hodrien – was driving, with myself and my brother Neil in the back. Our special guest was a Juventus supporter, Mauro Garino, a mate we'd first met in Dover when he was hitching back from Celtic in 1981. Mauro had been coming to Liverpool every year since then, usually staying at ours over Christmas. He loved everything about Liverpool – the city and the football club. He loved the Kop: the fervour, the colour, the atmosphere. Our friendship had survived the Heysel Stadium tragedy in 1985, and Mauro's one big ambition was to watch Liverpool in an FA Cup final at Wembley. It was his birthday on 8 April and I got

1

him a ticket for the next best thing – a semi-final between Liverpool and one of the best teams of the country, Nottingham Forest. We picked Mauro up from Manchester airport the day before the game – this was an era away from cheap flights into Liverpool – and lapped up his excitement as he opened his birthday card and discovered his ticket inside. Gradually, the penny dropped that he was going to one of the biggest matches on the football calendar. The boy was, to be fair, over the moon.

We headed off that fine spring morning with hope in our hearts, yet hopelessly unaware of a series of unrelated events that were already combining to disastrous effect. One such factor was a major hold-up between Hyde and Glossop, where roadworks slowed traffic to a standstill. This was bad news. Speaking for myself and Mauro, the pre-match atmosphere in the pubs was a massive part of the build-up to a big game. I loved it. I would usually try to get to the pub a couple of hours before kick-off and would always be in the thick of it, singing along with gusto after I'd had a few pints. Mauro, too, came to love the special flavour of the pubs around Anfield as, pint in hand, he'd urge the regulars to sing 'song of scarf'. On the one day you'd want to be there good and early to savour the big occasion, though, the long line of cars was barely moving at all, and we weren't even halfway there. It was starting to look like we'd miss one of the best parts of semi-final day, and I wasn't happy.

Eventually, we got through the Glossop bottleneck and headed over the sun-dappled Snake Pass, taking the Rivelin Road shortcut into north Sheffield. I had been to Sheffield Wednesday many times before and, from my days as a student in Sheffield, I knew the Hillsborough area well. I convinced everyone that we'd get served quicker if we avoided the popular pubs near the ground and went to the Freemasons

Arms, a famous old pub in the back streets of Hillsborough itself. So we parked up a fair old walk from the ground, and headed into the Freemasons around 1.30 p.m. So much for my plan, though – it was packed, with as many fans from Nottingham as Liverpool thronging the bar. The atmosphere was brilliant, everyone happy in spite of the prolonged wait to get served. Mauro tried to start his 'song of scarf' – a version of 'You'll Never Walk Alone' that, inevitably, consisted of him wailing various syllables – and was only mildly bemused when the Forest fans drowned him out with, 'What the fucking hell was that?' It was the last time we'd be laughing that day.

The pub started to empty out. I was agitating for us four to take advantage of the sudden lull so we could squeeze in one more pint, assuring the others I knew of a shortcut to the ground. Neil and Hobo were wise to my shortcuts, however. They checked with the bar staff, who confirmed that the football ground was a brisk fifteen-minute walk away, so that was that. At 2.15 p.m. we made our way towards the ground, cutting through the park to quicken our progress. Sheffield Wednesday's South Stand loomed into view ahead of us, yet, as we got closer, it became apparent that the way ahead was completely blocked. There was a backlog of Liverpool supporters, ten or twelve abreast, queuing up but, seemingly, going nowhere. Just like the traffic on the approach to Glossop, we were at a complete standstill.

This is no revisionist hindsight – the crowd was, in the main, good-humoured. There was still a good twenty to twenty-five minutes to go till kick-off, it was the FA Cup semi-final, everyone was eager to get in, and, at that stage, the isolated police you could see were viewed as a conduit to progress, not a hindrance. There was some ironic 'baaing' from fans imitating herded sheep, but very little antagonism at all. I'm hopeless at standing still. I went across to ask a policeman what was going on; why the crowd wasn't moving. The only reply I received was, 'What's up with you? Are you nesh?'

I think he was saying that a certain amount of pushing and shoving was only to be expected at such a big game, and I should get back in there and tough it out. There was a blind faith that, even though the overcrowding was so severe, everyone would find a way through, sooner or later. Lord Justice Taylor's Interim Report of August 1989 – to which I refer in this book – says that Chief Superintendent Duckenfield's second-in-command, Superintendent Bernard Murray, received a message from his commander on the ground, Chief Inspector Creaser, at around 12 noon. Creaser asked Murray whether the Leppings Lane pens should be opened, and filled, one at a time. Murray's reply illustrates a similar blind faith in what was, effectively, a type of self-policing among football crowds. He said that all pens should be opened simultaneously, as fans would 'find their own level'. What he meant was that, if it was too crowded in one pen we'd move to another until we found a satisfactory vantage point. That kind of thinking might have some plausibility in a huge, unsegregated end like the Kop but, with Leppings Lane sectioned off into pens by radial fencing, it was a huge risk assuming we would simply work things out among ourselves. It was the same outside the ground, too. The handful of police left to marshal the turnstiles just stood there, helpless and hopeless, as the crowd struggled to find its own level.

The problem that faced us was that there were only seven turn-stiles servicing that particular route into the ground. Yet many of the 10,000 Leppings Lane ticketholders, as well as the 4,500 with seats in the West Stand above it, would all be gravitating towards those solitary seven turnstiles. And, on the day, it was even worse:

because of the way the police were segregating fans, they blocked off access to the main road feeding the remaining sixteen turnstiles on the *other* side of Leppings Lane. This meant there were also North Stand ticketholders compelled to enter the ground via the same besieged turnstiles. It was turning into a free-for-all, and I was, by now, very glad that we hadn't stayed for that third pint. Thousands of ticketholders were converging on seven turnstiles with less than twenty minutes to go until kick-off. It was madness.

The atmosphere changed as the noise from inside the ground increased. One or two mounted police began to appear, but they had no information to give, nor any assurance that we'd make it inside for kick-off. They now became the focus of anger from fans who were stuck in the logjam – there were shouts of 'Sort it out!' and 'Let us in!' Up ahead you could see snatches of brick wall, blue gates, blue railings, but the crowd was eddying by now, spilling *en masse* left and right.

I was accustomed to the swells and surges of huge crowds on the Kop. For me, it was a part of the magic, especially at night matches – a crowd so tightly packed that you could see the steam coming off it. For the biggest games we were packed shoulder to shoulder in there, and the volume was often so loud that it would treble out into one long, distorted, oscillating sound wave. If you touched the crush-barrier, you could feel the current of the white noise vibrating through the tubular metal bars. At any moment, an exciting passage of play could see you propelled 20 yards forward, 10 yards to the side, often without your feet touching the ground. The popular description of the 'swaying' Kop was exactly that – a whole series of crowd surges and eddies all over the vast terrace, creating the impression of a swaying tidal wave. When David Fairclough scored his ultra-dramatic, late, late winner against St Etienne in 1977, a tsunami-force surge pinned my diminutive frame against a barrier, so that I was folded double on myself, my nose near-touching my knees. My midriff was trapped on the barrier and I could feel the air being squeezed out of me. I was delirious with joy – we'd surely just won one of the greatest games of my life – but, Christ, it was starting to hurt! These crowd surges never lasted more than a few seconds, but I could feel the pressure still piling down on me, long after the ball hit the net, more and more and more … 'Surely they'll start backing up, now?' I can only liken the experience to a kid having one of those giggling fits where they laugh and laugh, almost in fits. Surely they'll have to take in air any second, before they pass out? I was beginning to white-out when, finally, the crowd relented, everyone spilt sideways and backwards, and I was able to slip down from the crash-barrier I'd been trapped against. It was the worst crowd-crush I'd encountered, but by no means the only one.

Outside the Leppings Lane end on 15 April 1989, it was different. In spite of the dangers of that goal celebration against St Etienne, there was almost a protocol to the surges on the Kop. You knew you could ride it out, that it would only last so long before the sway changed course and took the crowd in a different direction. As kick-off time approached outside Hillsborough, though, it became a mêlée, the likes of which I hadn't encountered before.

With hindsight, the lack of turnstiles, added to the physical restrictions of the area outside the ground, are the main reasons for the insufferable build-up before the game. In simple terms, the geography of Leppings Lane dictated that there was no overspill, nowhere for the ever-growing crowd to go. But there are other factors, too. There was absolutely no leadership or direction from either the police or the Sheffield Wednesday stewards. Just two or three officials with loud-hailers organising the crowd into distinct columns and queues, assuring everyone there was still plenty of time to get in, would have calmed the agitation that began to fester. Similarly, experienced officers and stewards directing fans towards alternative entrance points would have relieved the pressure, too. None of these things happened, though, and as a result there was an ever-increasing logjam as more fans arrived, with insufficient space for people to queue in comfort while they awaited their turn. As more and more people tried to fit into the narrow confines outside the turnstiles, I found myself being propelled, feet off the floor, closer and closer towards a red-brick wall. I was powerless to change my direction, or the angle at which I was being carried. At any moment I'd be pinned against the wall, and then what?

My face was being pushed into the wall, when my brother, Neil, arrived behind me. He forced the palms of his hands flat against the wall, either side of my head, and used the leverage to push back, creating a little space for me to manœuvre in. At that exact moment, the concertina gate to our left opened. We stood back for a second – as did everyone else – expecting the police to eject someone, or police horses to come in or out. Then, slowly, people started to file in. Neil and I went through, and waited for Mauro and Hobo.

We stood to one side on the concourse, just inside the gates, where people were buying refreshments and match-day programmes. The concourse area was small, almost diamond-shaped, and would have seemed crowded with just a few hundred people standing around chatting, sipping Bovril and flicking through the programme. But with the steady flow of fans now coming in three, four or five abreast, sight-lines to the limited signage directing supporters to alternative entrances were almost completely obstructed by the ever-growing number of fans on the concourse.

Only one sign could be clearly seen. Directly above your head as you came through the turnstiles was the tunnel that led to the central pens, 3 and 4. This was the only entrance with visible, above head-height signage. It was unmissable, one big sign directly above the tunnel with the word STANDING. The tunnel shelved down to a steep, 1:6 gradient. Such tunnels in city centres, train stations and pedestrianised areas are typically flat, with 1:10 the accepted norm for a safe, gently sloping tunnel. But at Hillsborough, at peak, pre-match capacity, many fans would be swept down the steep Leppings Lane tunnel towards whichever pen the flow might take them. This is what was happening, right there, right then. Fans coming in through the turnstiles and the now wide-open gates could just about glimpse a swathe of green, green grass down that central tunnel. Hardly anyone thought twice. They headed right down it.

The Leppings Lane terrace had been divided into six sections, each closed off with radial fencing – pens, essentially – of which numbers 3 and 4 were situated directly behind the goal. The terrace was just about fit for accommodating a small-to-average 1980s away support. But for a major occasion like the FA Cup semi-final, with huge, ebullient crowds, the turnstiles, the concourse and the terracing itself at the Leppings Lane end were all woefully ill-equipped.

And Leppings Lane had already experienced a history of crowd problems, particularly in high-priority matches, and especially in the FA Cup. At the 1981 semi-final between Wolverhampton Wanderers and Tottenham Hotspur, Spurs fans experienced unbearable crushing on these same terraces. On that occasion the South Yorkshire police responded quickly to the danger and opened gates in the fencing to allow Spurs fans to spill out on to the pitch. After the problems at that game, Hillsborough was not used again as a semi-final venue until 1987, when Leeds United played Coventry City. Sheffield Wednesday had been promoted back to the top flight in 1985, and set about 'improvements' to the Leppings Lane terrace. But, rather than taking the (more expensive) advice of civil engineer Dr Wilfred Eastwood, who recommended more turnstiles and separate entrances and exits for the (then) three pens in Leppings Lane, the club followed the (much cheaper) advice of South Yorkshire police. They wanted to remove barriers and add more radial fencing, creating more pens, along with a 'sterile' central walkway. So, although Hillsborough had last received a safety certificate in December 1979, the club was reinstated as a venue for FA Cup semi-finals in 1987.

But the lessons of 1981 had not been learned. Despite Leeds having the larger support of the two teams, once again the South Yorkshire police insisted that the team coming in from the north were housed in the smaller Leppings Lane end. There was, once again, overcrowding in the central pens, and Leeds fans in the seats above had to haul crushed and fainting fans to safety.

Yet, rather than heed the warning signs and act accordingly, there was a school of thought within the police establishment that football supporters were a high-risk element who brought these problems upon themselves. The Hillsborough Independent Panel Report cites a 1987 document produced by the Association of Chief Police Officers that noted that it had 'become increasingly apparent that large numbers of spectators are arriving extremely late at the ground. This may be related to the restricted access to alcohol inside grounds and the prohibition on taking alcohol into grounds.' This gives an eloquent insight into the way the police were viewing football supporters at the time; their movements, in the view of the Association of Chief Police Officers, being governed by the availability of alcohol. Consequently, to avoid disorder, 'police ground commanders have occasionally requested that the kick-off be delayed', but 'this pressure should not be acceded to in future, the police should not be dictated to by supporters'.

We spotted Mauro and Hobo heading for the tunnel. I managed to weave my way through the crowd and grab Hobo's jumper, pulling him back and shouting 'Mauro' at the same time: 'This way!' I said. To this day, even writing this now, I cannot contemplate what might have happened had I not known the ground's layout as I did. Perhaps if I hadn't been so slight – I'm 5 foot 9 and less than 10 stone – I'd have taken my chances with the majority. But my instinct, especially after the scrummage outside, was to head away from the numbers and find a quieter 'spec'. Even as we made our way to the corner passageway, carnage was already unfolding on the Leppings Lane terracing.

What happened next has come to be known as 'the Hillsborough tragedy', and I feel the pain and the sadness of the day intensely. Yet the word 'tragedy' implies something accidental, a horrific turn of fate. But what readers will learn from the accounts in this volume is that Hillsborough was far from being a tragic accident; it was a man-made disaster. There were warning signs – many of them – and opportunities in the build-up to the game, and on the day itself, to avert the inevitable. These indicators and options were ignored, fatally, leading 96 innocent football to their deaths. So our sadness for that tragedy should be matched by our righteous anger at its causes.

Twenty-seven years later, we are still waiting for those responsible to be held to account. Compiling these accounts from those who were there and those most closely touched by the disaster has been the most difficult project I have ever taken on. For a period of eighteen months I effectively asked my interviewees to revisit the darkest episodes of their lives, and describe them all over again in unflinching detail. In speaking to these people I have come to understand just the tip of their pain; for many of them, this will never, ever go away. Ordinary men and women have taken on the carapace of warriors, the precise language of lawyers and the cynicism of those who have come to know so much disappointment that basic human hope is all but extinguished. I can pay these people no compliment worthy of their courage, their unfailing commitment to the ultimate cause of truth and justice. It has been a humbling and deeply humanising experience for me, and I thank each and every interviewee for their sincerity, their patience and their fortitude.

One of the first people to encourage my work on the book was Anne Williams. She opened up her contact book and spoke passionately over the telephone, never once believing that she would not get justice for her son Kevin. It is one more tragedy of the Hillsborough story that Anne died before seeing that day arrive. I thank her for the inspiration she provided. Anne Williams grew too ill to complete our interviews for *Hillsborough Voices*, and I am indebted to Peter Marshall for allowing me access to transcripts of the BBC's own very personal recordings with Anne for Panorama's 2013 film 'Hillsborough: How They Tried to Bury the Truth.'

My aspiration in accepting the invitation to compile this volume for Ebury was – and is – that each and every time the true story of Hillsborough is told it claws back the truth, for posterity, from those who sought to bury it. Each new reader who comes to understand what really happened on 15 April 1989 is another who can bear testimony to others less aware until, finally, the truth about Hillsborough is accepted as the truth.

The interviews in this book were conducted after the Hillsborough Independent Report was published in September 2012.

Since then we have had the monumental results of the new inquests, which have changed everything. But there's still a fight to be fought, and this book is a testament to why.

Kevin Sampson

CONTRIBUTORS

John Ashton was 41 in 1989. He was, at that time, a senior lecturer at Liverpool University's School of Medicine.

Andy Burnham, 19, was in his first year studying English at Fitzwilliam College, Cambridge University.

Peter Carney was a 29-year-old play development worker for Liverpool City Council, living in Kirkby.

Sheila Coleman, 32, was lecturing at Liverpool City College in April 1989. She left in September 1989 to start work as a researcher on The Hillsborough Project.

Barry Devonside was 42. He worked for the Prudential Assurance company and lived in Formby.

Jegsy Dodd was a 31-year-old performer, musician and poet from Moreton, Wirral.

Steve Hart was 29. He was working as a barman in Kirkby.

Peter Hooton, 32, was the co-editor of cult fanzine *The End*. He worked for Liverpool social services as a youth worker.

Damian Kavanagh was 20, and living in Skelmersdale. He worked for the Royal Insurance Company.

Steve Kelly, 29, was a taxi-driver living off Penny Lane in south Liverpool.

John Maguire was 13 in 1989; his friend Dan Nicolson was 4. They were founder members of Reclaim the Kop, the fan group that organised Truth Day in 2007.

John Mackin was 30 and worked at the civil service in Bootle, north Liverpool.

Tony O'Keefe, originally from Liverpool, was working as a fireman in south London.

Danny Rhodes, a Nottingham Forest supporter, was a 17-year-old Associate Postman from Grantham, Lincolnshire.

Steve Rotheram was at the time working as a bricklayer in Kirkby. He is now the MP for Walton, where Liverpool FC's Anfield stadium is located.

Martin Thompson was 19 in 1989, working in a frozen-food packaging factory.

Anne Williams was the 38-year-old mother from Formby who lost her son Kevin at Hillsborough. She spent the remainder of her life campaigning for the truth about the circumstances of her son's death.

Stephen Wright was a 20-year-old plumber from Huyton.

THE YEAR BEFORE ...

STEPHEN WRIGHT

It had become my favourite ground, Hillsborough. I first went there in 1984 for a League Cup game. They were in the Second Division but there was 50,000-odd people there that night, and I just thought, 'What a place, what a ground!' That big Kop end with no roof on ... it was a proper, old-fashioned footy ground. I just loved it.

ANDY BURNHAM

Third round of the Cup the year before, January 1988, Sheffield Wednesday v Everton. Wednesday are winning 1–0, Peter Reid equalises in the 80th minute ... I have never in my life experienced a crush like it. I've never been so uncomfortable at a football match, ever. I was hardly watching the game ... you know when something about where you are makes you scared about the situation? Well, I spent the whole of the second half with my eyes glued to the back of my dad's head, and my younger brother. I wouldn't let them out of my sight. I remember when we eventually got out we all, sort of, came round. It was as though we'd passed out and come back out of it, it had been so horrible in there.

DAMIAN KAVANAGH

I agreed with Bill Shankly's quote about the greatest day of the English season being FA Cup semi-final day. There's nothing quite like it – so much to win, so much to lose. For the previous season's semi-final I'd gone with my mates to Hillsborough for the first time. We popped into the first ale house we came across, but it was at the Forest end of things. We had a bevvy there, kept a low profile and there were no problems but you can't beat being with your own – especially our own – so we got off. We found this pub, the Horse & Jockey, which was sound.

There had been no noticeable police presence in the Forest pub, so it stuck out to me big time when they were showing up and were almost antagonistic when talking to the Reds' fans. They were a bit like them nightclub bully-type bouncers in the days before the registration cards; you know, 'What are you looking at, lad? I'll give you a smack,' all that. 'We're big and we've got this uniform and if you look at us the wrong way we'll stop you enjoying your day.' But, in a way, it was normal to be treated with disrespect by the police – in a way that I now can't explain to my son. If you wanted to go to the footy, you had to put up with that – and it was a factor in what happened. It's not the whole story, but everything is cumulative – trickle, trickle, trickle. And there's no doubt that the attitude of the police towards Liverpool fans was pre-set and, twelve months on from my first taste of Hillsborough, it was a huge factor in the way things happened.

But the year before, even though we'd won and we had a great day, I remember getting back and going to my mate's house, who was a big Blue. He said, 'Oh aye, come to gloat, have you?' And I told him about the coppers at the pub, how nastily aggressive they'd been. I told him I was only aware of the contrasting attitude towards us because we'd wandered into the Forest pub earlier that same day.

STEVE ROTHERAM

I was there the year before. At that time I was 27 years old: a bricklayer; an amateur footballer, and fairly physically fit. I went to the game with a mate who was a PT instructor in the navy. Both of us were physically pretty strong, yet both of us had felt peculiarly uncomfortable on the terraces of Hillsborough in the build-up to kick-off. I had a standing ticket for the terraces, in the now infamous pen 3. Despite being as fit as I was, there were times when the numbers in the pen caused me concern and I felt frighteningly constrained. For reasons I was unaware of at that time, the mounting crowd could be released at either side, and the crowds in each section appeared to find their own level. Obviously people had either moved to parts of the terrace that were less full, or headed out of the back of the pen via the tunnel entrance/exit to stand in a different pen.

DANNY RHODES

We went on the coach the year before, so it was all a little bit regimented. I was still only about 16 or 17, working as a printer on a YTS (Youth Training Scheme). We had our regulars who went week in, week out, but with it being a semi-final we filled six coaches. There were a lot of hangers-on, who were into making a day of it, having a lot to drink, but that wasn't really my thing. I just wanted to get inside and enjoy what was going to be my first really big game. So, anything to do with policing or anything like that – it didn't make any impression on me, either way. All I remember in real clear detail was that, once that big Hillsborough Kop filled up, you could feel it move underneath you, like being on a ship. Then the match started, Aldridge scored quite early on … then it was 2–0. We scrambled one back towards to the end, and there was an eight- or ten-minute spell when it was quite exciting, but, other than that, it was all a bit of a damp squib.

STEPHEN WRIGHT

It hurts me to think about 1988. Notts Forest were a good team in those days, one of the best in the country. And the FA Cup really meant something back then, so to beat them – what a joyous day! But, now, thinking back, it hurts. It meant so much at the time, beating them, getting to the final. But now … it's meaningless. It's nothing.

I was in the North Stand in '88, at the Leppings Lane end of the stand by that slightly raised bit of terracing near the corner – so I could see right across the Leppings Lane terrace. It was packed tight, but that was the norm. Being crowded, being squashed – you went on the terraces, and that was the absolute norm. I remember as a kid on the Kop being packed that tight that your feet haven't touched the ground. Big games, derby games, late seventies, early eighties; the sway of the crowd was that powerful I've been turned round, feet off the ground, so my back was to the pitch. Frightening, that – but you took it. You'd see people getting passed down over your head but you never batted an eyelid. It's how it was.

STEVE HART

At the '88 semi, you had to go through crowd control. It was all fenced off on the walk up to the ground and you had to go through barriers and ticket checks and so on. As you go through the turnstiles the first thing you see is the tunnel leading on to the Leppings Lane terraces. There's a big sign above the tunnel, you can't miss it, right in front of you: STANDING. Now, in '88, I had my dad with me and as soon as we came through we got directed to the side pens because they told us the central pens were full. They blocked off the tunnel and just kept people moving, either side.

JOHN ASHTON

I've got three boys, so at any given time there were different permutations of who I'd be able to take to the game with me. Myself, I'd been to Hillsborough many, many times since I was a teenager, so I was used to the conditions there. But at the 1988 semi-final we were in the corner of the Leppings Lane terrace and it was packed very tightly; abnormally so, I thought. So, for the 1989 game, I was determined to get seats.

PETER HOOTON

Everyone knew the Leppings Lane was a bad end. It was a case of, 'Not again!' I was in the North Stand for the semi-final the year before and, all through that game, Liverpool fans were being pulled up from the terracing into the seats. Afterwards, people I knew were saying they'd had to get out of there because it felt so tightly packed – it was uncomfortable.

BARRY DEVONSIDE

Nowhere, in any of the papers relating to this tragedy, will you find anything that explains or puts into context the removal of Chief Superintendent Brian Mole from his role as chief of police in the Hillsborough area. We now know, from public records, that he was hurriedly transferred to Barnsley only a week or two before the forthcoming semi-final, as part of an internal measure.

But there are two other things we know, too: one is that Mole was a hugely experienced police officer, accustomed to policing the biggest matches at Sheffield Wednesday FC. The second thing we know is that his replacement, David Duckenfield, had next to no experience at all, and very little time to get himself acclimatised. These two things added up to disaster. The decision to relieve Brian Mole of his duties, and the timing of it, right before such a high-profile, high-impact football match, was a mistake of the most profound magnitude. Everything we have subsequently heard from the police has been an attempt to hide this enormous error of judgement.

STEPHEN WRIGHT

There was a near identical situation before the 1981 semi-final, when Tottenham played Wolves. But there were no lateral fences, then – no pens – so the crowd could move outwards from the middle of the terrace, to the sides. Obviously Sheffield Wednesday removed barriers in response to the problems they had at the '81 semi, and divided the Leppings Lane end into pens. There were gates between the pens at the rear but, once the two middle pens were packed to capacity, there was no way of getting out of there for those at the front. There was nowhere to go. The ground had no valid safety certificate, the FA carried out no checks. They were basically playing Russian roulette every time there was a match. Every game played there once they took out those barriers, they were playing Russian roulette; with disastrous consequences.

PART ONE

THE DISASTER

15 APRIL 1989

PETER CARNEY

I was 29 – I turned 30 in the May of 1989 – and I'd been working for the youth services as a play development worker that past year, based out of Kirkdale Youth Centre. The week before the game, we'd taken a group of kids on a barge trip and, apart from the first day when it was glorious sunshine, the elements threw everything at us – rain, hail, even 6 inches of snow, one day. I was in bed most of the week leading up to the game with the flu.

Then, on the Thursday, my wife Tina told me she was pregnant. That was just … it was the best. It hadn't been straightforward, we'd been trying; it had been going on a number of years. So that was a big, big moment.

TONY O'KEEFE

I was living in Streatham. I'd moved to London for work, as so many of us did at the time. Football was my big link with home, with Liverpool, my family. I was with the fire service. By 1989 I'd done three years with the London fire brigade and two of those years were with the Rescue. So I'd seen a lot in that time. Obviously a detailed knowledge of first aid is a major part of your training but, above and beyond that, I'd had direct experience of several death situations. Our watch was at the King's Cross fire in 1987. I'd pulled bodies out of there, burned to death. I'd seen quite a lot in quite a short time. But, like I say, football was my release. I came up on the Friday night, full of excitement for the game.

DAMIAN KAVANAGH

I was working at the Royal Insurance in town, living at home in Skelmersdale with my mum and dad. Typical Liverpool lad, football mad, bang into it – I played on a Sunday and I watched the Reds every Saturday. I was watching the most exciting Liverpool team I'd ever seen, week in, week out. I loved it, and at 20 years of age I went to my second consecutive FA Cup semi-final at Hillsborough. Same ground, same opponents, and we were to wear red again. It couldn't get better!

JOHN MACKIN

The Leppings Lane end was widely disliked as a 'bad spec'. The sightlines were notoriously poor and the terracing was always packed tight. My season ticket qualified me for a terrace ticket – that is, the Leppings Lane – but, after the previous year's overcrowding, I wasn't keen. The system at Liverpool was that, if there had been any tickets returned, or if the players and so on hadn't taken their allocation, they would go on sale last thing, the day before the game. So I decided to take my chances. I left work at 4, went up to Anfield and hung around in a queue that was forming. After a bit, Peggy, the manager of the ticket office, chased off a couple of well-known ticket touts. Then, to my great delight, she sold the last few remaining tickets in the North Stand – one per person – to the small queue of regulars waiting there. That night I sold my Leppings Lane ticket to a friend of a friend in the Coffee House pub in Woolton. I was looking forward to the semi even more, now.

ANDY BURNHAM

The night before, I was in my local – the Cherry Tree, in Culcheth – with all my mates, a mix of Liverpool fans and Everton fans, all buzzing about the semi-finals the next day. I was with my best mate, Steve Turner – a Liverpool fan – both of us saying, 'Wouldn't it be great if our teams got to Wembley again.' But the conversation turned to the ticket allocation: 'How come Liverpool are in the away end again?' Because anyone who'd been to Sheffield Wednesday knew what that was like. And we were ridiculing the FA for this weird decision, based on the Hillsborough Kop vaguely tilting towards Nottingham.

DANNY RHODES

I'd just started as an Associate Postman – bit more money and, apart from the time you had to get up in the morning, I enjoyed that job. I remember in the run-up to the game, there was a lot of talk about Forest and Liverpool swapping ends; about us having the Leppings Lane end. Part of it was that Forest didn't have as big a support as Liverpool, but part of it was – yes, we had the big end last year, Liverpool should have it this year. Certainly among our little gang the thinking was – yes, it's only fair.

PETER HOOTON

So, after all the overcrowding the year before, my feeling was that the game should have been played at Old Trafford. We'd had to travel the furthest distance in 1988 so, in the interests of being fair, it should have been Old Trafford – which would have been more convenient for us. But not only did we not get Old Trafford, we also got given the same end again.

BARRY DEVONSIDE

It was a beautiful, sunny, spring morning. We were getting a lift to Sheffield in my friend Paul Edwards's car – me and Chris, Paul, his son Steven, and Chris's friend, Jason Kenworthy. Of course, Chris wanted to go behind the goal with his mates. The night before, he'd asked me and I'd said, 'No.' I went for a shower and he came back and asked me again, and again I said, 'No, Chris. You're not going in the Leppings Lane.' He left it fifteen minutes or so then asked me a third time. 'Dad, *please* can I go behind the goal with my mates?' I don't know why I relented. This decision will be with me for the rest of my life. Chris was an excellent son and if I had kept to the same answer as the first two times he asked, he would be at home with me now.

Jackie, my wife, wasn't happy about it at all. She had said to me some years previously, 'If you ever let any harm come to Chris, then you and me have got a big problem.' But I would always reassure her he'd be fine. So off we went.

JEGSY DODD

I was in a band at the time, signed to Probe Plus Records. We hadn't long got back from gigging in Europe – Holland, Belgium, Germany. Other than that, though, football was still at the centre of everything I did. I'd been to semi-finals before. I'd been everywhere with Liverpool, and that team, at that time, was beating everyone. Dare I say it, there was almost a sense of – here we go again. But, on the day, the sun was shining, it was the semi-final of the FA Cup … it gets you every time, doesn't it?

DANNY RHODES

Forest were playing some of the best football you'd ever seen, but it was always bloody Liverpool, wasn't it? The year before, we could have got Wimbledon or Luton. This time we could have had Norwich or Everton. But both times it was us against Liverpool. That should have been the final, both times.

DAMIAN KAVANAGH

I took my lucky scarf. No need for superstition, though; it was going to be the same outcome as last season: a win and the Reds to Wembley again! Nottingham Forest had a good side but we were better – better than anybody – and after a stuttering season we were right on Arsenal's case for the league title, which had looked lost on New Year's Day. Now we were just one step from the FA Cup final again. The double-double should have been done the previous season, but the Crazy Gang and a missed Aldo penalty meant that was not to be. We'd left it late this season but we could just do the impossible this time and make up for it.

It looked like Everton would get past a decent Norwich side in the other semi, so there was the prospect of another scouse final on the horizon. I actually hoped Norwich would win, though – the stress of derby day is bad enough without the added prize of the FA Cup and the massive bragging rights that would go with creating a bit of football history. The stick the losers would get would be unmerciful.

STEPHEN WRIGHT

In our house there's my mum and dad, our David, who lived away, and our Ann, who lived round the corner. Up until I was 13, me and our Graham slept in the same bed. So we were really close, every day of our lives. Anyway, in the week leading up to the game, our Graham wasn't going. He didn't have a ticket. Our David had been the year before, with me. So he gave him his ticket: 'Here you are – I've been before. You go.' So obviously our Graham was made up. I was going to games with the supporters' club coach in those days. We had a brilliant crowd on that coach: a really great laugh, great atmosphere. But Graham wanted to do his own thing. Him and his mate James Aspinall booked with Barnes Travel, down by Everton's ground.

IAN RUSH

Alan Hansen had been out for most of the season, but he'd come through a reserve match midweek. Hansen didn't think he'd be playing. I think everyone thought Phil Thompson would play. Me and Jocky [Hansen] both thought we'd be on the bench but Barry Venison fell ill and Kenny told Jocky he was playing. He wasn't happy about it, especially with it being a semi-final. He didn't feel ready for such a big game. He was a bag of nerves.

DAMIAN KAVANAGH

My Kop season ticket qualified me for a Leppings Lane terrace ticket; that suited me fine. I liked standing on the Kop and being part of the singing and quickness that had gone on to make us world famous. If I'd had the chance to buy a seat I'd have swerved it, anyway – and not just because it would have cost a few more quid.

I got up smart and went with Bailey, who had been my bezzie since school, to meet two more of my mates: Jamie, from work, and his bezzie, Scott. I'd managed to get a voucher from somebody who never went to the away games, and I used that to get Bailey's ticket. He was made up. Jamie was happy driving. He only lived in Aintree so it was no problem. We got down to Switch Island, Jamie picked us up, off we went.

STEPHEN WRIGHT

I went to wake our Graham up about 8 o'clock. All smiles, the usual big-game thing, semi-final of the Cup, 'Come on, we're gonna do it today!' And he was excited, like, but him and James were going on Barnes's coaches. He just goes, 'I'm not leaving till 9.30, I've got another hour in bed.' So I headed out then, off to get my bus. That was the last time I saw Graham.

MARTIN THOMPSON

It was one of those mornings where you open the curtains and the sun is shining and it just feels good to be alive. I was 19, it was a beautiful spring day, it was the FA Cup semi-final and I supported the best team in the country! And I *loved* the FA Cup – I used to get really, really excited before Cup games. I stayed at my girlfriend's house the night before, so I was up early and out to meet my brother and get our lift.

There were two cars going – five of us in our car: Sean Boardman was driving, Jason Kirwin, Simon Hughes, myself and my brother Stuart. We followed the other car to the Old Roan pub to pick up the lad who lived there, but he decided not to go. He hadn't been able to get a ticket. So we set off, both cars, about 10 o'clock or so.

DANNY RHODES

We'd started going to a lot of the games on the train by 1989. A lot of the lads wanted to make the awaydays more … I wouldn't say dangerous exactly, but it was richer, it was gritty, going all round the country on the train. It wasn't, you know – get on the coach, get driven straight to the ground, file into the ground then straight back home as soon as the game's over. Going on the train, you got to see the cities you were going to. Often, you'd end up getting a police escort anyway, straight from the train station to the ground. I really loved that – getting marched down the high street at Derby or somewhere, everyone singing, and all these people looking at us. It was all part of that gang mentality that you really wanted to be part of. Anyway, we decided we were going to Hillsborough on the train this time.

STEVE ROTHERAM

I remember distinctly the beautiful spring day as we set out for the match. We left on a coach from the Carters Arms pub in Kirkby and the atmosphere was the usual mix of high spirits, good humour and raucous singing. The expectation of a Liverpool victory manifested itself with claims that we would easily win 3–, 4– or even 5–0, and that Aldo would get a bag full.

Despite looking forward to the game, I hoped to avoid the same situation as the year before in the pens of the Leppings Lane terraces.

PETER CARNEY

On the morning of the game I was still a bit flat from the flu, to be honest. I wasn't looking forward to driving. There was meant to be four of us going in a Fiesta, but then my mate Mick phoned up, offering to drive. He had a bigger car, a Mondeo – so that's what we done. The only real snag we had getting there came around Stockport. There was quite a big hold-up with the traffic, but one of the lads had worked there, and he took us, literally, through the back streets of Stockport so we could shuffle past the roadworks.

JEGSY DODD

There was three car loads of us went – mainly lads from Aigburth, Dingle, Garston. All from the South End. I was the only one from the other side of the water. The youngest of us was Peter McDonnell, who was only 21; we were all quite a bit older, late twenties, early thirties. We drove across in convoy.

TONY O'KEEFE

I'm one of these who always wants to get there early. The others were more relaxed about it, you know, 'We don't have to go *that* early.' But Everton were playing at Villa Park, there was obviously going to be traffic, and I was driving, so that was that. It was me, my two brothers Kevin and Michael, and my brother-in-law Ian Jenkins, in the car. It's a good job we did set off at that time because there was roadworks and then, on the outskirts of Sheffield, we got directed the wrong way. We had to do this u-turn back on ourselves and, eventually, Ian just said, 'Come on – let's just park up here.' He'd been before and he said we were only about half a mile from the ground.

BARRY DEVONSIDE

There was a bit of congestion, quite a tailback, as you approached the Hillsborough area. Everyone had their car windows down, it was so warm. The car in front was having a bit of a laugh with a policeman, and the copper was laughing back, no problems at all. Next thing the lads get out of the car and the copper's letting them try his helmet on. It was all very good-humoured; give and take.

JOHN ASHTON

There was myself, my sons Mathew (16) and Nick (14) and their cousin Carl, who was 20. We headed over across the Snake Pass, typical Big Match feel: scarves flying out of the window; speculating about what starting eleven Kenny would pick; everyone pretty excited. There was a tailback for roadworks outside Hyde, on the Glossop road, but once we got through that it was fine. We stopped on the outskirts, had lunch in the King's Head pub, then made our way down to Hillsborough.

DAMIAN KAVANAGH

The delay in traffic seemed like no big deal. Thousands on the way to the match was bound to slow things up a bit, but we'd left in plenty of time. Above all else, it was just excitement – a car full of young lads on their way to an FA Cup semi-final! You think you know it all at that age – you think you're a veteran, don't you? But it was just anticipation. Excitement. Jamie parked up in Don Avenue, a little way from the ground, but not too far to walk, and off we went.

We eventually got to the Horse & Jockey – happy days! The sun was out, fans standing outside in their shirt sleeves, no hassle at all. The police didn't like so many being outside, they were growling, 'Back in, you! Get back inside!'

Like the year before the pub was chocker with Reds giving it loads with all the songs. 'A Liver Bird Upon My Chest', nice and slow and building up to a big, loud chorus. I'd been up to the league match against Sheffield Wednesday earlier that season, but this was a world away from that previous winter's cold draw. It was bouncing, just generally, a really great atmosphere – no hassle at all. Everyone up for seeing the greatest team in the world win their way through to another FA Cup Final.

We did an hour or so in the Horse & Jockey, then decided to get off down to the ground. I wanted the boss spec right in the middle, behind the goal. I always stood in the middle of the Kop where all the singing started, and I knew that if you got in the Kop after half-two you'd have no chance getting near the middle. And at away grounds I'd be looking for the same type of spec, too. The atmosphere at a semi-final was always brilliant, wherever you were in the ground – but I still wanted that spec ...

JOHN BARNES

The morning of the game, we did everything – as much as possible – exactly the same as we'd done for the semi-final the year before. We stayed in the same hotel, same coach company, left for the ground at a similar time. It was the usual big-game feeling as you get closer to the ground. Obviously the players' coach has to get to the ground quite a bit earlier, when there aren't as many people around – so we didn't notice anything different at all.

STEVE KELLY

I'm an Evertonian. Our Michael was the black sheep of the family! But I wasn't at Villa Park on 15 April because the following weekend I was due to run the London Marathon. I was a taxi-driver in those days, and your Saturday night is the busiest time of the week. There was no way I could afford to take the two consecutive Saturdays off, so that was that. I'd booked my hotel for London the following week, and my wife Christine and me were just going to have a quiet day shopping. We went down to Allerton Road, the high street near Penny Lane, where we lived, and were just enjoying a leisurely, sunny Saturday.

DANNY RHODES

Pulling into Sheffield, we were talking about how we'd get up to the ground. We knew that Hillsborough was a fair distance from the station, so walking it wasn't really on the cards. But, as it turned out, we had no choice in the matter. There was a line of buses waiting, and the police pretty much marched us straight on to them. They were quite officious: 'This is what you're doing, this is where you're going …' I'd come across that sort of attitude quite a lot – just a bit of an attitude towards football fans generally. Yet, in some places, the police were fine; it just depended where you went. South Yorkshire police were known for being a bit heavy, and the atmosphere on the bus going up to the ground wasn't great. The police were stood up on the bus watching everything you did, so you just sat there, really, looking out of the window.

THE TAYLOR REPORT

49. The nerve centre for police control is the control room or box situated at the south-west corner of the ground between the South Stand and pen 1 of the west terracing. The box is elevated and reached by a number of steps. It has windows commanding views across the pitch and straight along the line of the west perimeter fence. The box is very small and has seats for only three officers. Superintendent Murray was in control of it and was advisor to Mr Duckenfield, as he had been to Mr Mole the year before. Next to him sat Sergeant Goddard who operated the radios. The third seat was for Police Constable Ryan who operated the telephone and public address systems. At the back of the box stood Police Constable Bichard who was in control of the police closed-circuit television system operated by a row of consoles on a bench in front of him and behind the three seated officers.

58. At about 12 noon Chief Inspector Creaser asked Superintendent Murray whether the pens on the west terrace were to be filled one by one successively, but was told that they should all be available from the start and the fans should find their own level.

TONY O'KEEFE

We went to this pub for a pint and something to eat, and the atmosphere, inside and out, was just great. Loads were just standing outside, enjoying the sunshine, the big-match atmosphere starting to build. I took some photos of our lot, everybody cheering, everyone excited. But, again, it was me who wanted to make a move. Ian had got us seats in the stand above Leppings Lane. I was happy about that. I used to like going in with the crowd, too, but it was nice to have really good tickets for such a big match. You'd be able to see the game properly.

STEVE HART

We did everything exactly the same as the year before: same coach, set off from St Peter & Paul's in Kirkby at the same time; same route, stopped off at the same pub. This year, though, we got held up by roadworks, so the coach driver took us as close to the ground as he could get us. We all jumped off and the driver was going to park up. And the first thing you noticed was that there was no stewarding. Normally for a game like that you'd be filtered through barriers, there'd be ticket checks and so on, random searches – but there was none of that.

DANNY RHODES

We got to the ground and got off the buses. I remember going past Hillsborough Park and seeing fans sat out on the grass, all the colours, and I started to get the feeling at that point – that special feeling that makes you want to go to football. That adrenaline rush starts to build, you know? You're a couple of hours away before kick-off and you see the ground come into view, and it's just brilliant. You can see the younger kids picking up their pace trying to keep up with their dads, and you know just exactly how they feel. That feeling, that excitement – it never went away for me.

BARRY DEVONSIDE

We parked up around 1.30 p.m. in a side street near the White Horse Inn on Halifax Road and began making our way to the ground. A little way down the road there's the Gateway supermarket. They weren't actually letting people in. They were taking orders at the door and serving people one and two at a time. Again, it was all very good-natured. People queued up and waited to be served. I bought six cans of beer and two packets of crisps. We arranged the place we were going to meet up after the game, there on the Halifax Road, and that was that. We headed off down to the ground.

Christopher and I had a can each as we walked down, and we were feeding the crisps to a police horse. We had a convivial rapport with the police we encountered. It was a typical big-game atmosphere, lots of wisecracks and singing, everyone looking forward to the match. But the road leading down to the ground was very busy, and it was taking us longer than you'd expect to get to the exterior gates – the gates that lead on to the area immediately outside the ground, where the turnstiles are. So I placed the remaining four cans under a bush to pick up on the way home, and we continued on our way to the ground.

STEVE ROTHERAM

We made our way towards our end of the ground. There was the immediate feeling that things were very different than they'd been twelve months previously.

I often compare and contrast the policing of those two games. In 1988 there had been a cordon on the approach to Leppings Lane, but nothing a year later. Getting in to the match in them days was never an easy ride, and in 1988 the entrance into the ground included the usual hustle and bustle that was an everyday experience of getting into any football ground in those days.

However, there was definitely a visible mood change and a strange air about the stadium a year later, as large crowds built up outside the stadium. There was no hint of trouble, but things felt more chaotic than usual. I felt unsafe. Nothing seemed to be moving. Pressure started to build. Questions were being asked of police officers. We were looking to them for guidance, leadership and ultimately for protection. Nothing came other than shouting the odd instruction to nobody in particular.

TONY O'KEEFE

We started our walk down to the ground, just following the crowd and what have you. But straight away, Ian said, 'Oh, they stopped us for a ticket check here last year. I wonder where all the stewards are?' It was normal, wasn't it, for any big match to have stewards directing the crowds? But we thought nothing of it and carried on and, as you got towards the end of that sort of pathway, there was this big build-up, going nowhere, all seemingly trying to go to these turnstiles to the right. I looked at it and thought, 'It can't just be those few turnstiles for all our fans?'

PETER CARNEY

We got there not much later than we'd been expecting to, really. We parked up in a retail park on Penistone Road, and just meandered around the ground. I popped into a little shop, got some crisps, a Mars Bar and a pint of milk – classic flu-recovery menu! We sat in the sunshine for a bit, ate our crisps, watched the fans all excited, heading into the ground, then the two of us that were in the Leppings Lane end decided we'd go in ourselves.

MARTIN THOMPSON

We all walked down and, as we got nearer the ground one of Stuart's mates asked if anyone fancied swapping tickets. He had a seat in the North Stand but he wanted to go on the terraces with Stuart. They were 17 and they just wanted to be in the thick of it all and, to be honest, I didn't mind either way. Go on the terraces and you've got the atmosphere; go in the seats and you can watch the game! So I just said, 'Fine, I'll swap with you.' I pointed to the newsagent's over the road, with a Benson and Hedges sign. I said to Stuart, 'Go on, you go in with these. I'll meet you outside there, after the game.' So that was it – they went in, and I went round to the North Stand.

STEPHEN WRIGHT

The supporters' club coach always had a route they'd take, a certain place they'd park and a specially arranged pub or a social club they'd have boxed off; same routine every season, there'd be something organised for whichever club or ground you went to. We parked up and went to The Beehive for a couple of drinks, then walked down, as per normal, everyone in high spirits.

DANNY RHODES

Some of the lads wanted to go for a drink before the game, but I wasn't that bothered about going to the pub. Me and my mate went straight in; straight up the stairs. We went in virtually the same place as we'd been the year before. Right behind the goal, about halfway up the terrace – which is where we wanted to be. And it was quiet, you know? It was quiet for quite a long time. We just sat down on the terrace, waiting for the ground to fill up; waiting for the game.

And, again, that feeling was starting to build – excitement that, this time, we could really do it. Forest had been on this amazing run, something like 22 games unbeaten. There was talk that Hansen might be back but, even though Liverpool would always start as favourites, if Forest were ever going to beat them, then this was our big chance. We were convinced that this was going to be our day.

THE TAYLOR REPORT

59. By 2 p.m. it was apparent to those inside the ground and those monitoring events in the police and club control rooms that the number of Nottingham fans in their places greatly outnumbered those from Liverpool. The Kop and the South Stand were filling up steadily, but the North and West stands were half empty. It was noted about that time that the turnstile figures showed only 12,000 had entered, as against 20,000 at the same time the previous year. On the west terraces, although pens 3 and 4 were filling, the wing pens 1, 2, 6 and 7 were nearly empty. At 2.15 p.m. a Tannoy message asked fans in pens 3 and 4 to move forward and make room for others.

DAMIAN KAVANAGH

Me and Bailey bought a programme and went straight ahead and through the tunnel directly behind the goal. It was the obvious route to take – the clearly marked entrance that greeted you as you entered the stadium through the turnstiles – there were no conspicuous signs directing you to go anywhere else. Jamie and Scott didn't follow us. They didn't usually go right in the middle of the Kop and decided to walk around to the side. I noticed from the clock on the stand to my right that it was 2.15 p.m. Normally, this would be a little early for me. I always tended to head into the Kop at about 2.30 p.m., but this was the FA Cup semi-final and we wanted to part of it. The gradual build-up, the way the atmosphere got louder and louder as kick-off approached – that was what we loved.

PETER HOOTON

Walking down towards Hillsborough, we passed a well-known ticket tout. He said that there had been very little demand. His exact words were, 'It's on the floor.'

The last thing any football fan wants to see as you approach the ground is a mass crowd outside the turnstiles, rather than orderly queues. No one wants the hassle of every person for themselves – you want to see proper queues. But it wasn't like that outside the Leppings Lane. It was heaving. I'd been in several similar situations – I remember one terrible crush outside Molineux when Liverpool won the league in 1976 – and I didn't like that sensation. I didn't like being in the thick of a mass crowd like that.

THE TAYLOR REPORT

61. By this time [2.15 p.m.] the police Traffic Division reported that the Liverpool routes were clear, so the majority of Liverpool fans were in the Sheffield area. The numbers converging on the Leppings Lane entrance were increasing rapidly. Between the perimeter gates and the turnstiles the crowd became congested. There was no longer a separate queue at each turnstile but a single phalanx filling the whole approach area. Mounted officers in and outside the turnstile area were having difficulty manœuvring in such a dense crowd.

The police were beset by fans bemused by the ticket and turnstile labelling asking for directions. Many had been drinking but up to and just after 2.30 p.m. the mood remained good.

62. Superintendent Marshall was on foot among the crowd. He became anxious about the numbers coming down Leppings Lane and spilling out on to the roadway where buses and cars were moving. At 2.17 p.m. he radioed to control to have motor traffic in Leppings Lane stopped. This was eventually done at about 2.30 p.m. Up to this time, despite the large mass outside the turnstiles and the numbers still approaching, there was still no panic in the crowd; no perception of crisis by the police. In the control room Mr Murray, who could see Leppings Lane on the video, advised Mr Duckenfield that they would get everyone in by 3 p.m. Mr Duckenfield reaffirmed to him the policy about a delayed kick-off. It would be ordered only if there was some major external factor such as fog on the Pennines or delay on the motorway; not if spectators merely turned up late even in large numbers.

STEVE HART

As we started getting nearer to the turnstiles, I started to think that things weren't right. The pressure from behind was building up and building up and, even then, you could hardly breathe – it was bad. I got trapped up against the wall, by the turnstile, and I virtually couldn't move. There was people trying to push the crowd back and I managed to flip myself round into the turnstile itself. But the pressure from behind was so massive that I didn't stop. I just got propelled straight through. I still had the full ticket in my hand. People outside were getting pulled up above and over the wall by the turnstiles because it was that packed outside.

STEVE ROTHERAM

As things built outside the stadium, I looked on helpless as the police lost complete control and the situation became more and more unnerving.

It was claustrophobic: just very, very packed and uncomfortable. I had already decided that, if I could, I would swap my terrace ticket for one in the stands as I hadn't particularly enjoyed the experience in the pens the last time. Everybody was packed close together and, about fifteen minutes before kick-off, I overheard three lads deciding what to do when they got through the turnstiles. Two of them had enclosure tickets and one had a stand ticket. I suggested that we swap my Leppings Lane ticket for their West Stand ticket so they could be together and I'd pay the difference. I was pretty pleased when they agreed. I thought to myself , 'At least it saves the hassle of trying to get a good spec – if we ever get into this game.' There was obviously a logjam somewhere and it was really slow progress towards the turnstiles.

JOHN MACKIN

Even though I was in the North Stand now, you could only access your seats via the Leppings Lane turnstiles. It was just a seething mass of people swaying this way and that, but going nowhere. There was no system, no control. You could see the odd bobby on horseback, but they weren't issuing any advice or instructions. They were just *there*. Eventually I got through. Everyone was turning to each other and saying, 'Jesus, that was mad!'

JEGSY DODD

On the ticket it advised you to get there 30 minutes before kick-off, but it was chaos outside. I mean, football fans were treated like animals in those days anyway, you were used to overcrowding, but this was mad. It was chaos.

PETER HOOTON

I didn't want to go into the mêlée outside the turnstiles. It didn't seem to be moving at all. It was swaying from side to side, without any real forward progress. In spite of that, though, the general atmosphere was good. It was the semi-final of the Cup, everyone was excited – everyone just wanted to get inside the ground.

I tried to stand back and wait until the worst of the crush subsided, but the police were saying, 'Either you get in or you get right out of the way.' So I went to a corner shop just to get away from the police hassling you to join the mêlée. I didn't want to walk too far away from the ground, so I went over the road to this little shop on Leppings Lane.

JOHN ASHTON

Everything was fine until we got to that area immediately outside the ground. I mean, in the cold light of day it's terrifying when you consider just how small that area is between the turnstiles and the wall by the river. It's just a tiny, kind of triangular compound and it was complete mayhem, absolutely squashed and heaving. Now, I get claustrophobia at the best of times, so there was no way I was going into that chaos. I think Carl went in, but I just said to my sons Mathew and Nick, 'Let's sit back and let the crush die down.'

DAMIAN KAVANGH

The crowd built up steadily, like any other match. The singing was building up. Everything seemed fine. 'We're on the March with Kenny's Army ...' When you're in a large crowd you can't see what might be happening just yards away from you. A big open terrace like the Kop allowed you to roam wherever you liked once you'd entered it. This Leppings Lane end was a smaller terrace, split into pens with fences that were specifically designed to keep supporters in a particular area. Many or most fans wouldn't have realised that the area directly behind the goal was split down the middle into two pens, with radial fences preventing access either side. It was only later that I learned that the area we'd been in was called pen 4. The perimeter fence down the front was to keep fans off the pitch. Being a young lad and with grounds having looked like this since well before I started going, there was no sense of wariness at all about this set-up.

BARRY DEVONSIDE

Once we eventually got inside, Chris and Jason went off to the terracing and I took up my seat. I had a seat in the North Stand, which was to the side of the pitch. I went up there and found my seat and looked over to the right, and I saw Chris straight away. I could hardly miss him. Our supporters didn't really wear the football shirts, in those days, but Chris was wearing a Wales international rugby union shirt – bright red with a white collar. I could see him as clear as anything, there behind the goal, about 2.35 p.m. That was the last time I saw him alive.

JOHN ALDRIDGE

When we came out for the warm-up, you were aware that something didn't seem right – but your head is completely focused on the game. You could see that the middle section of our end was already packed, yet the side areas were almost empty. To me, that wasn't *that* unusual. I used to go on the Kop, I was used to seeing our crowd packed shoulder-to-shoulder; I was aware of the rituals, the excitement. Everyone has their 'spec', you know, but for the biggest games you all want to try to get in the middle. I knew how important it was to our fans to be right behind the goal, where you'd get the best atmosphere. So I didn't think too much more about it. I just thought, 'If that was me, that's where I'd be …'

JOHN MACKIN

I found my seat, about halfway up the stand, just on the halfway line: a great view. Someone then pointed out that Billy Liddell was sitting a few rows in front of us. I clambered over the seats and asked for his autograph. He signed my match-ticket stub with a beautiful copperplate signature, in fountain pen. 'Touch of class,' I thought, just like Billy. I told him I loved him, hugged him, and returned to my seat.

MARTIN THOMPSON

I was sitting with a few lads in the North Stand, about midway between the goal and the halfway line. We noticed that it was starting to build up a bit, in the middle. Now, you were used to seeing packed terracing, there was nothing out of the ordinary about that – but we commented on the fact the sides were almost empty. You could clearly see the steps of the terraces either side so, you know, I could see that from where I was … I'm sure the police officers who were right there must have been able to see it. But I thought nothing of it at this point. I wasn't worried at all.

DANNY RHODES

Because you've been to football a lot you know football grounds and football crowds – and if you've been there enough, you just know when things don't look right. And I distinctly remember about 25, 20 minutes before kick-off, saying to my friend – not only was our end a little less busy than I'd expected it to be, but their end, the Liverpool end … it was weird: from where we were standing, the right-hand pen and the one in the corner were virtually empty. And so were the pens to the left, and I remember my friend and me joking that Liverpool hadn't sold their allocation … At first I suppose it was just naïve amusement, I don't know – but the whole thing just didn't make sense. But we knew that something wasn't right – simple as that. If you knew football, you knew something was up.

THE TAYLOR REPORT

65. At 2.44 p.m. Mr Marshall radioed for reinforcements, for the Tannoy to request the crowd to stop pushing, and for a vehicle with loudspeaker equipment to come and request the same. Unhappily, at about 2.40 p.m., radio communication on channel 25 became defective. For a period of two or three minutes the control room lost contact. A communications officer came promptly and switched to the standby station. With the use of a handset at control, contact was restored. Despite this hiatus, two of Mr Marshall's requests were received. The Tannoy was used but with little effect. Reinforcements, including mounted officers from Penistone Road, were sent. The third request, for a Land Rover, was received direct by its driver PC Buxton who arrived at 2.46 p.m. and urged the crowd by loudspeaker not to push.

JOHN ASHTON

We were sat on the wall, by the river. All around us it was just one huge crowd, shouting and screaming. It was mayhem. There was a police Land Rover parked up and I went over and knocked on the window and said to the police guys – this is on record, it's in the notes, in the panel report – 'Look, you need to do something about this. Someone's going to get seriously hurt.'

STEVE HART

The first people I saw as I came through was a copper and a couple of stewards and I said to them straight away, 'You're going to have to do something, it's chaos out there. You've lost it, it's absolute chaos. Somebody's going to die.'

THE TAYLOR REPORT

66. Between 2.40 p.m. and 2.45 p.m. the crowd inside and outside the turnstile approach had swelled to over 5,000. At the head of the phalanx conditions had become intolerable. Those who got through were short of breath and sweating profusely. Many complained to police officers on the concourse inside the turnstiles and asked them in forceful terms to do something. Exit gates A and B were being shaken. It was clear the crowd could not pass through the turnstiles by 3 p.m. Police Constable Buxton radioed from the Land Rover to control asking that kick-off be postponed. The suggestion was acknowledged but rejected.

DAMIAN KAVANAGH

It's hard to say exactly how near the front we were; maybe halfway back, but still close enough to the front. We were leaning backwards on to a crush-barrier, like we would in the Kop. We were well used to riding the waves of the crowd surges. It's the reverse of what happens at grounds now. These days when somebody gets excited and stands up, it forces everybody behind to do the same in ripple effect if they want to see the action. Back in those days, somebody would strain forward to see the action, causing a domino effect that would stop at the crush-barriers. It could hurt going up against those barriers with the force of the crowd behind, so I always got my back to the barriers – and with plenty of people in front of me, whenever I could. Being young, fit and only a little fella I could wriggle my way around the terraces.

THE TAYLOR REPORT

67. Superintendent Marshall realised the crowd had become unmanageable. Although loath to do so, since it was contrary to basic police strategy, he decided to request the exit gates be opened to relieve the pressure. Otherwise, he feared fatalities would occur. Other senior officers outside the ground agreed. At 2.47 p.m. he radioed control to permit the gates to be opened. At 2.48 p.m., while Mr Duckenfield was considering the request, gate C opened to eject a youth who had climbed in with no ticket. Immediately, fans outside took advantage and about 150 managed to get in before a mounted officer enabled the gate to be closed again. Mr Marshall repeated his request. Still no response from control. He repeated it a third time, adding that if the gates were not opened someone was going to be killed. In the control room, Mr Duckenfield had not made a decision. Mr Murray asked him, 'Are you going to open the gates?' Mr Duckenfield gave the order and Sgt Goddard radioed to Mr Marshall, 'Open the gates.' Neither the club control room nor any police officers inside the turnstiles were told of this order before or after it was given or of any action it would require.

68. At 2.52 p.m., gate C was opened wide. Fans behind turnstiles A to G and from the concourse beyond came round to flow through it in large numbers.

69. About two minutes later the pressure outside gate A led Sgt Higgins to radio, despite the gateman's objection, for it to be opened. If it was not, he said, 'It'll go and someone will get killed.' Permission was given, but this time reserve serials were alerted to monitor the inrush towards the North Stand. Gate B was also briefly opened against the gateman's wishes and about 200 of those pressed at turnstiles A to G gained entry to their left.

70. The largest entry, however, was through gate C. In the five minutes it was open about 2,000 fans passed through it steadily at a fast walk. Some may have had tickets for the stands. No doubt some had no tickets at all. The majority had tickets for the terraces. Of these, some found their way either right, to pens 1 and 2, or left through the dividing wall to 6 and 7. But a large proportion headed straight for the tunnel in front of them.

PETER CARNEY

I didn't experience too much of the madness outside. It was well known, even then, that the stadium didn't have enough turnstiles for the numbers it was letting in, and that was a significant factor in why the disaster happened. The stadium was not fit to take the amount they were inviting in; but we were OK, at that point. I bumped into a lad I knew on the concourse. Him and his girl had just had a baby son not long before, so I spoke to him and congratulated them, and told him the good news about me and Tina. I actually said about the gate being open, I said, 'Look at that, they're letting all hands in, here.'

STEVE HART

I'd lost my mates in the mêlée outside, so I thought I'd just wait a while on the concourse, wait for them to come through the turnstile, then I'd go down the tunnel with them. So I'm standing there waiting, and I heard this police officer and a couple of stewards saying they were going to open a gate. I actually saw them unlock the gate and people started coming through. They never poured through, they weren't even jogging – it was a steady walk. When it all started being reported over the next few days, the police's official line was that a 'tanked-up mob' had stormed the gates and swarmed in. It weren't like that. People were walking. Loads came in, like, when the concertina gate was opened, but they were not running. There was so many coming in now, I thought, 'Well, there's no point in waiting for my mates here.' So I headed off straight down the tunnel.

JEGSY DODD

I got in without my ticket being checked. If you look at the footage – everyone's seen it now, the moments leading up to when they open the concertina gate – you can see a pair of white training shoes perched on a wall inside the concourse. That's me when I got inside the ground, so I saw everything that happened.

When the police and stewards opened the gates, most people headed straight down the tunnel to the middle section – but our little crew had this thing about not wanting to be with the singing mob. We always thought it was cool to do our own thing and stand to one side. Our little gang had all met on the Anfield Road end and the attitude there was to do the opposite of what the Kopites did. Even at away games, we'd always stand to one side. The cool lads who didn't wear colours never went in the middle, and that turned out to be our saviour at Hillsborough. We just automatically went to the right-hand side.

I'd been there the previous year and got so badly crushed that I'd climbed over to the seated area. As I climbed up to the seats I saw a lad I knew, Ally Edwards, and he was saying, 'You're all hooligans.' Even though I knew he was joking, I said to him, 'No, there's people getting badly crushed down there.' So I wasn't happy about going back in that end for such a big game anyway but, like I say, we stood to the right-hand side as you looked at the pitch. Even from where we were, you could see that it was really, really packed in the middle sections. That was the first thing that struck you.

PETER CARNEY

We heads into the tunnel, starts shuffling forward and there's more people arriving behind us. And at this point, the teams come out;

the players come out while we were still in the tunnel, edging our way forward. It was just a slow shuffle forward, inch by inch, but I was used to that. Then I lost my footing. I wasn't knocked over, nothing like that. I just lost my footing in the tunnel. But that was where I suddenly just went, whoosh! Because I'd stopped moving, I was just thrown by the momentum into the terrace – and I was facing backwards. And obviously I knew that was wrong, but when I was trying to get myself turned round to face the match I said to someone, 'Oh, it's just the start of the match, everyone jockeying, you know …' But it was hard. It was hard just to get turned round. And I never stood still from that point on. I was always moving.

STEVE HART

As you went down the tunnel there were two pens, 3 and 4. I went into the pen on the right. Again, it was packed but, you know, it was a semi-final, I expected that. I wanted to be behind the goal, it was the place to be. There's nothing of me anyway – I'm only thin – so I squeezed my way in. It was packed, like, but so what – it was the norm. But the pressure carried on building up. Now, I've been stood on the Kop for years. I've been to away games, everywhere. I was used to crowds, but I knew something wasn't right.

And everyone around us was thinking the same. The pressure was building and building and they're all saying, 'Push back.' And we're going, 'Where to? There's nowhere to go!' And it's building up and building up. And you could see people were starting to get really worried.

TONY O'KEEFE

We got upstairs and settled down. We were three or four rows from the front, looking down on to the terracing below. Now, we'd all been to big games, we'd been in the Kop – we knew that everyone liked to get as close to the middle as they could. It used to annoy me as a kid, the way the bigger fellas would just muscle you out of your spec when you'd be there for ages. I was only small, so I used to get inside the ground really early, get myself a great spec. I used to love the way the atmosphere would gradually build up; I loved seeing the teams come out on to the pitch. Then some big docker would come and stand right in front of you!

But straight away, this time, you're looking down and you can see this very, very tightly packed area right behind the goal, yet both the areas to the side are more or less empty. You could see the bare terracing by the corner flags either side. There was nobody there. I said to the others, 'That looks a bit hectic, doesn't it?' The sight of it made such an impression on me that I took some photos. Of course, we didn't know about the pens down there, the radial fences stopping any sideways movement. We were used to terraces where, if a particular spec became too crowded, you'd just move backwards or sideways or forward until you were comfortable again. We noticed a kid in a white shirt being taken out, and someone standing over him. He looked bad, you know, and I said to my brothers, 'He looks like he's had a heart attack.' We couldn't see the back of the terrace from where we were, just the front section behind the goal, and it was really, really, badly packed. We were just all looking at each other, going, 'That doesn't look right.'

JEGSY DODD

Not long after we took up our positions I could see a lad down behind the goal getting mouth-to-mouth, and I remember looking around me, thinking, 'There's something not right here.' I said to one of the lads who was with us, 'That lad is dead, look at him. He's dead.' And all around you, you were starting to hear these screams and you just knew then that something horrible was happening. I was starting to get a bit hysterical, thinking about the crushing the previous year and, even though you had no clear view of what was going on in those central pens, instinctively you knew: our fans were getting crushed.

THE TAYLOR REPORT

71. The initial influx through gate C, augmented by entrants via the turnstiles, came through the tunnel with great momentum. Fans spoke of being swept through, feet off the ground. The 1:6 gradient accelerated their progress.

JOHN ASHTON

We just sat on the wall by the river and, after a while, it all eased off, and we went in. I bought a couple of programmes from the little kiosk at the foot of the stairs, then we went up the little staircase to the right. We'd got seats for the West Stand, the seated area above the Leppings Lane terracing. There was no way I was going in there after the year before. We got to the top of the stand and couldn't get down the aisles to our seats because of the crowds of people coming in, up the front, from the terracing below. Carl was helping pull people up from below. So we had to clamber over the seats to get down to the second row, where our seats were. And once we eventually sat down, you could see this scene that was beginning to unfold on the pitch.

DAMIAN KAVANAGH

The crowd pressure was ever-increasing and the lads on the crush-barrier behind me were really struggling. There were just so many people in one condensed area, it was insufferable. There's no way in the world that the police or anyone else looking on and watching that end would not have known that crowd was in distress. It was chaos – as bad as I'd ever experienced – and it was getting worse. It didn't feel like a surge, more like steadily increasing overcrowding. I'd been to loads of matches when the crowd pressure had been uncomfortable and where, at times, you had no control over your own movement. There had been many occasions when people had fainted, or were just so overwhelmed that they were pushed upwards and carried over the heads of the crowd, then ferried down by outstretched hands to the front of the Kop for the St John's Ambulance gang to look after them – but this was something else again. I had never known a build-up of crowd pressure like it.

A man immediately behind one of my shoulders who looked about 30ish to me – slightly long, mousy hair and a dark blue shirt – was asking us to help push him back under the strain. He was trying to get under the crush-barrier. 'Come on, lads, help us here, push me back.' We tried to lean backwards towards him while he pushed at our backs, but our movements were restricted and he couldn't make any progress against the crowd behind him, anyway. He asked us to kick the soles of his shoes, so he could maybe spring over the barrier, but it was no use, he wasn't going anywhere.

A man immediately behind my other shoulder was in pain and couldn't even try to help himself any more. He was just pleading, 'Please … please … please …'

PETER CARNEY

Then there was a big surge, diagonally right – and I could see bodies on the floor. At this stage, the thought goes through your mind, 'This is bad news, this. Someone's bound to have got hurt. I've got to get myself steady.' So in the next movement – people stumbling, falling forward and we can't control where we're going – I managed to just work my way bit by bit to what I thought was a safe place. I felt the edge of a barrier and I managed to get just in front of it, with one line of people behind me. I thought I'd be OK there, but it didn't get any easier. It's like you're caught in a vice that's gradually increasing the pressure, getting tighter and tighter. All the time I was stood by the barrier, I was still getting moved around – I was never stood still. And this goes on for a while, like that: tighter and tighter. It goes on to such a point where I'm struggling for my breath. I was screaming out to the copper in front of us at first, but he was blanking us. I'm panicking and screaming out, and then I thought: 'I've got to conserve my energy here, just keep my breathing going.'

DAMIAN KAVANAGH

About six feet in front of me a fella said, 'Come on, lads, let's get this young girl out.' And people tried to help. She looked maybe 12 years old or so, with dark hair. I can't say I know what happened to her.

The singing had completely stopped around me by now, with everybody struggling. There were cries for help, cries of pain and cries to the police just a matter of yards in front of us to open the gates at the perimeter fence. The police were ignoring the requests, and I caught the eyes of this one policeman. Now, as a 20-year-old lad, I wasn't confident or worldly when it came to dealing with the police. In my experience, if you spoke to them, it only ended one way. But things were desperate – I was pleading with him, 'Open the gate.' He just looked at me, pointed behind me and mouthed at me to get back, which of course was totally impossible. At this point I thought, 'These people are not going to get me out of here.'

PETER CARNEY

I'm completely unable to move now – my legs have gone numb and my arms are trapped down by my sides. So I've tried to work my arms free, and I'm thinking, 'I'll just try to stay still and concentrate on my breathing.' And now, for the first time, you really are starting to think about, you know … it crosses your mind that this is really, really serious. The fella next to me … I couldn't move at all by now and he's right there, turning blue. Still the copper in front of us was taking no notice. We're shouting out to him, 'People are getting crushed here! Get us out!'

STEVE HART

This kid, just a few feet away, he just went. And everyone started panicking. Everyone started screaming at this copper to open the gate. He was just standing by the gate and basically just ignoring everyone. So people started trying to climb over the fence, but the fences then were angled backwards. They were designed to keep you in, so to get over them was virtually impossible anyway. And we're screaming at this copper to open this gate, and the pressure's building up and building up and everyone's screaming and crying now, it's horrible.

DANNY RHODES

About ten to three, there was a big influx of Forest fans. Where we were in our end it went from being comfortable to one of those feelings you get on terraces where, even among your own group, you're thinking, 'Should I move back?' But then it settled down a bit and the game started. And, even in that heat, it was played at a blistering intensity. Within the first few seconds Stuart Pearce kneed someone in the back and, if it was today, he'd probably get sent off. I don't think he even got a talking-to. But it was really fast-paced: Forest got a couple of corners, Beardsley hit the bar – even that made me think, 'This is our day. That would have gone in last year …' But then, at that stage, you started taking your eye off the game because Liverpool fans were starting to appear on the pitch, and it's obvious there was something going on, that end.

PETER CARNEY

Next thing, the match kicks off and all I can think is to try to keep breathing. I remember watching Garry Parker running, but it was a weird eye-line, like he was at the very edges of my vision. I felt detached from the whole thing. I was looking at the stand and looking at individual players, but inside I'm just trying to concentrate on keeping myself breathing. By now my legs have completely gone. I can't feel them at all. And my vision is just getting higher. At the time I told myself I was just trying to find things to look at, to keep my mind occupied, you know, 'Just concentrate on something and try to stay alert.' But looking back on it now, I must have been tilting my head back, trying to get air – like a fish dipping itself upwards, out of water. And that's why my eye-line has changed, too.

Anyway, my eye-line just goes higher and higher to the point where I'm just seeing clouds, but it's strange – it's like a pipe-vision of a cloud, like I'm viewing it through a tube, and all my vision is covered by this white cotton wool; it's even softer than that, it's just cloud. I start going down this pipe and it's now … I'm looking down on myself in the pen, surrounded by this group of people, and my head is lower than them, I'm sinking, below shoulder height to them, and they're this perfect circle, and I'm getting crushed; I'm going down. I'm above their heads watching myself getting crushed. And the next thing is that everything's black.

DAMIAN KAVANAGH

It was a very clear message in my head: the police, the St John's Ambulance, these people are not going to help you. The copper who'd told me to get back, he was only a few feet away. How could he *not* have seen the carnage that was going on? How could he have remained immune to it? He's there, he's watching people getting crushed, he can hear the screaming …

OK, so the investigative process is focused on the people at the top and their role in the tragedy, and rightly so, but I'd like to think that, whatever uniform I had on, if I can see people dying around me and I'd had orders not to open the gates … I think I'd have gone against orders. I think I'd have opened those gates and pulled people out. I don't think they froze. Either they were incompetent, or they were terrified of the consequences ... or they just didn't care. I am not having it that they didn't know, they didn't see what was going on – so I think some of those everyday bobbies who just stood there have got questions to answer, too.

STEVE ROTHERAM

My seat was a few rows back and to the left of the goal, so I didn't fully appreciate the way that things deteriorated so quickly on the terraces below. After nearly two decades of going to the game I sort of 'felt' when something wasn't quite right, even if I couldn't actually see it. A sixth sense, if you like. I don't think I was aware of anything serious until the game had started. To my right I could see a few people being pulled into the stand from below, but at first just put it down to someone pulling their friend up so they could sit together. At that stage it was a case of one eye on the football, with the occasional glances to the right.

There was definitely something going on below us, you could sense the agitation growing. But then people started appearing on the fences and actually on the edge of the pitch – and the atmosphere changed completely.

People were collapsing in front of your very eyes – and you were standing there, disbelieving what you're seeing. It was like a surreal dream, a nightmare; I saw a very young lad, a teenager, die in front of my eyes. There were other people who managed to climb out and who fell to the ground, distraught – not in physical agony but in floods of tears, traumatised by what they'd just witnessed. And then there were others, catatonic, just walking around in a daze, but not going anywhere, just … out of it. There was all of that, all going on at once and you're sitting thinking, 'What is this? What's happening?'

People in the seats around me, people I had never met before suddenly became confidantes as we tried to work out what was actually happening.

Wild conjecture raged, but we weren't sure what was happening despite the pitch now being strewn with people in obvious distress. Then I saw fans giving fellow fans mouth to mouth. I was simply stunned at the scale of what was happening.

IAN RUSH

The game started, and me and Phil Thompson had just sat down on the bench and, next thing, people started coming over the fences. At first it looked like the police were just sending them straight back in. But you could tell straight away it was something serious. We could probably see it better with being on the subs' bench. If you were playing, you might not have known what was going on. You wouldn't have seen as much of what was happening, but I remember Thommo saying to me, 'There's something seriously wrong, here.'

JOHN BARNES

I came back to help defend a corner. We were defending the Leppings Lane end, attacking the Nottingham Forest end. Now, even though Liverpool had such a big following, everywhere, you got used to seeing some of the same faces, week in, week out. Especially when you went out for the warm-up, they'd be standing in more or less the same place, wherever we went. And, standing there, defending the near post, you began to pick out familiar faces. I saw a couple of the girls we'd always see, cheering us on, and I thought, 'That doesn't look good.' They were squashed right up against the fence. Usually they'd be full of it, you know – excited, happy. Not this time. I looked at them and I thought, 'That just does not look good at all.'

STEPHEN WRIGHT

I'm in the North Stand, some distance from the Leppings Lane end, but I see people starting to get pulled up, up to the seating above. Next thing, I see this St John's Ambulance person walking this kid along the touchline and, straight away, you could see his arm was broken. From his elbow, you could it hanging down, then across. And I start thinking to myself, 'There's something going on here.' I looked down towards our end and, of course, people are starting to come over the fence by this time. Just ones and twos at this stage, and the Forest fans all start booing. And my hackles start going up then, you know – our Graham's in there. But then Peter Beardsley hit the bar and that diverted your attention.

PETER HOOTON

I got to my seat just as Peter Beardsley hit the bar. I was in the North Stand, towards the Spion Kop, the Forest end – more or less in line with the edge of the penalty area. I could see something going on behind the goal. Straight away, after what had happened the year before, I thought it must be overcrowding again. To me, it was obvious that what was happening had nothing to do with hooliganism. Anyone with even the most basic experience of going to the match would have known that. There was no way there would be Forest fans in the Liverpool end. Even from where I was sitting, towards the other end of the ground, my immediate reaction was that it was overcrowding.

DANNY RHODES

By now a lot of fans are spilling over the fences, on to the pitch, and the first reaction is, 'Oh, there's trouble.' And there's no getting away from it – there were chants and booing. A lot of Forest fans will tell you the same thing – you feel guilty, but it's just your initial reaction to what you're seeing. Football fans give each other stick. You're not thinking, are you? You're in that pack mentality and I think that, initially, most football fans would react the same. But then you start to wonder what is actually going on there. Because I'd never seen real trouble inside the ground. A bit between Forest and Leicester, plenty of incidents outside the ground, but *inside*? All I'd ever seen was the police or the stewards moving people from one pen to another, and that's what I thought was going on there. It was a boiling hot day, their end had become overcrowded, and the stewards were moving people out. Nothing out of the ordinary – it'll settle down in a minute. But, of course, it didn't.

JOHN MACKIN

The game started at a furious pace, end to end. It was only when the guy came on and started shouting at Bruce Grobbelaar that I really started to take notice of what was going on in our goalmouth. The trickle became a stream and then a torrent, as people clambered out over the railings and on to the pitch. The Forest fans began booing

– they thought it was a pitch invasion – and, even as the pitch was filling up with dazed, staggering people, bent double and clearly in distress, they continued to berate the Liverpool fans. We didn't know anybody had died at this point – but anyone could see that it was very, very serious. I can clearly still see one fella walking towards our stand, trying to hold his arm up at the elbow. His forearm had broken in two places and was now forming a letter 'z'. It was a shocking sight, yet still we had no idea of the scale of what was happening in the Leppings Lane.

TONY O'KEEFE

Some of our fans were screaming at Bruce Grobbelaar, and that was when I knew it was something serious. He kept turning round. Normally a goalkeeper will just focus straight ahead, eye on the ball the whole time – nothing will distract them. But Bruce kept looking back – you could see he was worried by what was unfolding behind him.

DAMIAN KAVANAGH

I then noticed somebody go to Bruce Grobbelaar and remonstrate with him but there still seemed to be no help coming to us. I knew I was really in trouble now, in great danger, and I remember thinking, 'I hope my mum hasn't heard about this.' Because she'd only have worried. I knew my dad would be listening to the match commentary back home on the radio.

Despite the pleading with the police to open the gates nothing was being done and I knew that I was on my own here, if I wanted out – and I knew that I *had* to get out. How on earth could what was happening to us behind that goal have been missed, or even worse … ignored? I was struggling to breathe and I remember thinking, 'Oh God, please get me out!', but I stayed very calm and focused on getting through this nightmare.

I didn't even notice that the match had been stopped. Me and Bailey saw a couple of lads going past us, over the heads, down to the gate at the front. We agreed that this was the only way out, but we were too restricted to make any progress. I had the use of my hands above my shoulders but a lot a people didn't. I always had my arms up this way at the match to help me move about. My dad had always told me to know where the exit to any place was, always know the way out of any trouble – and this is in my nature anyway.

I don't know how he did it, but Bailey got himself halfway up so his chest and shoulders were above the crowd. I lent my hand and pushed his foot up, and suddenly he'd made it on to the top of the crowd. I shouted, 'Get me out!', but he had no way of helping me. He crawled over the top of the crowd, to the gate down at the front. I saw him escape, which was a relief. I shouted after him, 'Just get out, Bailey, get out!'

PETER CARNEY

I'm getting thumped on the chest. I think what's happened is I've fallen under the barrier and I've found a pocket of air. And, in falling and hitting the terrace, that's what's given me the jolt and kicked me into action again. And I'm getting thumped all over my torso, belly and chest and, again, looking back, I'm taking that as people passing me over their heads down to the front, and I'm drifting in and out.

But then the next sensation I've had is just black, and noise. My vision is completely black, and there's this thumping starts to come into it. Now, it's most likely that this is someone giving me heart massage out the back, but the next sensation that I have is this echoing noise, and my limbs feeling completely stretched. It's like I'm on my back and there's someone on every limb and they're carrying me backwards. I hadn't been able to feel my limbs in the pen, but the sensation is coming back and, when I've woke, I'm looking at the wall. This red brick wall comes into view and I can see the sky beyond it and my first conscious thought is, 'I'm here. I'm here.' And the unwritten line is '… on this earth, still.'

MARTIN THOMPSON

I saw one fan running towards the halfway line. I thought to myself, 'Jesus! What's that idiot doing?' You didn't want the club getting a bad name. I had no idea, obviously, what kind of distress the fans in those central pens were in.

More and more people started spilling on to the pitch then, and it became clear what was going on. To anyone who'd been going to the match for a few years, it was absolutely obvious that it wasn't hooliganism we were seeing. People were lying flat out on the side of the pitch.

DANNY RHODES

A Liverpool fan appears on the pitch and comes right down our end, gesticulating at the Forest fans. You're thinking, 'What's this drunk idiot doing on the pitch, ruining it for everyone?' And there's more booing and chanting. *Now*, it's obvious what he was doing. He's trying to get the message across to the rest of the crowd – this is not what you think it is. But at the time …

TONY O'KEEFE

By now, our fans are starting to climb up the perimeter fences, some are beginning to spill over on to the pitch, there are people on the sidelines. Someone said, 'They're invading the pitch! What's going on? Why are they invading the pitch?' But I looked down and I said, 'No, they're not. Look, they're not even on the touchline, they're just milling around … something has happened.' Instinctively, I'm not sure why, but I began taking photos of what was happening down below. I don't know why – it must have struck me that what was unfolding was seriously bad. I could see the volunteers, you know – the St John Ambulance people all shouting to each other and gesticulating. They looked lost.

DAMIAN KAVANAGH

I managed to wriggle myself upwards, above the crowd. Some fella who was stuck there himself stretched out his hand: 'Here y'are, mate!' He held my foot, so I could drag myself upwards on to the top of the crowd. I crawled over people's heads down towards the gate at the front – about 20 feet or so in front of me, by now – so it came up very fast. As I got to the gate, I heard somebody shout to me, 'There's people dying here!' I already knew.

I grabbed the top of the frame at the opened gate and was about to haul myself out, when a policeman aggressively grabbed hold of me with both hands at my chest, stopping me going any further. He shouted at me, pushing me back, and I quote: 'You fucking twat!'

That's what he shouted at me. And I just thought, 'No way am I going back in there.'

I've seen his statement since, and to say he was batting for his side is an understatement. I didn't do that. Me, a traumatised 20-year-old man, declined the opportunity to make a complaint. I said no, because that copper has just witnessed hell on earth. That's the way I thought about it at the time, immediately after. That fella has just witnessed the most extreme scenes and maybe he's frozen and maybe the sight of us having to crawl over the top of people's heads to get out has sparked him into action, belatedly. I was prepared to think that. I was honourable towards that copper; I gave him the bounce of the ball. But now I've read his statement, and I know that he didn't give me the bounce of the ball. He batted for the conspiracy. So who's the 'fucking twat'?

Anyway, I knew I was in mortal danger in that pen. I knew he wasn't going to let me out, and I knew there was no way I was going back in there. Despite knowing that you don't go against bizzies if you want to stay clear of trouble for yourself, I knew this was very different, and I tried to force my way past him from my vulnerable position. It worked: as I tried to get through the gate he dragged me out and then threw me down on to the shingle track around the pitch.

TONY O'KEEFE

More and more people were spilling on to the pitch. I said to my brother, Kevin, 'I think I should get down there, see if I can help.' I think he was worried for me and we left it a few minutes, but the situation just got worse. People were getting pulled up from the terracing into the stands. Others started being laid out on the pitch-side; some of them looked gone. That was it. I started to make my way down from the stand.

STEVE HART

It was chaos. There's people getting pulled up at the back, up into the seats above, there's people screaming for the gate to be opened. I don't know what happened next but, somehow, in the overall push of the crowd, I find myself getting dragged out through the gate. I remember getting out on to the pitch and I literally fell over. I mean, the gate's not much wider than a door, it's about 3 feet wide and there's people screaming to get out. So I climbed back up the railings and we're trying to pull people out but it was virtually impossible. You're trying to get them up and over, the weight of me anyway, I'm not a big lad, I was struggling to get anyone over. I was shattered.

THE TAYLOR REPORT

75. At 3.04 p.m., Beardsley for Liverpool struck the crossbar at the Kop end. There was a roar from the Liverpool fans and at the same time a powerful surge forwards in pen 3. The several surges which occurred after the influx from gate C carried the pressure down the pens towards the pitch. The force became such as to twist and break two spans of a crush-barrier towards the front of pen 3. The evidence does not establish with certainty when this happened. Probably it was triggered by the surge at 3.04 p.m. But I am sure it occurred after the influx from gate C so greatly increased the pressure in the pen. When the barrier broke those whom it had supported were projected towards the perimeter fence. Many fell and the involuntary rush of those behind pressed them down. The crushing force was transmitted and dispersed so that all along the front of pen 3 fans were pressed hard up against the low wall and the wire mesh of the fence above it.

76. In pen 4 no barrier broke. Nevertheless those at the front were crushed against wall and fence. Further back, two barriers were bowed and some individuals succumbed to the pressure around them.

77. Surges on terraces are common. Usually, they go forward, then recede. Here, with the weight of numbers, there was no receding. The pressure stayed and for those crushed breathless by it, standing or prone, life was ebbing away. If no relief came in four minutes there would be irreversible brain damage; if longer, death.

TONY O'KEEFE

I went round the back and, already, they were starting to lay people out on the floor behind the central tunnel. They seemed lifeless – just laid out there, on the concrete, people trying to help them. I got down pitch-side – I think it must have been the side passage I went down, it was all a blur, but I was completely focused on getting on the pitch. I showed my ID to a couple of coppers and said, 'I want to try and help,' and they pulled me up on to the pitch, they seemed glad of the help. A first-aid guy gave me an armband and for a second I just kind of stood there trying to take it all in. I was thinking, 'Right, who do I go to first?' Some of those lying behind the goal had friends, or people, anyway, trying to help them. I'll never be able to stop thinking about that – how so many everyday fans reacted so quickly to what was going on. I'm standing there, watching all these people who had little or no knowledge of first aid, just *take over*. It was the fans, not the authorities, who took control of the situation: getting people on to stretchers, getting them to the first-aid point, getting them seen to.

The first person I saw was this lad leaning over another lad and I thought, 'Right, let's have a look at him,' and I went looking for a pulse. Checked his neck, checked his wrist, checked his groin. The groin is one of the strongest pulses, but no, there was nothing. I thought, 'What do I do now?' His mate was saying, 'Can you do anything?' I started giving him mouth-to-mouth, four or five breaths. You're trying to do your thing, looking down his chest, trying to listen out for a sign, but there's so much noise going on, it's so loud that you start to get a bit lost. Because when you're in the fire brigade you work with someone, there's always someone with you. And one of the first things you're taught is: stay with your casualty. So I tried chest compressions, more mouth-to-mouth. I was doing this for about a minute – maybe I should have given it longer – went back to chest compressions and, this time, it was stomach contents. And, you know, at that point that it's too late to do anything. I'm in this weird dilemma with his mate asking if he's going to be all right, and ... well ... he's not. It's not even a case of putting him into the recovery position. The recovery position doesn't come into it. He's dead.

PETER CARNEY

So, sound comes back – it's a different sort of sound. Before it was just this disconnected noise, but this is different. You can start to make things out – it's real sound. With that, I can start to focus on things. There's three coppers stood in front of me, by this fella with a bloated belly and a Wrangler jacket covering his face, right next to the wall. And I've thought, 'Much use you are, minding the dead.' Mick, the lad that I went in with, comes out and starts tapping me on the shoulder, walks around me and sees me crying, you know – I'm alive. Now, I don't know whether I've been put in the recovery position or I'm laid out on my back for dead. I don't remember any jumper over my head or anything, so I don't think I've been left for dead – but I don't know.

JOHN ALDRIDGE

You were aware that something was going on behind the goal. Something major. People were getting hauled up, people were climbing out, fans started sitting down behind the goal and along the touchline. It's been pretty well documented by now but Peter Beardsley hit the bar, and that seemed to trigger something even bigger. Suddenly, there was loads, you know – people were on the pitch, everywhere. Lads started pulling down the hoardings at the sides and, at that point, the ref stops the game.

DANNY RHODES

More and more police appear on the pitch, and one runs across to the referee and the next thing the game's stopping. The players go off and, again, you feel really guilty – but your initial feeling is, 'Ah, come on – how long is this going to take? This is the FA Cup semi-final. When's the match going to restart?' That's what is going through your mind. It's human nature, but you can't help feeling guilty when you think about it afterwards.

PETER HOOTON

More and more people started coming on to the pitch. The ref blew his whistle and began to lead the teams off the pitch. But, at that stage, most people inside the ground would have thought it would be a five- or ten-minute delay. But then, more and more people were spilling on to the pitch. The Forest fans were booing and singing, 'You scouse bastards!' It was pretty loud. So that was their initial reaction – not that the crowd was in danger, but that it was some kind of a disturbance. And then a small group of Liverpool fans ran towards their end. To some people it might have looked like a charge on the Forest fans, but they weren't giving it the Leeds Fingers; they weren't being aggressive. They were pointing and gesticulating back towards the Leppings Lane end, as though they were trying to tell the rest of the crowd what was going on down there. It wasn't 'You Scouse Bastards' – it was something much more serious than that.

THE TAYLOR REPORT

78. In the control room no one noticed the overcrowding or anything amiss in pens 3 and 4 until the first fans spilt out on to the perimeter track just before kick-off. Then, the officers in command assumed that there was an attempted pitch invasion. They called up reserve serials waiting in the gymnasium and all available officers elsewhere to go to the pitch. A request was made to HQ for dog handlers.

79. Superintendent Greenwood, the Ground Commander, was by the players' tunnel at the kick-off. He noticed fans on the track and went to the west end behind the goal. As he approached, he did not think the pens overcrowded until he was very close and saw those pressed against the fence. Even then, he thought the situation 'retrievable' if those higher up the pen relieved the pressure. He climbed on the wall below the fence and signalled with both hands to those behind to move back. Other officers joined him. It was impossible. Those fans who would have wished to comply were powerless to do so. Behind them, there were still many unaware of the crisis, watching the game. The football continued to joyous shouting and singing round the rest of the ground while those crushed and trapped slowly expired.

80. When Mr Greenwood's signals to move back proved fruitless, he tried to radio for the match to be stopped. At first, his message was not received by control, so he signalled with his arms towards the control box. Mr Duckenfield sent Mr Murray down from the box to have the match stopped via the linesman, the agreed emergency drill. Before he could do so, Mr Greenwood ran over the pitch to the referee who stopped the game. It was 5 and a half minutes past 3.

BARRY DEVONSIDE

I looked to my right and straight away you could see something was wrong. I had a clear unobstructed view of the pens, and I knew in about 30 seconds that this was not a public order offence. I immediately went cold, as cold as any time in my life. I was frightened for Christopher as I watched the disaster unfold. Liverpool fans were attempting to climb up into the stand above the terraces; others were climbing over the perimeter and radial fences. I saw police officers pushing fans back into the pens as people were struggling to get out. The Liverpool fans began ripping down hoarding to carry the injured. There were hundreds of police officers milling around, not knowing what to do. I saw some officers doing the best they could – three or four of them pounding on young supporters' chests – but what was needed was leadership.

My blood ran cold. I could feel the fear rising and I just tried to blot it out. But anyone, any parent, will tell you the same thing. You can't help yourself. There are people being carried out, but you hope that your own are going to be OK. I was looking over to where I'd last seen Chris, and it was clear to me by now that something was drastically wrong. And I was just gripped by this almighty fear.

TONY O'KEEFE

I was doing a sort of basic, on-the-spot triage, trying to look for people who, you know ... it wasn't too late to help them. I tried this girl for a pulse. No. Tried the next person. No. And then I saw this fireman in uniform, on the pitch, and he had a Maximan. A Maximan is the basic oxygen resuscitator you see in emergencies, with the mask. What happens is, you put the person in the recovery position and put the mask on them and you can set the Maximan to whatever mode – adult, child and so on – and it will breathe for them. So I asked this fireman, 'Where is everybody? How many of these have you got?' And he said they had fifteen appliances outside. I said, 'What do you mean, outside? Why aren't they here, now, being put to use?' He said they'd been told to attend a major disturbance. Most of the firemen were just sitting off outside, awaiting further instructions. I said to him, 'Major disturbance?' and we just looked at each other and looked around at all the everyday fans, orchestrating the rescue. His face said it all.

STEVE HART

We started ripping down the advertising boards and the coppers weren't too happy about that. So they started having a go at us: 'What d'you think you're doing?' All that. And I saw this lad just lying there. He'd obviously been passed out from the crush, and he was just lying there. And there was nobody with him and I started shouting, 'Christ, give us a hand, let's get this kid down the other end!'

JOHN MACKIN

Even as supporters were being ferried across the pitch on advertising hoardings-cum-stretchers, no one really thought there had been fatalities. Then the first one came by with his head wrapped in a jumper, then another, and another. My stomach turned. I think it was this awful, frightening sight that shook me from the kind of inertia that had gripped most onlookers. I made my way quickly to the front of the stand and watched in horror as another apparently dead body was carried by. Then a voice shook me to attention: 'Give us a hand.' It was a bloke trying to get another hoarding off the fascia of the stand, and struggling to unhook it. I leapt over the wall, grappled it off the wall, and we both then ran across the pitch towards what looked like the aftermath of a medieval battle. We dropped the hoarding on to the pitch and manhandled the body of young woman on to it. She was a dead weight. No life. The realisation then hit me and I felt like I'd been punched in the stomach. Her face was covered in a jumper, wrapped tightly round it so it wouldn't come loose.

MARTIN THOMPSON

We went down to the front, and we saw the first of them pulling the advertising hoardings down and using them as makeshift stretchers. We climbed over on to the pitch to see what we could do. I saw this lad, Tony Grier, who had gone in with Stuart and his mates. I said to him, 'Where's our Stuart?' He's a big lad, Tony, he's about 6 foot 4. He said, 'I was with him, I was right behind him, but I lost him in the crush.' More and more people started coming on to the pitch – there were a couple of thousand milling about, not really knowing what to do or what was going on. One by one, I started bumping into Stuart's mates. Then I saw my mates, and I thought, 'They all know him, they've all been together, they've all been in that pen with him.' And I started getting a bit desperate then.

DAMIAN KAVANAGH

I stood up and I was on the grass right behind the goal. It was the first time I'd ever been on to the pitch at a match. There were people lying on the floor, with others bent over them, trying to revive them – with mouth-to-mouth being given by those who knew how to do it. Some people had been sick. I saw one man whose trousers had been soiled. I knelt down on the pitch myself and started to cry as the enormity of what was happening all around me began to sink in.

I got up and got myself together. I noticed I'd got grass stains on the knees of my jeans. I started to look around for Bailey but, despite knowing loads of people who had gone to the match that day, the only person I saw on the pitch who I knew was Phil from work. 'Are you all right, mate?' I asked, and he was OK.

I noticed that some fans were carrying the injured to the other end of the pitch on advertising boards, clear from the chaos behind our goal and presumably to where they would receive medical treatment. I asked one fella to do the same with somebody who was out of it, but he said, 'Let's get him breathing first.'

I walked over to the side of the pitch and ripped down an advertising board myself, getting a small cut on the fingers of my right hand. The only other physical injury I got that day – which I didn't know until I got back – was a bruise on my back, in the shape of a hand. You could clearly see the finger and thumb marks. This wasn't from being struck but was evidence of the pressure in the pen.

I walked over to one man lying on the floor who was unconscious. I'm sure he was dead, in fact I know it in my heart – but you hear of people getting revived when all seems lost. A couple of young men were standing with me, including one policeman without his helmet on. For a second or so – that lasted for ages – we hesitated, then I dragged this poor Reds fan on to the board myself, thinking, 'Come on, mate, you can make it.' He wasn't tall and seemed maybe just a little older than me, with dark hair. His mouth was open and his eyes were closed. As I dragged him, his trousers came down to just above his knees, showing his underpants – but this didn't matter.

The young constable collected his helmet from the floor at this point and went off, leaving us to it. I got the impression he was relieved that somebody had taken over from him. He might have been going to assist somewhere else, I don't know. We carried the Reds fan as quickly as we could to the other end of the pitch, into the left-hand corner where others were being taken, and left him for the attention of the St John's volunteers. If I'd known how to do mouth-to-mouth I'd have done it.

JOHN ALDRIDGE

The teams go off, but a few of us just stayed out there. We couldn't take it in. Steve McMahon's a scouser, I'm a scouser, we're just, 'What's going on here?' The ref asked us a couple of times to leave the pitch and eventually we start walking off. Graham Kelly appeared and I think we gave him a bit of stick, you know: '*Now* do you understand why Liverpool should have had the bigger end?' He didn't say much.

TONY O'KEEFE

I looked round and saw three or four people standing over this lad on a hoarding. They're starting to lift him, so I jogged over to help – three fans and two coppers, and we ran him down to the other end. We put him down and I couldn't believe the abuse from the Forest fans, all booing and singing, 'Get off the fucking pitch.' I looked up at them, and I caught this copper's eye and … I don't know what I was expecting but I didn't think it'd be naked hostility. His face … he just grimaced at me and I thought, 'You just haven't grasped this, have you?'

JOHN ASHTON

So we're right at the front of the upper stand, and I'm looking down as people start appearing on the pitch; people being laid down, and our fans are starting to make these makeshift stretchers out of the advertising hoardings, and I turn to the boys and I'm pointing down, as injured fans are being laid out, and I say, 'I think he's dead, you know?' And I point down at another. 'I think *he's* dead. He may be dead, too …' And my antennae were up. There's some being laid out on the pitch, in the goalmouth, and you can see they're still alive. Then the announcement went out over the Tannoy for any medics to go and help. So I took the boys to the top of the stairs and told them, 'You wait there.' And I went down to the back of the stand.

STEVE HART

All the injured were getting taken off down towards the Forest end of the ground. The gym, which was by now the emergency first-aid point, was behind the stand at the side. But with all the chaos down our end, the quickest way in was round their end, by the left corner flag. That's where we were being told to take them, so we had to run the length of the pitch with these homemade stretchers. I didn't know any of the people there, who were helping at the time, but we rolled the kid on to the advertising board and we started running him down the pitch. But as we got towards the Forest end, all the coppers were just standing around, looking at us. And I said to them, 'You're no use standing round here, you should be down there, helping people.'

When we got the kid down to the corner, there's already people lying there and there's a couple of first-aid people walking round, probably St John's Ambulance Brigade, with their kit bags and what have you. And some of the people lying there, they were blue. They were dead. It was obvious they were dead. But the kid we carried down – Kevin Williams, as we now know – no way was he dead. It was like he was asleep; but you knew he just needed someone to help him.

So we ran him down there, and I said to this copper, 'Here, look after this kid, he needs help.' And his exact words to me were: 'You just fuck off back down the other end.'

Looking back now, I should have stayed with him but we'd got him down there and that was the right place to get him looked after. There was six of us who carried him, and one of us was an off-duty fireman. We just thought he'd get attention, you know, so me and him just legged it back at that point, to see what else we could do.

TONY O'KEEFE

So we left him there. At that stage, you think you've done the important part. You've got him to where the medical effort is being co-ordinated; you think, 'OK, he'll get looked after, now.' I mean, he wasn't well, but his colour was good, he was breathing. I didn't know, at the time, that the lad was Kevin Williams. But he was alive – him, and others. And I just think that, if I'd … if we'd put them in the recovery position, if they'd had the Maximan, then perhaps they would have had a chance. No matter how I try, I can't *not* think that thought.

PETER HOOTON

Then the police line comes across. I thought, 'They've got this badly wrong, here; they've completely misinterpreted this.' It was a solid line of police from one side of the pitch to another. It was an obvious attempt to prevent this perceived pitch invasion. At first, it was in line with the penalty area, but they moved forward and moved forward, until they got to the halfway line. Again, if you had any basic understanding … there was no way in the world this was a pitch invasion. You'd seen pitch invasions on the telly in the seventies. Ironically, one of the most famous was the Newcastle versus Nottingham Forest game – in the FA Cup quarter-final – where the game had to be replayed after Newcastle fans swarmed on to the pitch. This was nothing like that. Anyone with any football experience would have known that.

STEPHEN WRIGHT

People are all over the pitch by now and I said to myself, 'Our Graham's in there.' So I got down to the front, jumped over, got on to the pitch. The Forest fans by now are all booing, like it's a pitch invasion or something. They're these singing anti-scouse songs – 'There'll be no scouse in Europe' – and booing us, and that really got my back up. But other than that, I was just wandering round in a daze. And I now know that where I was in the penalty area, our Graham was no more than ten feet away from me, lying there, dead, in the corner of the eighteen-yard box. But I was just in a daze.

MARTIN THOMPSON

I was panicking by now. I had that same feeling that anyone will know if they have a younger brother, and they haven't come in when they're meant to. It's pure panic, yet you're almost more scared about how your mum is going to react.

So I started to look all over place, really searching like mad for Stuart. There were people slumped everywhere, bodies being rushed across the pitch on all these stretchers made out of boards – and you could tell. You could see arms flopped down, lifeless expressions, and I just followed to where the bodies were being carried.

They all seemed to be heading for this corner. I didn't know it was the gym, then – I just followed where everyone was going. This copper stepped out in front of me. 'Where do you think you're going?' I told him I was looking for my brother. He just said, 'You're not. Get back there.' But I just went past him. He didn't come after me. He wasn't really bothered. I don't think the police had any idea what to do. They were probably thinking the shift would be over soon, looking forward to their chips or whatever.

So I carried on in there and there were already bodies laid out with blankets covering their faces. I knew they were dead – obviously they were dead – yet it wasn't registering with me. There was something holding me back from accepting that they were dead; and part of it was, I was thinking to myself, 'One of these could be my brother.' So I pulled back one of the sheets, then another – and at that point a copper came over and threw me out.

DANNY RHODES

Next thing, all the stretchers – well, they weren't stretchers, were they? It was fans trying to rescue fans. And this is where it really starts to hit home. They started treating the injured down our end. They were trying to take them out down that exit, to the right, but a lot of injured fans are being laid out on the pitch down our end. And now the atmosphere is changing. Now, if anyone is chanting or being abusive, people are telling them to shut up. There's little scuffles breaking out in our end between lads who've maybe had a drink and are still in that rivalry mentality and others who are telling them to shut up, something's going on down here. You still don't really know what's happening. And then I look down and there's one guy lying there, and someone put a black leather jacket over his face. And … it's shock. They only do that when someone's dead. You've seen it in films, you've seen it on TV, you know what it us, but … someone said, 'Fucking hell – that guy's dead.'

And that's when it all closed down.

DAMIAN KAVANAGH

The police had formed a line across the pitch to keep us apart from the Forest fans – they were still thinking about containment of trouble. They were totally blind to what was going on. I walked over to one policeman who was an officer, not a constable. I asked him if there was anything he wanted me to do to help. He replied, 'No,' they were looking after everything now, 'Thanks.'

JOHN MACKIN

About eight of us lifted the hoarding up. I could feel my leg shaking as we drew ourselves upright. Then we turned and started as fast a walk as we could manage, before breaking into a trot. I'm certain we were all mindful of the body on the hoarding and the trot evened out to a pace where we felt safe we wouldn't drop her. We headed off towards the far corner of the ground, the gap between the North Stand and the Kop end. I remember being aware of a hole in my shoe, and how the damp pitch was now soaking my sock. I suddenly felt awkward at the thousands of faces watching us, and looked down at the girl's body. I concentrated on trying to see if she was breathing. There seemed to be no sign of life. Even now, what she was wearing is etched into my mind. I've often thought of trying to trace who she was, but I've never taken it any further. Perhaps I'm scared to know.

When we reached the corner of the pitch, there was a sharp turn to the left as we tried to guide the hoarding into a room under the stand. But it was too awkward a turn and, as we tried to twist the hoarding to let us enter, it tipped slightly, and her body slid and hit the floor with a thud. If there had been any doubt in my mind as to her condition, it was immediately discarded. We picked up the body and moved her into the large room where someone directed us to lay her down on the floor. There were dozens of other bodies in there, with dazed people walking among them. I got out as quickly as I could and went back out to look for someone else I might be able to help.

PETER HOOTON

I went down on to the pitch. The word was starting to get out that fans had been crushed, but there was no mention of deaths at that stage. But there was a lad I recognised from Liverpool games, Warby, and he was on the pitch, crying. He wasn't the sort to cry, so I began to realise that something very serious was going on. Still, though, it didn't for one moment enter your head, the extent of the crushing or that there had been fatalities.

Liverpool fans were racing to the emergency point with stretchers and the mood had completely changed. The Forest fans could see that this was a rescue attempt, and most of them now started to applaud the Liverpool fans in their efforts.

I went over to the corner. I could see people getting CPR, the kiss of life; there were people who had wet themselves – I tried to convince myself that they'd fainted but I think that, in my heart of hearts, I knew. I felt totally inadequate. I was scared. I could see all these people, Liverpool fans, mainly, and some St John's Ambulance

Brigade, all working desperately, trying to help these people who were flat out, and I froze, I'll admit that. I didn't know what to do. I had no first-aid training. I didn't know what to say to anyone, so I went back to the police line. I told this policeman what was going on and asked him why the police weren't helping. He said, 'We're waiting for orders. We can't move until we get orders.' That is what he said. That is fact. I thought to myself, 'You know – as a human being, why don't you just break rank? Why don't you just do something to help?'

THE TAYLOR REPORT

98. At about 3.15 p.m., Mr Graham Kelly, Chief Executive of the FA, Mr Kirton also of the FA, and Mr Graham Mackrell, Secretary of Sheffield Wednesday, went to the control room for information. Mr Duckenfield told them he thought there were fatalities and the game was likely to be abandoned. He also said a gate had been forced and there had been an inrush of Liverpool supporters. He pointed to one of the television screens focused on gate C by the Leppings Lane turnstiles and said, 'That's the gate that's been forced: there's been an inrush.' Inevitably, Mr Kelly was interviewed a little later live on television. He spoke of the two stories concerning the gate: the fans' account that the police had opened it, and the police assertion that the fans had forced their way in.

STEPHEN WRIGHT

I got to the eighteen-yard box and there's carnage going on all around. Now, thinking back, when it happens … you're in a bit of a dream state. You're not taking anything in, you're in a daze. I heard someone shouting at me. I looked up and I saw one of my mates, Peter Warnick, in the first row of the West Stand – the seats right above the Leppings Lane terrace. And he's shouting down, 'Look for your Graham, look for your Graham,' and, obviously, I'm looking everywhere. I couldn't find him. I mean, the problem that I had, he was in jeans and a denim shirt. I was in a denim shirt. Half our support was wearing denim shirts – it was the fashion at that time.

The police just lined up right across the halfway line. They didn't know what they were doing. I remember saying to one copper, 'What are you doing? There's people dying there. There's people dead.' But they were just, you know, 'You just get back down there.'

DANNY RHODES

There was just this sudden hush. Word started to spread around the terrace and even the lads who'd been mouthing off shut up and, it's weird … I mean, we're just stood there, watching what's unfolding in front of us and … it's what you've done for years and years, you're stood on the terrace watching the action on the pitch but what you're watching is a tragedy unfolding before your eyes. And there's nothing you can do.

JEGSY DODD

I made my way back out to the concourse area and there were people being laid out, lifeless. There were bodies just lying there and people were wailing – everyone was starting to lose it. I remember seeing this one fella, an older man, laid out on the floor, and a doctor was leaning over him. This doctor – I know he was a doctor because I've seen him since, he's been on TV a few times, talking about Hillsborough – he was right next to me, trying to revive this man. I said to the doctor, 'What can I do, what can I do?' And he said to me, 'Undo his trousers; undo his top button on his shirt.' He was going blue, this fella. Like I say, he was older and, all around me, people seemed to be more, you know, saving kids and the younger ones.

So I had to basically undo this fella's flies and undo his shirt so he could breathe, and a copper came up to me and he goes, 'Get out of the fucking way,' and all that. I said to him, 'I'm trying to help here.' But he was having none of it; it was, 'Get out the way!' So I stood up and stood back, and this copper threw a coat over the man's face. He'd given him up as dead. There were bodies lined up out there by now – their heads and faces covered with coats or pullovers.

JOHN ASHTON

Already there were casualties being laid out in that area directly behind the tunnel – it's a kind of baseball-diamond shaped area, by the turnstiles. So I started to engage with what was happening – and what was happening at that stage was that there was no emergency response from the ambulance service. I think there was one ambulance attending at that time. This was about 3.30 p.m., and by now the police were starting to take people out, in any order. I could see straight away that no one was applying triage at this stage. If you compare it to a war situation, triage is what military medics would do with casualties. It's basic medical training, where you separate victims into three groups. If people are dead – it's brutal, but we're talking saving lives here – there's no point in taking them to a MASH station. You may as well leave them until later. Then there's the group who have minor injuries and, again, you can see to them later. The group you need to identify, quickly, is the group in the middle, where it's critical; those whose injuries require immediate, high-quality attention. So that was my priority. I wasn't thinking about resuscitating people at this stage, although there were various first-aiders and other volunteers who had responded to the call for medics, all administering mouth-to-mouth and CPR. This was all taking place right behind the stand, at the entrance to the tunnel. There were other medics and volunteers out on the pitch who began trying to resuscitate people as well.

I spent the next hour or so going round in circles, trying to sort the casualties into triage groups. But there was no leadership, no emergency plan. I imposed a leadership of my own on the situation and, bit by bit, the police started to do what I told them to do. And then more ambulances appeared as things progressed, and I was going round the casualties saying, 'That one needs to go to hospital. That one needs to go to hospital. He can wait ...' and so on. And there were five people who were dead; who I certified dead.

BARRY DEVONSIDE

There's a fella sitting nearby with a little transistor radio, and people are crowding round, trying to find out what's going on. And he tells us there's ten dead and I just go weak. I can't describe it other than that it was just this foreboding, this dreadful fear: what if Chris is one of them? And down on the pitch you can see that our fans are doing everything they can to help. Everything they possibly can. They're making stretchers, they're carrying the injured to get medical attention. And, to be fair, there are police who are trying to help, too. There's a small minority who are helping with this make-do rescue operation.

But the majority of them were worse than useless. A group of our fans ran past with this body on an advertising board, lifeless, his arm flopping down and, at that point, I was gripped by this stone-cold fear, an all-consuming dread. And I had to get out of there and find Chris.

PETER HOOTON

There was this surreal kind out of out-of-body cacophony down on the pitch. Neil Fitzmaurice described it as being like the sound you get inside the swimming baths, and that's exactly right. It was this disembodied babble. And I went back into the seats and just sat there – but with my back towards the Leppings Lane end. It's like a time-lapse here: I just sat there, I couldn't move. I didn't want to leave. But then there were the announcements for people to leave the ground, and I sort of came round. There weren't many people left inside the ground. I went back down on to the pitch and, I don't know why, but I went out through the Leppings Lane tunnel. I suppose I just wanted to see with my own eyes what had happened. I can't explain it, but I jumped down from behind the goal on to the terracing and I saw where the barrier had buckled. I knew then that it was much more serious than we were being told. And I went up the tunnel. I remember being surprised how steep it was. That wasn't really mentioned at first, but you see it much more clearly when the tunnel is empty. It was surprising how steep it was.

JOHN ALDRIDGE

There were fans trying to get into the dressing room, trying to tell us exactly what was happening. That stopped after a while. I don't know if Wednesday put security on the door, but we were just sitting there, not knowing if the match would be re-started or what, waiting to be told. But outside you can hear this shouting and screaming, and what you keep hearing is: 'There's people dying. There's people dying out there.'

IAN RUSH

We're in the dressing room, and we still think we're going to go back on. After what happened at Heysel, you still think you're going to go back out and play. I think the referee popped his head in and told Kenny he would leave it five or ten minutes. He said that, if the decision was taken to go back on, he'd let the players warm up again before re-starting the match.

So we didn't really know what was happening at this stage, but then there's this corridor by the dressing rooms, and people start being brought down the corridor. They're carrying bodies down the corridor, whether they were alive or dead, we didn't know at first. But there's their friends and family with them, and they're coming into the dressing room saying, 'There's people dead out here. There are a lot of people dead.' Some of them were losing it, shouting at us, 'If you lot go back out there and play that game, you're [such-and-such] ...'

Kenny [Dalglish] went out to talk to them. You know Kenny, he'll always go and talk to the fans, but you could see he was very concerned. I think he knew this was bad. After a bit he comes back in to the dressing room and says, 'We can't go back out there. No way.' So we knew, by then, it was something awful.

JEGSY DODD

I'd gone to that game with some pretty tough lads, and I'd never seen them show much emotion before – but this was terrible. We started to meet up, and the word was going round by now that this thing had been enormous. There'd been deaths. Some of us were crying, holding on to each other. It was worse than a death in the family in many ways, because it was communal, and it had happened right there, in front of you.

STEVE HART

We started carrying more people down to the first-aid point, leaving them there, coming back for more. I remember talking to this lad who was splayed out in the goalmouth. He'd broken his leg and he was waiting to be seen to. There were people just milling round, and they were blank. Everyone was walking round and it was like they weren't there, they were in a dream or something. They were walking past each other and there was nothing in their eyes. It was weird, surreal. It was mental.

TONY O'KEEFE

We did this a few more times – get the casualty on to a stretcher, a hoarding, run them down the other end, leave them at the medical point, to be seen to. We'd just laid someone down, and a medical officer came up to me, saw the armband and said, 'Here, come with me, you might be more use over here.' And he took me into the gym. He says, what we've got to do now is prioritise. We've got to find out who is injured, who is going to survive. It was a bit chaotic, there were all sorts in there – civilians, police, all trying to help – and this doctor was basically saying that we've got to go through the victims and, if there's no sign of life, we've got to cover them up, pull an item of clothing over their face to show that they're dead. And I did this a couple of times and I just stopped and said, 'I can't do this. I'm not a doctor. It's not up to me to pronounce who's dead and who's alive.' I'd been called to jobs on the London Underground where the person has been absolutely cut in two, but I can't say they're dead. That's not my job. That's up to the doctor. So after doing this a couple of times, I … I just couldn't do it.

DANNY RHODES

Our end started to empty out, but we stayed quite late. My mates and I made our way down to the front left. We wanted to do what the Liverpool lads were doing. We wanted to get involved, try to help in some way – but there was no way that that was going to be allowed. The police down that corner wouldn't let us on the pitch. So we just sat down on the terracing in that corner. There was nothing we could do to help, but we didn't want to leave.

STEVE HART

Next thing I remember, one of the lads off our coach comes up to me in the goalmouth. He's been in the North Stand, to the side, so he hasn't got a clue about what's gone on. And then another lad comes over, he's got a radio. Quite a few people had radios because Everton were in the other semi-final. He says to me, 'Oh, they've put the gates through, haven't they? It's all over the radio. Our lads have put the gates in.' And I'd been right there. I'd seen exactly what happened, and I told him, 'They did *not* put the gates in! The police opened the gates.'

But that was within minutes. It was being reported that Liverpool fans had charged the gates. I was that adamant, I took the lads round to show them. I was going, 'Look, there's no buckle. There's no foot marks. No way did our fans put those gates in.' And then these coppers come over and one of them had the flat hat and the cane – you know, the long truncheon – and he wanted us gone. I gave him a bit of stick. I was shouting at him, 'You lot opened those gates! You fucking know you did!'

And he just tells my mates to get me out of there, or he's going to lift me.

JEGSY DODD

Some of our group started to get news that young Peter had been caught up in the worst of it. They went off to try to find out what had happened to him. I couldn't remember where I'd parked the car. I went into this fruit and veg shop and they let me use the phone to call my mum and my girlfriend. The people in the shop were great – they were asking if I was OK, asking if I needed anything, but I was coasting through it, really. I was in a daze.

JOHN ASHTON

After a while we'd certified fifteen dead. The police were just providing torn-out sheets from their exercise books for me to write a kind of informal death certificate, and safety pins to pin these sheets of exercise paper to the peoples' clothing, and I just wrote on it, 'CERTIFIED DEAD' and the time, the date, my name and my signature. And each of the dead was allocated a number by the police. I came to believe that those informal death certificates had become separated from the bodies and lost. But I subsequently discovered from the Hillsborough Independent Panel's report in September 2012 that my statement to Lord Justice Taylor in 1989 was annotated with those numbers each of the deceased had been allocated at that time. So the death certificates can't have been lost.

It was very hard to identify most of them. If it was today, you'd have a credit card, a mobile phone, multiple forms of verifying someone's identity. But most of the people we treated just had their match ticket and their money. This was all around 3.30 to 4 o'clock. Whether any of those I certified dead were still alive at 3.15,* I don't know.

----

* The 3.15 p.m. 'cut-off point' was to become one of the most controversial elements of the subsequent campaigns for truth and justice. The usual procedure following civic or public disasters that have led to large-scale loss of life is for a series of mini-inquests. The purpose of a mini-inquest is to establish the identities of the dead and the bare circumstances of their death. A mini-inquest will not seek to apportion blame. Once the Director of Public Prosecutions has looked at the results of the mini-inquests to establish if criminal proceedings should ensue, there then follow the more detailed 'resumed inquests' with a much wider remit. Prior to the resumed inquests, the coroner, Stefan Popper, ruled that he would not allow any evidence relating to any event, observation or incident after 3.15 p.m. His reasoning was that, by 3.15, all those who subsequently died would have received the injuries that killed them. The 3.15 cut-off point was never accepted or acknowledged by many of the bereaved families, and it remained a point a conflict throughout the twenty-seven-year campaign. To the day she died, Anne Williams refused to collect her son Kevin's death certificate – a protest against the coroner's verdict of accidental death, and his imposition of the 3.15 p.m. cut-off.

STEVE KELLY

So we're walking along Allerton Road and there's a crowd gathered outside a Colorvision shop, the telly shop, used to have all the TV sets in the window. And as I looked, I could see there was an incident occurring on the screens, at Hillsborough. Straight away, let's be honest, it's the 1980s, I thought, 'Crowd trouble. Let's get home, see what's gone on.' So we get in, turn the TV on and find out exactly what's beginning to occur. And I think by about 4 o'clock there's a helpline you can ring, to see if any of your loved ones had been lost. Well, I knew my brother had gone to the match, but even at that point I'm thinking, you know, 'He's a very, very experienced football fan, he's been to every game you can name – he'll be all right.'

JOHN BARNES

We went up to the players' lounge. Both sets of players were there, Forest and us. Everyone was just numb. Remember this is a time before mobile phones. There's no live coverage, no Sky Sports or whatever, no real way of knowing exactly what is going on, just the old tele-printer bringing the scores in. And, along with the Norwich v Everton game, and certain other scores, there's the tele-printer clicking away, updating you on how many are injured and dead.

JOHN ALDRIDGE

It was horrendous. A lot of the players' wives were up there, and they were in bits, crying and holding on to each other. You just couldn't take it in. Every few minutes it seemed like more were being reported dead. You felt helpless, you know – it's just a football match.

Something like this – it's beyond comprehension. It shouldn't happen. And perhaps there's a little bit of guilt there, too? They've come to watch you. They've come to watch Liverpool. They've come to watch a game of football, and now they're dead.

IAN RUSH

You were looking at the telly, but not really taking it in. It was all a bit unreal. Then Kenny's on the pitch with Brian Clough, trying to explain to the fans what's happening. We didn't realise at the time, but the Tannoy wasn't working. There were people milling about all over the pitch, and an ambulance slowly working its way through. It was only then that we really started to understand the size of what had gone on. Even though you'd been hearing all these shouts from the corridor – fans trying to tell us how bad it was – somehow, it didn't really sink in. Then we're up there, seeing it all unfold on the TV like it's news from somewhere else ... but it's here. It's us. That was the first time, for me, that it really sunk in. Most of us were just solemn. We were in shock, I suppose. John Barnes was in a terrible state.

JOHN BARNES

When I saw some of the footage, people lying at the side of the pitch with their faces covered with their own shirts, fans trying to revive other fans on the pitch-side, the way they were carrying their own on these homemade stretchers ... there was something so horrifically sad about that image. The fans' own rescue attempts. I don't know, it just hit me, hard. I broke down, and there was nothing anyone could say to me. I was in shock, yes – but, more than anything, I just found the whole thing impossible to understand. It was a football match. A football match.

DAMIAN KAVANAGH

I left the pitch using the players' tunnel. I walked past Gerald Sinstadt from the BBC. I went past the away team's dressing room to my left, and saw Des Walker and Lee Chapman, who both looked at me, and seemed uneasy doing so. I saw a payphone and took the opportunity to call my parents to let them know I was OK, but I didn't have any change. Another Reds fan behind me gave me a £1 coin without any second thought – thanks, mate, whoever you were.

I spoke to my mum and told her I was fine and asked her to call Bailey's parents. I told her we had been split up, but I definitely saw him escape from the pens. He had survived unhurt. A steward then said no more people could use the phone! Why? What harm were we doing? Was it because we were only fans, we weren't good enough to be where we were, in the stadium using the phone – even during this hell?! Some Reds fan then started shouting at this steward that his brother was behind the goal in all the chaos – why shouldn't he use the phone? I left the stadium through a nearby door.

I walked around the ground back towards Leppings Lane. Some fella stopped me, saying I shouldn't pass that way as what I would see was going to be too upsetting. I told him I'd be all right, but he insisted in the nicest possible way that there were badly distressing sights behind the stand, so I left it and took a detour.

My lucky scarf had somehow stayed on throughout all of this but I took it off now and hurled it away. For the first time I heard a noise coming over the Tannoy at the stadium but couldn't make out what was being said. From where I was walking I could see down into the stadium, through the gap between the West and South Stands. I saw an ambulance on the pitch by our goal. The game surely wasn't going to re-start, was it? I wasn't having this, there was no way I was going to watch any game if it did re-start. No, I knew there was no way, and I just kept heading for the bookies to meet my mates.

PETER CARNEY

My next memory of it is that I'm in an ambulance and they're taking me to the Northern General Hospital. I'm stripped naked and they examine me and everything. They told me I was staying in overnight and allocated me a bed and I told them I didn't want to – I wanted to go back to my wife. So they said, 'OK, we'll give it an hour, rest you up. See how you are.'

MARTIN THOMPSON

I was really starting to worry by now. I found some of my mates and we started to make our way out of the ground. We went to the newsagent's where we'd agreed to meet, but I was starting to get this deep foreboding that something was badly wrong. I wasn't expecting Stu to be there, and he didn't show up.

I thought, 'OK, I've got to phone my mum now. But the queues for the phone boxes were stretching literally all the way down the road. We carried on walking. The Sheffield people were at their front doors, asking if anyone needed to use the phone, making cups of tea for us. That was really, really good of them. I phoned Mum and told her I couldn't find Stuart. I don't think she was fully aware of the scale of what had happened, and I suppose I must have played it down a bit – 'He'll be all right, don't worry,' that sort of thing. She told me to carry on looking for him. So we split up; some of the lads went to the hospitals, and I went down to the boys' club* with one of my mates.

STEVE ROTHERAM

As we walked along the road you could hear car radios. The media were already starting to speculate how many were dead. You'd go past one car and they were saying ten had died. Then, just a few yards up the road, another would be saying fifteen. And the desolation that swept over you was unreal. Men were crying in the street, fans with pained expressions were saying they had seen terrible things first hand. A sense of dread hung over crowds of people as they waited by coaches and cars, fearing for their fellow supporters.

I walked in the same haze as others and quietly stood in one of the queues forming along pathways leading to houses where the good people of Sheffield had thrown open their doors to allow fans to phone loved ones at home, to let them know that they were safe.

BARRY DEVONSIDE

I remained in the North Stand until a message came over the loud-speaker saying that no game would be played today, and for all fans to

---

* The disused Hammerton Road boys' club, opposite the police station, was used as an information centre for those trying to trace friends and relatives who were unaccounted for. A team of social workers was called in to help with the mechanical process of finding and identifying the injured and dead, and with grief counselling.

leave the stadium. As we filed out it was as if it was a funeral; the fans were so quiet, nobody was saying a word.

Outside, it was chock-a-block. There were police cars, fire engines, everyday civilian cars, bumper to bumper. You could have made better progress walking up the road over the car roofs.

As I'm getting further away from the ground, back towards the place we've arranged to meet, every phone box I pass has got a queue outside, at least a hundred people, presumably all wanting to call home and let their relatives know they're safe.

But my heart is in my mouth. The closer I get to the rendezvous point, I so desperately just want to see Chris's red Wales top. See his smiling face. I just want him to be there, safe. And as I come up the road, this shocking dread deep inside me: I can see Jason there, but no Chris. It's all over Jason's face. He can barely speak, but he says,

'You're going to have to prepare yourself for the worst.'

I can't take it in. I'm just standing there. 'What do you mean, "prepare for the worst?"'

He tells me Chris is dead. Jason's carried him to the gym. And, I don't know, none of this seems real. The next thing I'm making my way back to the ground, and I ask a WPC, or a traffic officer, to direct me to Sheffield Wednesday's gymnasium.

DAMIAN KAVANAGH

I saw this lad who I knew from Sunday league training – Bally; he had his foot in plaster. 'All right, Col,' I said to him. 'Did you do that here?' But he hadn't. He'd come there with his foot in plaster. We both stood there, waiting for the people we'd come to Sheffield with. I waited for what seemed like ages and, eventually, just assumed that the lads have gone straight back to the car. So I walked back there. As I turned into Don Avenue I saw Jamie's car – but none of the lads.

The weather was still beautiful, but the car was in the shade on the other side of the road. I was stood right by the car. I had a cold shiver. I had no jacket, only my away shirt on. I could have waited on the other side of the street where it was warm, but I didn't want the lads to see the car but not me – even if only for a second or so. A group of Reds were meeting across the street at a minibus and just waiting for the rest of their group. They had the commentary of Everton's match on – force of habit, I suppose – but nobody was listening. Nobody was interested.

ANDY BURNHAM

It was a scrappy game. Pat Nevin scored and the Holte End went mad, as you'd expect. Norwich weren't threatening much and Everton were looking good for the win, everyone was bouncing. But the other end, the Witton End had this massive scoreboard. I remember it coming up about ten minutes from the end: 'Six dead at Hillsborough.' And in that moment the whole thing just changed. All the Everton fans were turning to each other, asking if anyone had a radio. Our game just kind of *finished* but there was none of the jubilation you'd seen in '84, '85 or '86. Everyone was muted. We just sort of filed out of the ground, completely preoccupied by what was going on at Hillsborough.

DAMIAN KAVANAGH

A fella came out from the house I was outside of and asked if I was OK. I told him I was. I told him that I knew we'd get the blame in the media over this, but that he mustn't believe it – it was not our fault. He said he knew that already. He'd spoken to his brother, who was a steward at the match. He asked me, did I want a cup of tea? – but I didn't want anything. I wanted to see Bailey. I wanted to see my mates come round the corner, into that street.

He asked if I wanted to use his phone and insisted that he wouldn't take any money from me (this was typical of the compassion shown by many Sheffield people that day). I took the opportunity to call Bailey's parents personally. I went back outside and waited for my mates. Everton had won by now.

Finally, my three mates came around the corner together and rushed towards me and hugged me. We didn't really hug in those days, but we held on tight. They'd been worried that they'd never see me alive again.

JEGSY DODD

We waited for the others. The death toll was going up with each news bulletin, and it was just horrible – people were wailing. We'd decided we'd stay, however long it took, and go back together. It was hours afterwards when the last of our lads came back to the cars. Peter wasn't with them. They'd had to go to the gymnasium to identify his body.

JOHN ASHTON

We carried on in that vein for some time, trying to make the best of the situation. I subsequently discovered that there were some twenty medics – off-duty doctors, nurses, firemen, paramedics – who had helped on the day. I spoke to one of the ambulance men who, eventually, attended, and he told me that it was very much left up to the clubs to decide what sort of level of ambulance support they wanted. They usually used St John's Ambulance Brigade, but St John's was operated on a voluntary basis. They were very much dependent upon a donation from the club. I mean, St John's are good, but the point is that in an emergency situation like this you need a full-scale response. And, of course, we later discovered that the 'major disaster' had not been declared – or had been misreported. The emergency services arrived expecting to deal with a riot situation.

THE TAYLOR REPORT

18. PC Bichard's call to police headquarters at 3.13 p.m. for the fire service to bring hydraulic cutting equipment to cut metal fences was heard by Chief Inspector Edmundson. He went into the adjacent operations room to give instructions for the message to be passed to the fire service. There, a temporary control-room assistant was already speaking to the fire service about a house fire. Mr Edmundson interrupted the call and asked the assistant to tell the fire service that cutting equipment was wanted at Hillsborough. There followed a conversation between the assistant and Miss Davies at the fire service in the following terms:

> Police: Can we have cutting gear for Hillsborough, please – straight away?
> Fire Control: Just a minute. Right – what's the address?
> Police: Cutting equipment for Hillsborough football ground – straight away.
> Fire Control: Hillsborough football ground?
> Police: Yes, Hillsborough football ground.

Fire Control: What road is that on? Do you know?

Police: There has been a major accident, all the ambulances are up there.

Fire Control: What road is it on?

Police: I have no idea; Hillsborough football ground.

Fire Control: What road is it on? Do you know?

Police: 'Hillsborough football ground – what road is it on?' [this was asked to someone in Police Force Control] – 'Penistone Road' [to Fire Control].

Fire Control: Penistone Road.

Police: Penistone Road, OK?

Fire Control: Penistone Road, just a minute – what's exactly involved?

Police: It's football, a big match; Liverpool v Notts Forest.

Fire Control: Yes, but why do you want us? You said it was an RTA [Road Traffic Accident].

Police: No, no, no; major incident inside the ground.

Fire Control: Major incident inside – do you know exactly what it is?

Police: No, I don't; they want all the cutting gear.

Fire Control: For what? Do you know?

Police: Hang on a sec—

At that point Chief Inspector Edmundson intervened and spoke for the police. The conversation concluded as follows:

Police: Hello!

Fire Control: Hello! Now you want some cutting gear – what exactly is it for?

Police: There has been a major accident at Hillsborough football ground, where the semi-final is; the crowds have forced their way in, they have broken fences and gates down. I don't know exactly what it is but there are people trapped.

TONY O'KEEFE

I went round the other side of the curtain and there was rows and rows of people, and there was this young lad lying there moaning and groaning. I went over to him, and he says, 'Am I going to die?' I said to him, 'No, you're in a safe place, you're talking to me – you're not going to die.' He didn't look very well but he was breathing, he was conscious enough to ask me if I could phone his mum. So I went and found a pen and I wrote down his number, his name, on the match-day programme – Gary Unsworth, Southport supporters' club – he even told me where his coach was parked. This is all going in my head, I'm trying to visualise it, remember it all, and all I'm thinking is, 'I've promised the lad. I've got to do this.'

STEPHEN WRIGHT

When I look back on the day, I think I was one of the last to leave the pitch. Like I say, I was in my own dream state, but I remember there was a scarf just hanging there, hanging down off the fence. So I got it and I put it right up at the top of the fence, where everyone could see it, and I tied it really tight. It seemed symbolic, somehow. I couldn't find our Graham on the pitch or anything, but I tied the scarf tight to the railing – and it gave me comfort.

SHEILA COLEMAN

I'd been to Great Homer Street market with my partner, and my son, who had just turned 11. We were walking back to my mother's house and I remember this old guy running out of some flats, saying, 'Isn't it terrible, what's happening at Hillsborough.' I was the only Red in a family of Blues, and I was worried. I used to go in the boys' pen from I was 7 years of age. I knew people who were there. So I just hurried back to my mother's to find out what was going on and, already, it was being reported as hooliganism.

ANDY BURNHAM

We headed back to the car. Jim Rosenthal (the sports presenter) was running the other way, shouting, 'This is terrible, terrible ... this is awful.' And we were just completely in shock: 'What's going on?' And we drive back in utter silence as it begins to filter through, over the airwaves. I must have known at least twenty people who were at that game but, going back to the night before, my first thought was about Steve Turner. Is he OK? The death toll is mounting as we drive back up the M6, and they're saying the Liverpool fans have charged the gates and forced their way in. Then my brother says, 'They're in that away end, aren't they?' And we knew straight away what he was talking about. That ground, that end – we were all thinking about the Cup game there, the year before. So, on the radio they were saying the fans had forced their way in but, straight away, we were saying, 'No way. It's that away end, those pens. It's not safe ...'

TONY O'KEEFE

There were a couple of coppers having a cup of tea, and they looked up at me – they knew I was going to say something. I said, 'You lost it, today. You completely lost it.' And I didn't mean them individually, but … how difficult can it have been to shut off the entrance to that tunnel? What would it have taken? A few police – one copper on a horse: 'These pens are full; plenty of room left and right.' Because, when I saw those barriers, twisted like that … that must have taken some unbelievable pressure for them to bend and buckle like that.

JOHN ASHTON

It all went quiet around 5 o'clock. I went down to the gym to see what had happened to the people who were dead. They were laid out there, on tables, in the gym. Now, since then, people have often referred to Polaroid photographs of the dead. But my memory is of a large gallery of photographs of Liverpool supporters along the wall, which I took to be people they were on the lookout for, on the day. Which plays into the notion that the police mindset, on the day, was that there would be a hell of a lot of scallies arriving, intent on causing trouble, so they had this gallery of mugshots to look out for, in the gym.

But after a short time – it must have been about 5.15 – all sorts of police began to arrive from all over the ground, and we were asked to leave. We were chucked out and the doors were closed, and that was that. We had to go away. Whatever was going on in there – and I now understand that what was going on is what the police call 'a hot debrief' – they didn't want any non-police to hear any part of it, at all.

PETER CARNEY

I rested up in the hospital, but all I'm thinking is, 'I want to get out of here. I want to get back and see Tina.' I hadn't had a chance to phone her but, at that stage, I had no idea just how bad the thing had been. I think my blood pressure must have been sky high when I'd first been brought in, because when the medics came back and gave me another check-up they said, 'You're OK, you can go. There's no broken bones, no major injuries – just make sure you rest up.'

Now, who can say if I was in shock or whatever? I was conscious of what I was going through there and then, and that I was being cared for, but I think I was still just going through the motions. I was aware of what had happened in the ground, but I had no idea of the extent of what had gone on. I had no idea there'd been fatalities. I was aching all over, and I was just relieved they'd said I could go home.

MARTIN THOMPSON

We waited at the boys' club for ages. There were people just milling round, sitting there drinking tea and coffee, smoking; everyone desperate for news. The lads who had been up at the hospitals looking for Stuart came back – no sign of him. Social workers started to arrive. They began to take down details and offer advice and counselling to all these distraught people who just wanted basic information. Then the chaplain came and sat with us – Reverend Gordon Wilson, the chaplain of Sheffield Wednesday Football Club. I'm not religious at all, but he was great – very comforting, very reassuring. He stayed with us, just talking. By this time people were being told to go back to the gym at Hillsborough – the morgue, as it turned out.

BARRY DEVONSIDE

I found my way to the gym and it was pure pandemonium. There's an absolute scrum of journalists and photographers, at least 20 of them, all trying to get in, and one policeman on the door.

I told the policeman on the gymnasium door what I was there for and he let me inside. I'm completely mentally lost by now, absolutely terrified. I don't know what I'm doing, or what to ask, or what I'm going to be shown. A lady approached me and asked me very gently if there was anything she could do to help. I wasn't making much sense, I was mainly just very, very frightened. The lady told me her name was Betty Thorpe, she was just a local resident who had seen what was unfolding and had come down as a volunteer, to see if she could help. I told her I thought my son might have been killed, and she pointed me towards a solitary door at the far end of the room.

I went and knocked at the door. It seemed to take an eternity before anyone came to answer. The door opened and what must have been the biggest policeman I have ever seen in my life was standing there in front of me. He was incredibly off-hand with me.

'What do you want?'

I told him. I said, 'I think my son has been killed. I think he's been brought to the gymnasium.' I gave him as detailed a description as I could, and he just said, 'Wait there.' He was gone about twelve or fifteen minutes before he came back and said, 'Nobody of that description.'

Well, I was completely lost at this point. I didn't know what to say. I wanted it to be true, but Jason had told me he'd carried Chris to the gym himself. He couldn't have made a mistake about something like that. Chris was in there. I asked him to look again.

'I've just told you,' he said. And he slammed the door in my face.

I walked over to Betty and told her what the ignorant copper had said to me, and the manner in which he had spoken. I was shocked – I never expected to be spoken to by a police officer in such a cold, rude manner.

I said, 'Is there a phone around here, I have to speak to Jac, my wife.' I was dreading it but, equally, there was no one I wanted to speak to more. At this moment a police sergeant came along and Betty approached him and told him of my situation. He was much more sensitive and took me off to a little room behind the gymnasium.

There was a phone in the corner and the police sergeant sat me down and asked for my number – but my mind just froze. Everything was numb, it was all just one big blank. I couldn't remember my own phone number. The policeman tried directory inquiries for me, but they told him my number had come up as ex-directory. I knew that wasn't right, I said – I've never been ex-directory in my life.

The police sergeant said to the telephone operator, 'Are you aware that there has been a disaster at Hillsborough and that many people have lost their lives?' He gave them his name, his rank, and told them how critically important it was that they put me through to my wife, but at that point the line went dead. The sergeant put the phone down, and that was that.

In the end, they got hold of my brother-in-law, John, and he went and picked up my brother, and they both drove over to our house, and told Jackie what was happening.

STEPHEN WRIGHT

I went and looked on the Barnes's coaches – couldn't find Graham. So I tried loads of coaches. Then I thought that, in all the chaos, he might have just jumped on the first coach he saw. Couldn't find him.

So, next thing, I'm thinking, 'I should phone home, tell them what's going on.' But there's big mad queues for all of the phone boxes. All of them. No chance. So I knocks on a door, ask if I can use the phone. And this wasn't just me: next door, the house after that, there's people queuing up outside to use their phones. They were great, the Sheffield people, letting us into their houses, letting us use their phones. They were brilliant.

So I phones home, said, 'I don't know what's happened to our Graham.' They were made up to hear from me, and they just told me to come home. They said, 'You know Graham, he's probably jumped on a bus, or got a lift off someone. Come home.' So I headed back to our coach.

TONY O'KEEFE

A priest came up to me on the pitch and he was telling me, 'God is good,' God is this and that, but I didn't want to hear it. I walked away, got off the pitch by the corner flag and got out of the ground. I knew my brothers and my brother-in-law would be wondering what had become of me. I had the car keys and I knew they'd be waiting, but there was only one thing in my mind, which was this lad in the gym. So I went and found his coach – Southport supporters' club. There were a few people standing by it and I said, 'Any of you lads know Gary Unsworth?' They were waiting for quite a few of theirs to come back, so they were relieved to know that Gary was OK. They said they'd let his mum know, but I thought, 'I've told him I'd phone her,' so I said I'd phone her anyway. That's another thing that will never leave me. As I'm walking back down the hill, there's all these Sheffield people outside their houses and they were just great. Are you OK? Do you want a cup of tea? Do you need to use a phone? So I got through, this lady answered and I said, 'Mrs Unsworth?' And straight away she said, 'It's Gary, isn't it? I'm a nurse. Tell me!' And I said, 'I'm a fireman, I've just been with your lad.' She said, 'Is he dead?' I said, 'No, he's not going to die. He's not very well, but he's breathing. He's conscious. He's going to be OK.' I started to make my way back to my car after that and, somehow, I felt ... that was one, at least.

BARRY DEVONSIDE

Betty Thorpe, the lady who had been helping me, suggested that, if Chris wasn't here in the gym, perhaps he'd been taken away in an ambulance. She offered to take me round the hospitals. I can't speak highly enough of this woman for what she did for me over the next few hours, driving me around Sheffield to different hospitals and mortuaries. She was an angel. She'd seen what she'd seen on the news and, even though, at this stage, she'd come to understand that the situation had been caused by hooliganism, she still wanted to do whatever she could to help.

We got in her car and she drove me to the first hospital – the Hallamshire, where we were taken up to the canteen. It was already overrun with distraught Liverpudlians, 80 or 100 people or more, all shouting for information. I was witnessing scenes the likes of which I had never seen before and don't want to see ever again. I could only liken what I saw to the aftermath of, say, the Israeli conflict or one of those major atrocities you see on the news, people running around in abject panic, crying and screaming.

Eventually someone from the hospital's administration jumped up on a table and shouted in a very loud voice, 'We have x number of people here. Please stand back and try to be patient. We will list the people we are treating, as soon as possible, in alphabetical order.'

He started listing the dead and injured, and people were literally collapsing with grief. I shouted above everybody, 'Do you have a young man by the name of Christopher Devonside, wearing a Welsh international rugby shirt?' The reply came back very quickly – no. Chris wasn't on any of their lists. I said to Betty that Chris *must* be in the gym. And you can't help yourself. I started to hope that perhaps Chris was still alive; but surely Jason Kenworthy could not have made a mistake like that. Nobody makes a mistake like that. At this point we were told that we should go to the mortuary at the Northern General Hospital.

TONY O'KEEFE

We got in the car and, at first, they were, 'Where have you been? We've been waiting here ages!' And I was, 'You do not want to know. Seriously, you do not want to know where I've been!' And we put the radio on and they're saying there's twenty people dead. I said, 'And the rest, there's over a hundred dead, at least.' My brothers are saying, 'No way – a hundred dead at a football match,' and I'm, like, 'I'm telling you. I've just come from there. There's at least a hundred people laid out in that gym …'

STEVE HART

All the way home, nobody said a word. Not one word, from anyone. It was the weirdest journey I've ever been on in my life. We just sat on the coach and obviously the radio was on and, the closer we got to home, the numbers of confirmed dead were going up, and up, and up ...

JOHN ASHTON

After a major incident, you have debriefs – police, medical, council; each agency will have its own debrief, then everyone will pool together for a multi-agency debrief, so you can try to understand the lessons of what's happened. But the 'hot' debrief is the first one, and, just after they chucked us out of the gym, I'm pretty sure that is where the narrative that ultimately fed through to the Prime Minister and to Bernard Ingham began to be formed.

MARTIN THOMPSON

I said to the Chaplain, 'Look, I'm not making this up: I haven't seen my brother since half-one. I couldn't find him on the pitch, he wasn't in the hospitals, the people at the boys' club have got no trace of him, what shall I do?' He told me to phone my mum again, see if Stuart had called. By this time, Anne Williams was round at our house to see if Mum had heard anything. Our Stuart was 17, Kevin was 15 – they both had their own group of mates, but they knew each other well. Kevin was someone who played football on the local field – typical, cheeky young lad. If they'd have seen one another inside the ground, or whatever, they'd definitely have stood together to watch the match. I told Mum we still hadn't found Stuart. At that point a bus arrived to take everyone back to Sheffield Wednesday.

JOHN ASHTON

After we came out of the gym, I passed a very young policeman, very upset, on his way in to the debrief. He was in tears, he was totally distraught, this young bobby, and he said, 'They're going to blame us, now. The officers are going to lay the blame for all this with the ordinary bobbies.'

I took that to be a reference to the dysfunction between the command structure and the lower ranks. Because we all saw those scenes where the serving front-line bobbies were waiting for permission to open the gates on to the pitch. And that young police officer was certain that it would be the lower ranks who carried the can for their bosses' inadequacies on the day. Which was interesting because, as it transpired, they didn't blame their own junior officers at all – they laid the blame squarely with the Liverpool supporters. And that narrative was commencing, right there, right then.

MARTIN THOMPSON

We got back to the ground and everyone was filing towards the gym. Then Colin Moynihan turned up – he was the Sports Minister of the day. So, suddenly, the police blocked off the entrance to the gym and told us we couldn't go in, because Colin Moynihan was making an official visit. We'd have to wait outside until he'd gone.

By now, you're not just starting to fear the worst; you *know* the worst. In your heart of hearts, you know what has happened. And I just wanted to … Well, I said to the copper on the door, 'Look, I've been at that boys' club and I've been here for hours and I just want to find out what's happened to my brother.' And they were just so … they didn't care. I would hate to ever be like that with someone who was obviously distressed. There was no empathy at all. To him, the lines were clear – I'm here, you're there. That's how it is. You'll wait there until we tell you that you can come in.

JOHN ASHTON

Around 8 p.m. the coroner, Dr Stefan Popper, arrives at the ground, and I think this gets you to the very heart of the questions that still need to be answered. There are layers to the onion that have gradually been peeled away over the years, taking you closer and closer to the core of the cover-up. And this, for me, lies at the very core of it. Why did Popper choose to go down to Hillsborough, at that time, on a Saturday night? Was he asked to come down there? Now, you have to take this in the context of the government of the time. Margaret Thatcher *despised* Liverpool. She hated the place. We know, now, about her views on managed decline and so forth. So when the lies began to be put to her, she was receptive. She was pre-disposed to believe the South Yorkshire police version of events and, straight away, this thing of the 3.15 p.m. cut-off begins to emerge. You have to ask yourself, 'How high did that chain of command go?' Did Thatcher head directly to Whitehall with this briefing, putting the pressure on other people in the Health Service? Leaning on the coroner to say 3.15? And the other big issue we may never get close to the truth about, is: how much of a role do the Freemasons play in this? How many of those people in Sheffield belonged to the same lodge? We know that a lot of senior police officers are Freemasons, and there's this very clubby crowd in South Yorkshire with the city council and the MP, Irvine Patnick, and Sheffield Wednesday Football Club. So that's another stone that has to be lifted.

STEVE KELLY

We carried on watching the news coverage. By then the situation had become very grave. There'd been thirty or forty confirmed dead and many hundreds of injuries but, still, I thought our Michael would be fine. He'd been everywhere. He was at Heysel and I remember him telling me, when he got back from Belgium, that he'd had a second sense that something bad was going to happen, and he got off. That wasn't like him, to turn his back and walk out when his beloved Liverpool were playing, but the point is, he was a seasoned, well-travelled fan. He knew when to walk away. And he was a big, strong lad, too. He had two inches on me; big shoulders. I didn't really give it a second thought, at that point. So I went to work. Like I say, I was a taxi-driver. It was Saturday night, busy night, it never really came into my thinking that Michael would have come to any serious harm. I went to work.

STEVE ROTHERAM

The coach home was almost completely silent, punctuated by howls of dismay with each update about the fatalities. The closer we got to home, the more the total was rising. In those days everyone was in an amateur football team and, when we got back, we started making plans to hold a match and a charity evening to raise funds. I told the main fella who was organising everything that I'd do whatever I could to help.

PETER CARNEY

While I was being seen in the hospital, Mick went back to where we'd left the car and brought it back to the Northern General. It must have been close to 8 o'clock by the time we got going. He puts the radio on and it came over the news: '93 dead at the Hillsborough stadium disaster.' And my mind is just racing away: '39. 93. 39. 93.' My head is going, '39 died at Heysel; 93 died today.' That was my reaction – what goes around comes around. We switched the radio off and drove home in silence. He dropped me at the house.

DAMIAN KAVANAGH

We drove home subdued, listening to the news on the radio. When we got to the outskirts of Skem, I told Jamie to drop me and Bailey at the Derby Arms so he could get back home a little more easily. As soon as we got out, some fella commented, 'Bad up there, eh, lads?' 'Yeah, mate, terrible.'

We walked back towards ours and met Linda and Audrey on the way. They were stood outside Audrey's, worrying and waiting for their husbands, Dave and Geoff. Dave and Geoff were long-time mates and neighbours who we'd grown up with. Young fans always look up to the guys who've been there and done it before them. Geoff, like Dave, had been a sound source of vouchers for away matches for me and my mates. When the children were born, Geoff stopped going to all the away games like he had done. I always enjoyed talking to him about the Reds; he knew what he was talking about and loved the club just like me. As for Dave, I had got his ticket for Hillsborough. It was easy for me to pick his up at the same time I got mine, when I nipped up to the ground in my dinner hour. When I knocked to give it to him he was out and I'd left it with Linda.

Audrey had had a call. She'd been told that Geoff was all right, but they hadn't yet heard about Dave. I tried to make them feel better, telling them there were delays coming back, and that we'd heard that the demand for the phone lines had brought them down. We left them, and as we walked around the corner I commented to Bailey that I didn't like the sound of it: Dave and Geoff would have been together, so why would they know about one and not the other? I felt that anybody who survived would be well on the way home, if not already back by now. If they were in hospital, surely someone there would make contact with next of kin? I was worried for him.

I walked the short way remaining to ours and my mum just hugged me and cried. It is only since I have become a dad myself that I can fully understand how my mum and dad must have felt.

STEPHEN WRIGHT

Nobody off our coach was hurt. Everyone made it back. But the journey home was done pretty much in silence. We got to the Rocket (a famous landmark Liverpool pub next to the M62 motorway) and we saw some of the Everton coaches pulling up, and their faces were as shocked as ours. There was no joy for them, getting to the final or whatever. They looked as shocked as we were.

ANDY BURNHAM

The first thing I did when we got back was phone Steve's house. His mum picked up. 'Steven! Thank God ...' But it wasn't him – it was me. Steve wasn't back. And that must have been going on in hundreds of homes, all over Liverpool ... families waiting and hoping to hear from their loved ones. We just sat there. I didn't know what to do. In the end I just said, 'They should all be getting back by now. I'm going to the Cherry Tree.'

JEGSY DODD

Driving home, listening to the radio – it just felt like the end of the world. It was the end of football, the end of everything – almost like you'd imagine if you'd been in the First World War, in the trenches. It was the first time I'd ever seen dead bodies. Plural. And, driving back, we were numb, in the end. Nothing mattered. I'd say that at least half the lads I went to the match with that day never set foot in a football ground again.

I got back to the Millhouse, my local, and I was the last one of all the regular match-going lads to make it back. It was very, very emotional; everyone was just breaking down, crying and hugging each other.

BARRY DEVONSIDE

We went to the Northern General Hospital and, again, there were similar scenes of hysteria. This time we by-passed the crowds of people all shouting for information and assistance, and went to find the mortuary. I knocked at the mortuary door and the attendant answered – I asked him if they had a person called Christopher Devonside. At first he said he wasn't sure – he would have to check. I was much calmer by now. I reasoned with them, told them I used to work in a mortuary, which was true. I don't think they would have let me in otherwise, but I assured them I wouldn't be shocked or sickened by anything that I might see, and they let me in. Again, there were very, very distressing scenes. There were about a dozen or so bobbies all sitting around with their helmets off, and you could see it, they were shell-shocked. They knew.

There was a pile of clothes in the middle of the room. Clothes from people who'd been killed. I could hardly bear to look but, even at a glance, there was no bright red Wales rugby union shirt. I asked the guy who seemed to be in charge, 'Do you have a Christopher Devonside?'

'No.'

'Was anybody brought in who was wearing a red Wales international rugby union top?'

'No.'

Perhaps the guy was just mentally fatigued. Maybe it was all taking its toll on the everyday staff whose rota just happened to throw them into work on a Saturday evening. But there was no real interest; no compassion. It was just, 'No. Nobody matching that description.' Next.

MARTIN THOMPSON

We finally got into the gym and they said to us, 'You're now going to see a board, with photographs.' There were only a few female victims, but they'd put the girls on a separate board. So, on the other board, the male board, there was what looked like hundreds and hundreds of Polaroids, this big mass of faces. And I had to look through them all, over and over. I couldn't see him, I couldn't take anything in. But he was there. Eventually I saw him. It was him. Number 53.

BARRY DEVONSIDE

By now it's about 9 p.m., and we're getting nowhere. I'd been told to go to Hammerton Road boys' club. If Christopher isn't in the gym and he's not in the hospitals then I had to try the boys' club. But it was a similar story there. We got down there about 9.30 – it was a sort of church hall – and they didn't have any details of anyone matching Chris's description. And you'd think that, OK, there's carnage going on. There's hundreds and hundreds of casualties, there's people dead. But a young man in a red rugby shirt – I'd have thought that someone of that description would stand out, somehow.

STEPHEN WRIGHT

The coach drops me off in Old Swan and I jump a cab home, back to Huyton. Obviously the taxi-driver had the radio on and he was telling me how many were dead. And I just broke down in tears in the taxi. I was in a terrible state, not knowing where our Graham was and seeing what I'd seen, it was all spinning round in my head, you know?

So I gets home and all the family are there, my mum, my dad, our David, our Anne with the baby, Louise. We had the radio on and it was playing all sombre music, like the death of a monarch. Every now and then there'd be an announcement: 'Sunspan Coaches are back; Home James are back.' Then they go, 'Barnes Travel. They're all back.' So we thought, 'We'll leave it a bit. Leave it an hour. He's on Barnes Travel, it'll take him an hour to get back from Walton – at the most.' No sign. This was well gone 9 o'clock by now, and we started getting really worried.

BARRY DEVONSIDE

My brother Roger and my brother-in-law John both arrived at the boys' club about 10.30 p.m. My brother said, 'Are you OK, Will?' That was his nickname for me – Will. I suppose Betty must have gone home by now. It was getting very late.

A constable came over and said to me, 'You'd be better off going back to the gym. There's a bus service been laid on to run people down there. It'll be back in a minute; go and wait for the bus and they'll take you back to the gym at Sheffield Wednesday.' So we went back there. Inside the gym there was a big board with photographs of the victims. I couldn't see Christopher there. I suppose that, in my heart, in my head, I didn't *want* to see … But then Roger put his arm around me and he just pointed to his photo, right there. There's Chris. And it all came out. I just broke down, crying.

ANDY BURNHAM

I must have known at least twenty people who'd been at Hillsborough. They started coming back in dribs and drabs, and you started to get the first-hand reports. Some of them had seen some pretty awful things. The whole atmosphere in there was subdued, sombre. Contrast it with twenty-four hours earlier when we'd all been full of hope and excitement. Even when we'd been having a go at the FA over giving Liverpool the Leppings Lane end again, it had been a bit, you know, 'What do they know? … stupid old farts.' Now it was anger. I'll never forget it. Steve walked in there in the end, and we just looked at each other and shook our heads.

BARRY DEVONSIDE

We went back to the door at the far end of the gym and told them we'd seen Chris's photograph. So these two detectives showed me through and asked me to wait. Then they pulled back these curtains and there was a black body-bag, zipped up. They unzipped it and there he was. They asked me if it was him and I must have nodded. I just wanted to kiss Chris. I bent down to try and I was pulled back by the Sergeant. I turned around and pushed him back – and then I was able to bend down and kiss our son.

MARTIN THOMPSON

They took me through to another part of the gym and pointed out this trolley, and I knew straight away it was Stuart. There was one leg hanging down with a bare foot, and his other foot sticking out with a Reebok training shoe. In the late eighties everyone started wearing Reebok trainers and Stuart was made up with this new pair he'd bought. Just seeing his foot hanging out … I put it back. The chaplain was still with me. He said he'd give Stuart his last rites.

But then, literally within a few seconds of that, two coppers came over and sat me down. That part of the gym was laid out like a school exam hall – there were rows of tables like exam desks. They sat me down at one of these desks and said they needed to take a statement from me. There was no sensitivity about the way they spoke to you, no 'Do you want to take a few minutes to collect yourself?' or anything like that. It was straight into it – they slapped this sheet down and looked at me and said, 'What have you been drinking?' Not, 'Can you tell me if you've had a drink, Mr Thompson?' – which would have been bad enough. I was in shock, I was in a daze.

I couldn't take it. You could hear people wailing and breaking down all around the gym. It was a bit surreal. I got up out of the chair and said I had to phone my mum. They said, 'That would be withholding evidence. We need to get your statement down straight away. What have you had to drink?' I said, 'Tea, coffee. I've been here all day.' They said, 'Are you sure that's all you've had?' And I started to lose it a bit, at this point. Now, I'm quite a placid person, I'm usually very calm – but I was snarling at them. 'What do you mean, you murdering bastards!' That must have come from somewhere, me saying that ... I got up and told them I was going to phone my mum. 'I've just identified my brother's body and I need to speak to my mum.' Again, there was no arm around your shoulder or any remote gesture of sympathy. They said, 'Look, you – sit down and shut up!' If the Reverend hadn't come back, I don't know what I would have done.

He took me through and I phoned my mum and ... that was just the hardest ... the hardest thing. She said to me, 'Come home, son. Just come home.'

STEPHEN WRIGHT

As the night went on, people were starting to turn up at the house. Have you heard anything? My mate Peter Warnick – the lad who'd been shouting down from the seats – he came round. Next thing, they say on the radio that there would be taxis laid on for any relatives who were worried about missing relatives. They'd be leaving from town to take people back to Sheffield. So I said to Peter, 'I've got to go back. I can't stand this.' And he says, 'I'll come with you.' So we headed back to town, to Hatton Garden, where the taxis were meant to be leaving from.

We gets to town. Nothing. Not a taxi in sight in Hatton Garden. In my mind I was expecting a queue of people and a fleet of taxis, but there was no sign of anything. So we walks down to Radio City in Stanley Street. We said to them, 'You made an announcement that there'd be taxis to take people back to Sheffield.' And they sorted it. Radio City got on the phone and organised a taxi for us, from there.

JOHN ASHTON

As soon as we got back, I went straight into Radio City. In those days I used to do regular spots on the radio about health matters, so it was normal for me to just go in – I knew everyone there from the receptionist to Brian Harvey, the producer. In the car, on the way home, it was becoming apparent that the supporters were getting the blame for what had happened, so I wanted to set the record straight. I dropped the boys off and headed into town, to Stanley Street, and I went on the Radio City news.

BARRY DEVONSIDE

So I'm in shock, I'm utterly beside myself, I don't really know where I am or what is going on, but I identify Chris. Following identification, I'm taken over to a table where two plain-clothes policemen asked me to confirm who it is I've just identified. I replied that it was our son, Christopher Barry Devonside, and that he lived at home with his mother, my wife Jac and our daughter Vicky. I confirmed his address and his date of birth.

And then – 'Mr Devonside, could you tell us how you got to Sheffield today?'

I responded, 'What has that got to do with identification?' His reply was that they were trying to piece together what the fans' day had consisted of. I told him we had travelled to the game by car, with friends.

'Did you stop for a meal, or have a drink?'

Already, distraught as I was, I could sense something about the questions they were asking. But he just said they were routine questions, the sort they'd always ask in a situation like this. So the next thing he asked me was, 'Did you have a meal? Did you have a drink?'

Again I replied, 'What has that to do with identification?' At this point my brother nodded to me and I left the table to speak with him.

He said, 'You know what's happening here, don't you?'

I said, 'Yes, they're going to blame us.' My brother wanted to have a word with the coppers, but I said to him, 'No. Christopher never put a foot wrong, in life. He was always respectful. He was a credit to his family, to his city, to his team and to himself. And out of respect for Chris, we're not going to have a scene.' And I went back to the table and saw the procedure through. But I knew from that point on that the police already had their agenda. I thought to myself, *What a bunch of bastards. Those who have been killed are still warm and the police are already trying to cover their tracks.*

SHEILA COLEMAN

That Saturday night was horrible. It was one of those occasions when you feel like you've got to be around people and everyone stays together, but you don't want to talk or anything. Everyone was very, very subdued.

STEVE KELLY

Town was flat. I was picking up lads who were starting to come back from the game and, Everton as well as Liverpool, there was no jubilation. There was nothing.

I had Liverpool fans in the car and they were telling me about the hysteria, about how disorganised everything was, how good the people of Sheffield had been, helping. And, as daft as it sounds, you felt like you were just giving basic counselling there, just by listening. Obviously you couldn't charge anyone, it was a case of trying to do what you could to help. You drop them off and it's, 'No, you're all right, you just get yourself inside.'

JOHN ALDRIDGE

It was only once we'd been dropped off, and we got back home, me and my wife, and we slumped down and put the news on ... it's only then that it really starts to hit home. Up until then, I don't know whether I'd blocked it out, or the full enormity of it hadn't sunk in for whatever reason, but all of a sudden I'm back in our front room and it comes on the news – it *is* the news – and me and her just break down. I couldn't stop crying. I just couldn't believe what had happened, couldn't stop thinking about it. I didn't sleep at all. My mind just wouldn't switch off.

DAMIAN KAVANAGH

My mate Terry had come to ours waiting for me, worrying. He told my mum he'd take me out when I got back. He came back later and took me out for a drink. I suppose I needed it. We went to the Toby and I was glad to see Derek in there with his scarf around his neck – he looked like he was in a daze. Back then I used to go to the Oakfield before and after the match with Derek and his mates, and his two young sons; one of them, Leon, now plays for Everton. After that, Terry drove us to Southport. On the way, I told him I was starting to fear the worst for Dave. I can't remember much else about the evening but I'm sure I wasn't a barrel of laughs. When I got home I cried myself to sleep.

BARRY DEVONSIDE

We finally got home at about 1.30 in the morning. All the family had arrived; there were cars parked everywhere – family, friends, relatives – but I was terrified to go in. I knew how much Jac loved our children … I was frightened. When the door opened, Jac just stood there. For a few moments we said nothing. We put our arms around each other. Jackie told me there were 17 dead so far. I said, 'No, Jac – it's much worse than that …'

STEPHEN WRIGHT

It must have been about 2 o'clock in the morning by the time we got back to Sheffield. We went to the Northern General first. Gave his name and description. Nothing. Went to the Hallamshire and it was pretty much the same again. Gave his name in, description, they went away, came back. Nothing. But they said, at the Hallamshire, go back to Sheffield Wednesday. Go to the gymnasium. They didn't elaborate. I just thought I'd be going to some kind of information point or something.

Gets back in the taxi, went down to Hillsborough. Copper on the door, I tells him, 'We've been sent down here from the Hallamshire Hospital.' He says, 'OK, come in.' It's like a little side room off the gymnasium, sort of thing. And on the wall there's all these pictures – Polaroids – of people yet to be identified. It's hard to quantify how many, but it was a lot of pictures. A lot of faces.

I was in shock at this stage. There's all these pictures, all these Polaroids, but I may as well have been looking at a blank wall. I'm not taking anything in. I turn to Peter and I say, 'He's not there.' And I go to walk away, but Peter stays there. Doesn't move. He just goes, 'There he is.' And it is. It's him. Denim shirt. Suede collar. It's our Graham. I didn't know what to say. I just nodded and I said, 'Yeah, that's him.'

So they takes the picture down, the police, and, it seemed like in the blink of an eye, they take me round this corner, through these doors, into the gymnasium. And there's like a stretcher in front of us, with a green body-bag. So he unzips the body-bag and there's our Graham lying there. But he only unzipped it to just below his neck, and I wanted to be sure it was him. So I unzip it a bit further down, so I can see his clothes, and … I lean closer, go to speak to him, you know? He's bruised, a bit swollen … I was looking at him, I was touching his face … I was low. I was low.

They zipped him back up and wheeled him away.

MARTIN THOMPSON

It was about four in the morning by the time we got back to mine, but I couldn't go in. I just sat outside. Do you know the way you got blamed for things when you were a kid? It was like that. But I hadn't …

Even now, there's no safety mechanism to shut that feeling out. Whenever I think of that day, those two things haunt me. Number 53. And having to tell my mum.

STEVE KELLY

It was after 4 a.m. when I got home from work. I'd had the radio on every now and then, when I was light. The death toll had mounted, I think it was over eighty by the time I called it a night. But still, it didn't enter my head that Michael would have been in any danger. When I got in from work there was a note on the coffee table. My sister, Maureen, had phoned to say there was still no word from Michael. But I just took the dogs out for a walk. I thought, 'Maybe he's seen some terrible sights. He'll have taken himself off for a pint or two to forget about it, get away from it all. He'll be fine.' I went to bed.

STEPHEN WRIGHT

Your mind is racing. I could see all these body-bags on the floor, but your mind isn't really taking it in, it's jumping all over the place. You don't settle. Next thing the police are back and they're saying, 'We're going to do an interview with you.' They sit me down at this table and at first they ask me who our Graham was, confirm his address, stuff like that. Then, straight away, really, it's, 'Where did he go before the match? Did he have a drink?' I'm saying, 'I don't know. I wasn't with him.' So they ask me, 'What about you? Did you have a drink?' I said, 'Yeah. I had a few pints.' At the time I was mystified. 'Why are they asking me all these questions?' But you can see where they were going. I was in bits.

And they got his name wrong. His name is Graham John Wright. That's his name. But it went out as Graham Sean Wright. They probably couldn't understand what I was saying ... But that all caused distress to the family, too. That went out all over the world. Even that first banner on the Kop, the tribute to all those who'd died, every name stitched, embroidered into the flag – they had his name as G. S. Wright. So they must have got his name from the papers.

I'd never known death up until then. Nothing like this had ever happened in our family. And now I'm having to phone up and give them ... tell them all what's happened. And I can't see the dial. I've got the phone in my hand but I can't see to dial.

Our David answers. I just go, 'Dave. He's dead.' Our David goes, 'No ...' Next thing I could hear my mum screaming in the background, absolutely screaming ... I just slumped down at the table with the phone still going. I hear my dad on the other end, so I picks it up again and he just says, 'Come home. Make sure you get home safely.'

So we left, then. Me, Peter and the taxi-driver left the gym and we drove back, through the countryside. Not a word was said. Not a word. In my head, I'm talking to our Graham. I'm saying to him, 'Just give me a sign. Let me know you're not suffering.' These two magpies suddenly just flew up, right in front of the taxi. Two for joy. I thought, 'Yeah!' I was happy about that.

THE TAYLOR REPORT

109. By commendable hard work, a team of pathologists headed by Professor Usher completed post-mortem examinations on all the deceased within forty-eight hours. They found that 88 of the victims were male and seven female. Thirty-eight were under 20 years of age, 39 were between 20 and 29 years and only three were over 50. In virtually every case the cause of death was crush asphyxia due to compression of the chest wall against other bodies or fixed structures so as to prevent inhalation. In all but nine cases that was the sole cause.

In one, pressure on the chest had been so great as to rupture the aorta; in six cases there were also injuries to the head, neck or chest; in the remaining two cases, natural disease was a contributory factor. In 18 cases bones were fractured. Thirteen of those were rib fractures. However, one was a fractured femur, one a fractured radius and the remaining three involved fractures of bones or cartilages round the voice box. These injuries suggest the victims may have been trodden while on the ground.

110. Blood samples were taken from the dead. No alcohol was found in any of the females. Of the males, 51 had no more than 10 milligrams per cent in their blood, which is negligible; 15 had over 80 milligrams per cent and six over 120 milligrams per cent.

111. Although the great majority of those who died were in pen 3, at least five were in pen 4. Most deaths occurred at the front of the pens but there were a few fatalities further back.

THE NEXT DAY

BARRY DEVONSIDE

I didn't sleep at all. As soon as it started getting lighter, I went out. I wasn't walking anywhere in particular, just walking, aimlessly, walking and thinking, 'What have I done, what have I done?' Mentally, I was lost. I was in a very bad way. I got down to Formby Beach and the sun came up and I just broke down in terrible floods of tears. About 7 a.m. I went and knocked at Jonny and Kate Kennedy's house. Both of them worked at Radio City and I knew they would have been at the game. I was lost, and I think I just wanted to explain what went on. I knew the police had failed on the day.

STEVE KELLY

I woke up, violently. Shot right up, stone cold, awake. It was about seven in the morning. Christine, my wife, said, 'What's up? Are you all right?' I said, 'I've got to find out what's happened to Mike.' So I went straight downstairs and put the news on. It was all Ceefax, then – just the bare facts, latest death toll, how many injured, and the helpline number. I waited till about 9 o'clock and started to ring the helpline. I couldn't get through at first but I kept trying, and eventually I got through. I gave a description of Mike. Now, Mike was my brother, I knew every inch of him. I still do. But the police said, 'No, there's nobody of that description. All of the dead have been identified. If he's injured, the hospitals will be your best bet. Ring round the hospitals, check with his friends.'

So I started ringing round a few hospitals, gave his name, gave his description and got the same answer. He wasn't there. So I started thinking at that point, 'Oh, he must be OK. He'll have got his head down somewhere.' So I phoned my ma and said to her, 'You know what Mike's like. He'll be fine. He'll turn up like the bad penny that he is.' I regret saying that, now. Obviously.

MARTIN THOMPSON

Me and Stuart shared the same bedroom. I woke up, like I was jolted out of a really bad dream. I sat up, looked around and the sun was coming through. It was another beautiful sunny day. I looked over at my brother's bed. It was empty. And, on some deeper level, you know that something terrible has happened – but it's just not real. You cannot take it in. I just sat there, staring at his bed.

But I could hear the radio or the telly on downstairs. After a while I went down. Everyone's just sitting there – but nothing gets said.

SHEILA COLEMAN

As soon as I got up, the first thing I did was put Radio Merseyside on. They'd started listing the names of those who'd died. I was sitting there, listening out for the names of my friends and not wanting to hear them. I remember feeling pleased because there was no one I knew, but then feeling guilty because the names they did read out were someone's son, someone's husband, someone's daughter ...

In the immediate aftermath, there was this almost tangible outpouring of grief, this instinctive, collective thing – the way everyone gravitated towards Anfield; the flowers, the messages. I think that showed Liverpool in its best light.

PETER CARNEY

The next day one of the lads came round and we went straight to Anfield. We were there at the ground before they even opened the gates. We bought some flowers, left them outside – and I remember seeing two of the kids from the youth centre, there with their nana. People were starting to arrive at the ground in numbers. I don't remember any announcements being made on the news or from the club – it just seemed like the immediate, obvious thing to do.

JOHN ASHTON

The Radio City report was repeated throughout the night, emphasising not just the innocence, but the critical and heroic role of Liverpool supporters in their response to the unfolding crisis. And on the Sunday morning the whole media thing went into overdrive. This thing of being a doctor, having been there at the match, being from Liverpool, being able to coherently recount what had happened – they came from everywhere. I went on the BBC's breakfast news, with Jeremy Paxman interviewing me live. I was angry and very emotional, and I laid it out in emphatic terms that it was incompetence that caused the disaster; incompetence ran through the tragedy on every level, from the FA to the police to the lack of a 'disaster plan' and the lamentable inadequacy of the emergency plan. Any attempt to shift the blame on to the supporters was a smokescreen. So there was me in the BBC's Liverpool studio, Paxman in London and a guy from the Sheffield fire brigade speaking from outside the Hillsborough gates, and it was difficult to rein in the anger and emotion.

From that newscast, the requests came thick and fast. Canada, Australia, the Far East – they just descended from everywhere. My sole interest was in getting the truth out as widely as possible.

DAMIAN KAVANAGH

My mum woke me up in the morning to tell me Dave had died. He had lived in our street, a well-thought-of family man who'd followed the Reds for years. The last conversation I'd had with him was the day before I went up for his ticket. Our season ticket vouchers gave us a few days where we would be guaranteed to be able to buy a ticket for games like this. He phoned me up: 'Where's me ticket, la?' in his usual jovial style. 'Don't worry, mate, I'm getting it tomorrow,' I'd told him. I remember in 1985 he couldn't make the Newcastle match – just a regular league game, this. He came around to give me his ticket from his Kop season-ticket book – this was the season before I managed to get my own first season ticket. It was typical of him, not wanting any money from me: 'I'm just glad it's going to good use, lad,' he said. Dave and Geoff had taken me with them to Wembley too, introducing me to their mates and their in-joke word 'rancid'. Mum confirmed that Geoff had survived.

My dad went to work on the Sunday but came home early. The phone was constantly ringing with friends of our family asking after me. I walked up to the shop to get sympathy cards for Linda and the kids. I couldn't stop crying – everybody was affected. Everybody knew somebody who had been at the match. This disaster had struck at the very heart of our community.

STEVE KELLY

Mike lived in Bristol. He'd quite often travel up to the games with the local branch of the supporters' club. But, just as often, if it was a Saturday game, he'd stay at my ma's, see us lot and make his own way back to Bristol the following day. So he'd travelled up to Hillsborough on the supporters' coach but, when he wasn't there for the journey back, nobody thought any more of it. 'He'll have gone back to his mother's,' sort of thing.

Anyway, I phoned Radio Bristol, asked them to put out an announcement, an enquiry, for Michael – or anyone who'd seen him – to get in touch. I'm starting to panic a bit by now. He's a fully grown man but you'd have expected him to be in touch by now. So I tried the helplines again. I gave a very full description of him. Our Mike was the least fashionable person in the world. I used to have a laugh with him – he had these Mungo Jerry sideburns. They weren't even fashionable in the seventies, let alone the end of the eighties. I gave the helpline every conceivable detail; the ring I'd bought for his birthday, which he wore on his middle finger. Most importantly, he'd had a serious operation about eighteen months before. He had this one long scar running from his throat right down to his stomach. You couldn't miss it. It was like one big tattoo. There's no way you wouldn't see it – you couldn't *not* see it. And still they said, 'No, there's no one like that here. Don't worry. All the dead have been accounted for. Try not to worry about it any more.' But I was starting to get a bad feeling. So, in sheer exasperation, I said to Christine, 'I'm going over to Sheffield to have a look.' She came with me and, as we were driving along, I says to Christine, 'I'll kill him when I find him.' It's the sort of thing you say, isn't it? But of course I regret that, too.

STEPHEN WRIGHT

My dad was sat in his chair, my mum was in hers. Silence. It was such an empty, empty, soulless place. The house was gone. There was nothing. It was never the same place after that. I went and sat on the arm of my mother's chair, like I'd done since I was a child, but, already, all that had gone. Everything had gone.

Our Ann came round. She'd only just found out, and she was hysterical. She was screaming, crying – she was shouting at me, saying this and that.

I went out of the house. It was another lovely, sunny day. I went down the road and, without really thinking about where I was going, I ended up at St Aidan's church, the church I'd gone to all my life. Our Graham used to go, too. James Aspinall, his mate, who he went with, he used to go. We knew, by then, that James had died, too. Him and Graham were well known to the priest; to the church. We all were.

There was a mass taking place. It was standing room only. It was absolutely chock-a-block. I was stood there, at the back. Of course, everyone knew. Word goes round very quickly, doesn't it? It was already known that two parishioners had died in the tragedy. I'm just standing at the back and I'm in bits again, I've gone – tears streaming down my face. There's people looking at me, people who knew me, all sorrowful. This fella who'd just taken communion, he just put his arms around me. I was lost. Completely lost.

DAMIAN KAVANAGH

I went to mass on the Sunday for the first time in a good while. I was told two lads from our old school were in hospital in Sheffield. Little Robbie, a lad whose sister had been in my class – he'd been in real trouble, but he pulled through. And Steve, from the year above me. Steve, then and now, is a teammate in our weekend footy league. He too, while very seriously hurt, was going to be OK.

STEVE KELLY

I couldn't think where best to look for him, so I drove straight to the ground and headed directly for the Leppings Lane end. It was already being adorned with scarves and flowers and tributes. Not just from Liverpool – from every club you could name. There was a policeman on duty in one of those big overcoats. He must've been boiling! It was another lovely sunny day. I parked my car right there and the copper came over, on the front foot right away: 'Move your fucking car! Have you got no respect?' I don't know, I should have moved, but I don't like being spoken to like that. I told him I wouldn't move. He swore at me again, so I threw my keys over the wall and said, 'What are you going to do now?' He began to arrest me. Christine was crying. It wasn't an ideal start. His sergeant came over to see what was going on and I explained why I was there, and this sergeant was much more reasonable. He said, 'Let's find your car keys first, then we can start looking for your brother.'

STEPHEN WRIGHT

I ended up at the priest's house for a bit. You're looking for answers, aren't you? Why has this happened? What's going on? And then, I'm walking back to ours and, already, the press are camped outside. It's uncanny how they get to know everything. They're there, like, within hours of me identifying our Graham.

I've stopped outside our next door neighbours' and there's a procession of them, door-stepping every house. Does Graham Wright live here? Did you know him? Which house was his? Someone must've pointed me out because next thing I'm getting followed into our house. They're knocking on the door. I don't even know these people and they're shouting through the letterbox, asking for pictures. It was easier just to give them a photograph. Once they've got that, they're off. And when you think back, you're thinking, 'Who were those people?' They never even gave us the pictures back. But that's the kind of daze you're in. You're not thinking straight.

IAN RUSH

Next day, I was still numb. I couldn't take it in, what had happened. I got a phone call from Kenny – I think he phoned round everyone, just to make sure we were OK. He said he was organising a coach to go up to the hospitals in Sheffield. There were people in a bad way, and he thought it would be good if we went to see them. It wasn't an order or anything, it wasn't, 'You have to do this.' But I'm sure that

Above: As the Leppings Lane terrace becomes increasingly overcrowded, play is suspended. Liverpool goalkeeper Bruce Grobbelaar and Alan Hansen can only watch in horror as the events unfold.

Right: Some fans are able to climb onto the pitch, but many are penned in by the crush.

Below: Supporters in the West Stand help pull fellow fans up from the crush to safety above.

Above: Kevin Williams is carried on one of the advertising hoardings used by fans as makeshift stretchers. Steve Hart (wearing a Liverpool scarf) and Tony O'Keefe (immediately behind him) were among those trying to save Kevin's life.

Left: Liverpool manager Kenny Dalglish watches in anguish as the gravity of the disaster becomes apparent.

Below: An ambulance finally makes it onto the pitch.

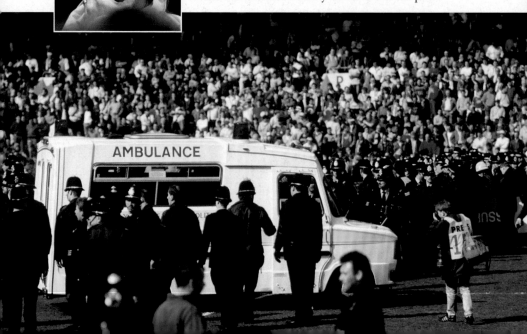

Above: Prime Minister Margaret Thatcher and Home Secretary Douglas Hurd visit Hillsborough the day after the disaster.

Left: A collapsed barrier in the Leppings Lane terrace, the snapped and twisted frame telling its own story.

Below: An inconsolable fan mourns at the scene of the tragedy.

Above: John Aldridge pays his respects as mourners gather outside Anfield, 16 April 1989.

Left: Within days of the disaster, the Anfield pitch is covered in flowers, scarves and banners sent from people all over the world, including fans from other clubs, players and politicians.

Above: Thousands gather for a requiem mass, held outside Liverpool Metropolitan Cathedral.

Above: Kenny Dalglish attends the requiem mass with his daughter Kelly, his son Paul and Liverpool FC chairman John Smith.

Above: Kenny Dalglish and John Barnes at the funeral of Gary Church. Kenny organised it so that the club was represented at every funeral.

Above: Angered by their treatment by Sheffield Wednesday, who had failed to erect a memorial to the 96 by the tenth anniversary of the tragedy, the Liverpool fans publicly campaign for a boycott of Hillsborough.

Left: Since opening up on its new site in August 2003, the Hillsborough Justice Campaign shop has provided a focal point for the campaign, offering everything from stickers and pamphlets to counselling and legal support.

Below: Truth Day. Eighteen years after Hillsborough, Liverpool fans demonstrate against Kelvin MacKenzie and the *Sun*'s smear campaign at LFC's FA Cup match against Arsenal.

Above: MP Andy Burnham's speech at the twentieth anniversary of Hillsborough, attended by over 37,000 people, is seen by many as one of the pivotal moments in the campaign for justice.

Below: Supporters gather for a vigil outside St George's Hall after the disclosure of the Hillsborough Independent Panel's report on 12 September 2012.

Left: Anne Williams, who fought tirelessly for a new inquest into her son Kevin's death, at the twenty-fourth anniversary memorial service at Anfield. She died just days later, having suffered from cancer, and was honoured with the Helen Rollason Award at the BBC Sports Personality of the Year ceremony in December 2013.

Below: Justice at last. On 26 April 2016, following the verdict of unlawful killing at the Hillsborough inquests, St George's Hall in Liverpool is lit up to commemorate the fans who lost their lives. They will never be forgotten.

basically every single player went. And that's how it was. Everyone just wanted to help.

STEVE KELLY

They took us to this church hall – the Hammerton Road boys' club. They put us in with three social workers, and the one who eventually sat down with us – Christine, her name was, coincidentally – she's saying to me, 'Can you give me a description; what was he wearing? Does he have any distinguishing features?' And I'm, like, 'No disrespect, Christine, but I've already been through this half a dozen times. We've established that all the dead are accounted for. I just need to find out where my brother is …'

She's very patient, this Christine, and she apologises and says she realises it must be frustrating, but could I just, once more, give her a detailed description of what Michael looks like. So I tells her, and as I'm telling her all this I notice a youngish constable looking over. He comes a bit closer. He's wearing one of those light blue denim shirts they used to have, with the epaulettes, and their number on the shoulder. I carry on with my description. Christine, the social worker, is jotting things down, but out of the corner of my eye I can see this young bobby is taking serious notice of what I'm saying, and, I'm thinking, 'Aye-aye, what's going on here?' But I still felt confident because, you know, they'd told us: all the dead had been accounted for.

The young bobby comes over, taps Christine on the shoulder, she has to follow him to the centre of the church hall, out of earshot. There's lots of hand gestures and, whatever they're saying, it looks important. By now it's starting to get to me. I can see that they're talking about me and there's a massive change in the policeman's body language. They're looking over and she's nodding her head and it's really starting to worry me. And then he takes Christine over to a phone in the corner and, for the first time, this dread came over me. I felt then that something horrendous had happened.

So they came back over and you can see it on their faces; the bobby says to me, 'Would you be prepared to come and look at some bodies?'

Plural. Bodies. I says, 'What do you mean, identify some bodies? There's only one person I can identify and, anyway, haven't all the dead been identified?'

No, he says – there's a male and a female still to be identified. My heart sinks. I must have known. But, still, I said to him, 'Why would I want to look at a woman, then?' And he says, 'Fair enough, would you please come and take a look at the man?' And, inside, I'm going to pieces. I feel so weak, so scared … he must have repeated the request a couple of times and, in the end I said, 'Yes, OK, if it helps to clear this mess up, let's go.' He said, 'We need to take you to a place called the Medico-Legal Centre.' And, again, I said, 'OK.' And I went to get out of the chair, but I couldn't move. My legs had turned to jelly.

JOHN ALDRIDGE

It was heartbreaking. It really brought it home to you. There's all our fans who've come to Sheffield to cheer us on, and they've ended up in hospital, like this; some of them in a coma, you know? For myself, it was very hard. Brucie was clowning around, trying to put a smile on their faces, but I just couldn't … I'm looking at some of these kids and you just know they're not going to make it; or, if they do, then their lives are going to be very, very different to what they were yesterday, when they set out for the match.

MARTIN THOMPSON

In the end I just went down to the pub, but it was unearthly. Usually, Sunday afternoon is one of the best times at our pub, but it was just full of people sitting round, hardly speaking. It was like that for days, weeks afterwards – people just sitting there. I tried to get drunk but I don't know if it was adrenaline or something else counteracting it, but I just could not get out of this dazed, surreal state of mind. I couldn't get drunk. I didn't feel anything.

STEVE KELLY

So they took us to the Medico-Legal Centre – it was only a few minutes' drive away – and, as soon as we walked in there, that's were all the niceness ended. It was cold; it was suits, suspicious, poker faces. The way they spoke to me, their stance, everything – they made me feel like I was there to defend myself.

We went to another room and we went through the whole process, all over again – the ring, the scar, the Mungo Jerry sidies. And then, with no warning, no preparing you, no 'Are you OK, Mr Kelly?' they just pulled out this Polaroid and threw it on the table in front of me. And I mean *threw* it, like he was dealing a hand of cards. It span round and came to a stop in front of me, upside down. I picked it up and turned it round and there he was. It was Mike. Dead.

I said, 'That's him.' They said, 'Are you sure?' I just nodded and went to put the photo in my pocket, and his hand came over and held me by the wrist. He said, 'You can't take that. That's the property of South Yorkshire police.' I said, 'Sorry.' I was on autopilot then. I was numb. I said, 'What happens now?' They said, 'We'll take you down to the morgue.'

By now my head's all over the place. The social workers had gone, it was just all these corridors and, the next thing, we're in this very small room. It was claustrophobic, it was so cramped in there, and in the centre of the room was this window, with purple curtains. I must have frozen because one of these coppers sort of ushered me forward, towards the curtains. Again there was no preparing you, no 'Are you OK, Mr Kelly? Are you sure you're ready?' and the curtains are pulled back and, God bless him, there's our poor kid, lying there on this trolley.

I took a step back and I fell to my knees. I couldn't believe it; I wouldn't. I crawled back towards the window and pulled myself up, so my face was level with the trolley, and I remember just murmuring, 'It's him.' It was sinking in now. That was our Michael, dead. I turned round to them and said, 'Can I go in?' They said, 'No.' I said, 'He's been on his own all night. I want to go in and give him a kiss.' He said, 'You can't go in. You can't touch him. He's the property of the coroner.' I said to him, 'He's my mother's son, he's the property of no one. I want to go in and give him a kiss.' He said, 'You can't.' He took me back outside, and I just thought, 'Jesus Christ. I've got to tell my mother, now.'

STEPHEN WRIGHT

Our Graham's girlfriend, Janet, was at the house and obviously she's in bits. I didn't know what to say. Our David was back. It was his ticket, wasn't it? He's thinking, 'That should have been me. Maybe if I'd have gone, instead ...' All that.

Then Janet said she wanted to go to Hillsborough. She wanted to go to where our Graham had died.

STEVE KELLY

So I went to phone my mother. I couldn't remember her phone number. My mind had just gone blank. Eventually I got the number from directory enquiries and my cousin answered, put my ma on. And I told her. I said, 'I've found him … he's dead.' I can still hear the screams down the phone, the howling, the wailing …

I went back to find the policemen who'd taken me there and I told them I wanted to go back in and see my brother again. They told me that wasn't possible. I'd identified him, and that was that. Again, there was no basic sympathy. Not once did any of them offer me a cup of tea or put their arm around me. In a time of sadness like that, it's a basic human thing to put your arm around someone, try to comfort them. But I think that, even then, the police were getting their game-plan together. They were seeing things how they wanted to see things. And I was on the other side. I must admit, I became quite aggressive at that point. I thought, 'I don't care what they do to me. I want to go back in and see Michael again.' And I kicked up that much of a fuss that they backed down and let me see him again.

After a bit they came in and said, 'That's enough now.' So I told them, 'I'm going home now; I'm going to see my mother. But I'm coming back to see him again tomorrow. And the day after. And I'll be coming back to see him every day until we bring him back home to Liverpool. He's not your property.' And I drove back home to break it all to my ma.

DAMIAN KAVANAGH

I went in the Toby again with my mates on the Sunday night. Some of them had been to the match and were in the crush. Carl and Bomb

Head were as relieved as I was to find out each other had survived. Carl confirmed that the other lads, the ones we went to the Oakfield with, were all OK. Bomb Head had a photo of himself from a Sunday paper, helping to pull people up into the West Stand above the terrace – he'd survived himself that way.

But it was in the Toby that it was confirmed to me that Sef had died. I broke down again, in public – young men don't do that, do they? Me and Sef hadn't been best mates or anything, but I knew who he was from school days. It was more the casual tragedy of it. He'd gone to the game with his mates – Steve, Robbie, Tony and Jason – who had all thankfully come back. But Sef didn't. Jason wrote a beautiful poem about the five of them, which I've kept to this day.

THE FOLLOWING WEEK

MARTIN THOMPSON

I just walked around. For two or three days, that's all I did – I'd walk around, go down the beach, sit on the sand dunes, trying to work things out in my head. One thing that really got to me was that they didn't even close Hillsborough after the disaster. Can you imagine what would happen if you owned a nightclub where 96 people died? The club would be closed immediately, it'd have its licence revoked and the owners would be in the dock to answer manslaughter charges …

It was hard. I couldn't come to terms with any of it. One moment someone is here, they're with you, every single day of your life – and then they're gone. Where had he gone? I couldn't stop thinking about that: *where* had Stuart gone?

I'd been working in this frozen-food factory trying to get some money together to go travelling. I'd been planning this big Inter Rail trip around Europe. None of that mattered any more. For those first few days I was in a dark, dark place.

PETER CARNEY

I recognised John Ashton when he came on telly, because he helped with my rescue. When I was first brought out the back, he examined me and had me moved. I remember him being interviewed, I think he was on *Newsnight*, and he gave it the full bifters. He told it exactly how it happened and he was absolutely right. And, again, hearing John Ashton – it only confirmed for me that the only accounts you could rely upon were those of the ordinary fans, the people who'd survived the crush, or people who had helped with the rescue. Everyone else was just covering their tracks. From our side, it's always been this one consistent account, all the way down the line. From the other side, well – it's completely full of holes, isn't it?

JOHN ASHTON

On the Monday morning, 17 April, I took a phone call from Richard Alderslade, the Regional Medical Officer in Yorkshire. He said, 'John, you need to stop going on the media and criticising the emergency response. I remember putting the phone down and thinking, 'Where has that come from?'

JEGSY DODD

On the Monday, I was watching all the coverage on the BBC news and I couldn't believe what I was looking at. The old fella we'd been helping – the guy the copper had thrown the coat over to pronounce him dead – was sitting up in bed in hospital talking to Margaret Thatcher. He was alive. His name was William Mylchreest, from Wavertree. I tracked him down through the telephone directory and spoke to his daughter – told her how made up I was that her dad had made it. It was strange – very emotional. Making this connection with a complete stranger in the most desperate of circumstances, and yet this one had a happy outcome.

DAMIAN KAVANAGH

I went into work on the Monday morning. I can even remember the name of the scheme I was looking at – Kontak Manufacturing. Obviously everyone at the Royal knew I'd been at the game, so you can imagine what the reaction was. Everyone was coming over to check I was all right, hugging me. When they heard what I'd been through, they were amazed I'd come in.

Two of my mates were in tears in the toilets. I was trying to counsel them, just basically talking to them, trying to calm them down, but it was horrendous. They were broken.

I remember looking at this case and just staring at it. I wasn't taking a single thing in. Then I went on my dinner break, but I couldn't eat a thing. I don't think I'd even felt hungry since I got back on the Saturday. My mate said, 'You should go home, you know?' I said I was OK – I'd rather be doing something. But I was just sat there, staring out into space, and one of my work colleagues came over and said, 'Come on – you're going home.' And I was off all week, after that.

PETER CARNEY

I went down to the toy shop on County Road and bought a football. Anfield had been opened up to the public by now and there was this spontaneous thing where people were congregating at the ground and leaving tributes. So I bought a ball and took it to the ground. I put it on the penalty spot.

And I'd had this idea for a flag for a while. The original plan was to do something like the Roma fans had in the '84 [European Cup] final, that huge floater flag that covered about half their end. So, leading up to Liverpool's centenary, I'd been planning a massive big flag like the Roma one – one that would celebrate LFC's achievements. After I'd been to the ground I went to see my mate Fred Brown, who lived a few doors down from the Shankly Gates. He's an artist, and I said to him, 'We've got to do that banner.'

JOHN ALDRIDGE

I headed straight up to the ground, under my own steam. It had already become the focal point for all the tributes, and I just wanted to get up there and show my solidarity, pay my respects. I was having real difficulty coming to terms with what had happened and, looking back, I think you just wanted that connection. You wanted to be there, among people who understood. And there were nods and let-ons, people saying hello and wanting your autograph and what have you, but mainly they left you to it, you know? Everyone was going through the same thing. Everyone knew.

STEPHEN WRIGHT

Anfield became a shrine. The queues were two miles long – some days longer – as people waited to lay their wreaths, leave their scarves and messages, and pay their respects. As a bereaved family, we were able to go straight in. They had a lounge, one of the directors' rooms, where the families could go. I was in there with Peter, and he idolises Dalglish. Kenny's the greatest thing that ever walked the earth, you know? And there we are in this lounge in circumstances of the most extreme grief, and there's Dalglish and Peter just taps him on the shoulder and goes, 'Kenny, how the fuck did you score that goal against Belgium?' I think it was what was needed, to be honest. Kenny's face, that smile – we all just laughed out loud, and it felt like this big release.

And walking out there … the Salvation Army band playing, half the pitch was taken over by this carpet of flowers. The smell of those flowers, it still comes back to you, at times. Dalglish again, I think it was him who described it as the most tragic but the most beautiful sight he'd ever witnessed.

I walked across the Kop, reading all the tributes that had been left, from everywhere. Everywhere. And our Graham used to have this Liverpool tea towel hung above his bed. I took it down and laid it on the pitch.

PETER CARNEY

Fred Brown worked at the Centre for Arts Development Training, by Exchange Station, and he sorted it for us to work from an empty office in CADT. So, on the Tuesday, we just got down to it – somebody drew a trophy, someone got a list of names. The material came from one of the window dressers at Lewis's in town. She used to give all their unwanted off-cuts and roll-ends of fabric to the Merseyside Play Action Council. All these odds and sods went into the store room there. I found three pieces of 10 x 24 foot material and I'd already made a start (before Hillsborough). I'd sketched it all out on A3 and I had a good idea how the flag would look.

The original idea we had was to stitch the three big pieces together to make this one banner which would celebrate the club's history and achievements. But now, for this flag, I turned all the achievements to black. The trophies were going to be black; and there'd be a red European Cup in the corner to represent Heysel. The Liver Bird was going to remain white.

So we just set to it. John Fay did all the stencils for the lettering, Fred did the trophies, someone got a list of names, and we literally made the flag on the floor there at Peter House. All day every day, the Tuesday to the Thursday, people came and helped out until the flag was ready.

At that stage we hadn't embroidered the names – we'd painted everything, because we wanted it ready as soon as possible. On that original flag – I made a new one for the twentieth anniversary – we only managed to do their initial and surname. I know now that we made all sorts of mistakes – some of the names were wrong, some of them we repeated – so when I re-made the banner I was able to correct those mistakes, and we put their full names, too – surname and Christian names.

MARTIN THOMPSON

I went down to Anfield with three or four friends and they were just closing up the ground. A steward said to me, 'You can't go in now. You'll have to come back tomorrow.' I got really upset. I broke down. It was everything – anger, grief – and the girl on reception, Karen, came out and put her arm around me. She said, 'It's all right, he's coming in with me.' The penalty area was already covered with flowers. By the end of the week the whole pitch was this sea of flowers.

Karen was great – red hair, looked after everyone. She took us up into the players' lounge, and Craig Johnston had just arrived. He'd jumped on a plane from Australia to come to Liverpool and try to offer support. Karen introduced me and he said he'd written a poem about the tragedy. But he just burst into tears. He was in bits, absolutely crying his eyes out. It ended up that I was comforting him! It was all a bit surreal – there were all your heroes, who you'd put on a pedestal, serving you tea and coffee. Bruce Grobbelaar, Ray Houghton, Peter Beardsley – their wives were coming over to see if you were OK. It must have been really hard for them, too. It must have been strange.

JOHN ALDRIDGE

In the days after the tragedy we were down at Anfield all the time, talking to the people who'd been there, or who'd lost their loved ones. I found it hard. I wasn't the most talkative in those days and, when it came to people whose lives had just caved in on them, I didn't really know what to say. There are people, professionals, who've had years of training, specialist counsellors, and *they* don't know what to say! Yet you also knew that, just being there – I'm sure it made a difference. Us players being there for them definitely helped in some small way.

STEPHEN WRIGHT

So we went back to Hillsborough in two taxis; myself and a couple of mates, some of our Graham's mates, and his girlfriend Janet.

We took some flowers, wreaths and so on. Sheffield Wednesday were OK, it was open door; there were clergy there and social workers and so on.

We get shown out on to the pitch, and I take Janet to see the terrace. So we're sitting there on the Leppings Lane terrace, and our Graham's girlfriend's crying, then the next minute this official came over and he goes, 'You're going to have to move, now. The Duke of Kent's here.' I just said, 'I'm going nowhere, mate; I'm staying right here.' I don't even think my legs could have moved anyway. I was bad. He didn't know what to do so, in the end, he left us alone. The Duke of Kent and all these sort of dignitaries are being shown around the ground, and they just walked right past us, like we weren't there. Not even a nod; nothing.

A priest came over and sat down with us. I asked him if he'd hear my confession. He says, 'Of course.' So I gave my confession there on the terrace, asking for forgiveness for all the bad things I'd done to our Graham throughout his life. So I was absolved of my sins on the Leppings Lane terrace that Tuesday after the tragedy …

MARTIN THOMPSON

I heard about the *Sun*'s headline straight away. Everyone was up in arms. At first, what they were saying didn't fully sink in. Then I started to think about it. 'Pick-pocketing the dead?' Well, I was round the side, by the gym, lifting blankets to see if Stuart was … that could have been me they were talking about. That copper could have looked over, seen me and – you know what their mindset was like – he'd have drawn his own conclusions, wouldn't he? That was my first thought. Then you started to hear more: Liverpool fans assaulting the dead. I mean … just try to imagine that. They'd be lynched. Did people really believe that could possibly have happened?* I've got to be honest, I reacted to it in a purely selfish way: is this what they're saying about *me*? I had to get out of the house.

DAMIAN KAVANAGH

When I heard about the *Sun*'s headline, I was livid. I was really, really, really angry. Did they not realise that, if even one person had been out of line, the evidence would have been all over the telly, all over the papers? If there really was mass drunkenness, where's the footage? If people were smashing their way into the ground and beating up coppers, where's the footage? Where's the photos? Because I guarantee you, if *anything* like that had happened, it would have been proper front-page news. Instead, they had to make it up, didn't they? The rage that that rag provokes in me is untold. It's had such a profound effect on me that I can barely even look at the word in any context. On holiday in the Lake District, I found myself walking past a pub called the Sun Inn.

Up until that time I hadn't even thought about making a complaint or a legal statement or anything like that. Then I started thinking

---

* In its edition of 19 April 1989, the *Sun* newspaper led with a front-page headline of 'THE TRUTH'. Underneath were sub-headers:

- Some fans picked pockets of victims
- Some fans urinated on the brave cops
- Some fans beat up PCs giving kiss of life

In spite of lead reporters counselling their Editor against such an approach, Kelvin MacKenzie went ahead. As a result, the *Sun* was removed from the shelves of hundreds of Merseyside newsagents in protest at the story. In many outlets, the boycott of the newspaper is still in place, 27 years later.

about Dave, who'd died. Sef, who'd died. The way the fans had responded to the unfolding tragedy, compared to the way the police and the authorities had just stood there, doing nothing. I could not believe they'd write something like that. I just said to my mum and dad, 'That's it – I'm going to sue the bastards.' And, at 20 years of age, that was the first time my mum had ever heard me swear.

TONY O'KEEFE

Working on the Rescue, you develop a thick skin. There's a certain sense of humour. It's how different people cope with certain things. But when the *Sun* came out with its headline on the Wednesday, I just lost it. There were a few of my colleagues, people I worked with, people who knew me, and they were repeating this crap they were reading in the *Sun*. This one guy made the wrong remark at the wrong time, and I just completely lost it with him.

STEPHEN WRIGHT

To be honest, we were in a daze. We were in our own environment, trying to cope with things as best we could. One of my workmates knocked at ours and said, 'Don't buy the papers, they're writing terrible things.' But, effectively, we'd had a media blackout in the house anyway. We didn't have the telly on, we weren't getting the paper. We were hardly even going out. Friends, neighbours, were bringing round meals, everyone trying to do their bit. My uncle told us about the AC Milan fans giving a minute's applause during the sixth minute of their game, but other than that we wouldn't have known. I wouldn't have seen the *Sun*'s story.

ANNE WILLIAMS

They weren't sparing us, they were making it more complicated for us, and I think the families were treated appallingly. We were bereaved, they didn't care about us; all they wanted was to make sure it was covered up. I mean, the *Sun* newspaper, that started it all, and we all knew that wasn't true. That did a hell of a lot of damage, and that spread everywhere. Even my auntie coming over from Canada once said, 'Oh, those drunken Liverpool fans,' and you have to put people right.

JEGSY DODD

In the immediate days following, everyone was trying to organise concerts and fundraisers, but I just couldn't think straight at first. I had to book a holiday and get away from everything. I couldn't even answer the phone, so we just got off to Majorca for a week. It didn't help that much, to be honest. The whole thing was massive – the coverage was everywhere. And then this whole thing of the *Sun*'s headline broke: THE TRUTH. And it wasn't just the *Sun*, either. I'm sure that the *Star* and the *Express* ran with similar sorts of stories too – it was just that the *Sun* was the first of them, and the most extreme. It wasn't a good time. The cover-up had started. As far as most people were concerned … give a dog a bad name … we'd done it, we were to blame, we'd killed our own fans. For ten, fifteen, twenty years we've had to live with that and, in so many respects, the city still hasn't lived it down to this day.

JOHN ASHTON

What I subsequently learned is that a series of letters were sent that week – letters to, and between, the very top management of the Sheffield Health Authority, the Chief Executive of the NHS, the Regional Medical Officer for Trent – and letters sent by members of the Royal Family and by prominent government ministers of the day. Between 17 April – the day I received the phone call from Richard Alderslade – and 21 April, letters of commendation were sent from Margaret Thatcher, Kenneth Clarke, the Prince of Wales, the Duke of Kent to, for example, Stanley Speight, Chairman of the Sheffield Health Authority, praising the emergency medical response. A pattern emerges in these letters – the use of the same, identical superlative adjectives in applauding the medical effort. 'Magnificent … professional … dedicated … pride … fortitude,' each of these letters uses the same terminology.

Who can say if there was a template, so to speak, or a briefing? We know that Stanley Speight personally escorted Margaret Thatcher around the Sheffield hospitals. Was there an orchestrated narrative about the emergency response? What is for certain is that these letters were all cited as 'disclosed material' in the Hillsborough Independent Panel Report. The letters are all there on record in the repository documents for anyone who wants to read them.

PETER CARNEY

We brought the banner down to the ground on the Friday and hung it on the corner of Anfield Road and Kemlyn Road. People started adding things, pinning things on; a ribbon, a badge. There was a sticker of John Aldridge, and next to it was a badge in the shape of a crown. Not so very long afterwards, Aldridge left to join Real Sociedad – whose club crest is a crown. So I took that to be symbolic; it was a message.

The ground remained open over the Friday, Saturday and Sunday – it had turned into a shrine. We went to pick the banner up on the Monday, and it had been moved inside the ground. It had been laid down right by the away team's bench, on the pitch. It was spread out on the grass and Phil Thompson was stood over it, looking at the banner. He couldn't get over how many Thompsons there were on the flag.

MARTIN THOMPSON

I was still distraught about it – not just about the *Sun*, it was the way *all* the papers were now starting to report the tragedy. I was there. I was on that pitch. I knew what had gone on.

Someone said to me, 'Make sure you don't buy *Hello!* magazine.' *Hello!* magazine? As if I'd buy *Hello!* magazine! So, of course, what do I do? I go and get a copy. And it had, as its centre-page spread, this fully blown-up image of the central pens at the moment where nearly a hundred people are about to lose their lives. You can clearly see Stuart, and he looks dead. And there's Kevin Williams, right behind him. And he's still alive.

Now, today, I don't know, if you were looking at a photomontage of a mining disaster or a factory fire, or a building that's collapsed with people inside, you'd mainly just see it as news, wouldn't you? That photograph of the little girl in Vietnam, burnt to bits with Agent Orange – it's photo journalism, isn't it? You feel sorry for the victims, but you don't feel as though you're intruding. Live coverage of the tsunami, you can see bodies floating past and you don't think, 'That's somebody's mother.' You don't personalise it. But that's what was happening to us, with that image. The photographer who took the picture is possibly thinking of that moment as news – he's capturing a man-made catastrophe, as it happens. His picture is now a historic document. But, at the time, my God, I was destroyed.

STEPHEN WRIGHT

We got our Graham back on the Friday. He was resting at Craven's, the undertaker, in Page Moss. My mum and dad couldn't face going down. I went numerous times over that weekend. He looked a lot different to when I'd identified him. They do them up, don't they? The funeral was arranged for the Wednesday, but on the Sunday they had to close the lid. It had been over a week and the body was beginning to smell and they had to close the coffin. I'd still go down there, but it wasn't the same going to see him, after that. It was just a coffin.

JOHN ALDRIDGE

There was one hospital visit. It was awful; haunts me to this day. We were going around the wards, talking to the kids. Then we went upstairs to another ward and this one kid, he's in a coma. The doctor says to me, 'Will you just come and sit with him? Just have a word in the young lad's ear?' And you say, yes, of course you'll go and sit with the kid, it's no trouble at all. So you whisper in his ear, 'When you come out of this we'll all take you down the dressing room and there'll be signed shirts and footballs for you, you can meet all the players. I promise you, we'll sort it all out, make it happen.' The doctor steps over and says, 'Thanks very much. That'll mean so much to the kid's mum and dad.' I says, 'No problem. When do you think the lad is going to wake up, like? When is he going to be OK?' The doctor said, 'Oh, no – we're cutting off the machine this afternoon.' You could have cut me in half. I couldn't take it in. I think … I don't think I ever really got over that.

MARTIN THOMPSON

I went round to my gran's. She was a proper, wise old woman, my gran – worked every day of her life. She said to me, 'After the First World War there were young soldiers walking back in their bare feet. They'd been in the trenches for four years, watching their friends and comrades die, only boys your age, watching boys die. And this is the truth – it's not just you. Every second of every day, children are dying and parents are crying. So what you have got to do is, you've got to be strong. You have to be strong for other people. Because, if they can see that you're standing up to it and you're coping with it, it will help them to cope, too. You've got to deal with it.'

So, I think it might have been the night before the funeral. I went in the pub and all Stuart's mates were sat around this big table, sombre. No one was saying a word. So I went over and said, 'Fucking hell, you'd think someone had died.'

I think that helped. Obviously I was hiding my true emotions, and it was obvious to them that I was concealing how I really felt. But, nonetheless, the fact they could see that I was doing that, it was like, 'Well, if he's trying to put a brave face on then what right have we got to be sitting round moping like this?'

STEVE KELLY

I don't think my mother and I were ever the same, after that. That incident, the circumstances; our Michael was her first born, she doted on him. And I was the bearer of bad news. It wore me down, eventually. I don't know if either of us ever recovered from it.

PETER CARNEY

God love all the people who'd volunteered to come down and help clear all the tributes from the pitch – I couldn't have done it. I can't say 'cleared up the mess' because it was one of the most beautiful sights I've ever seen. I'd been on the terraces a couple of times through the week, but I think they closed it off on the Wednesday. People left their most treasured mementoes and possessions there. One in particular was a 1965 FA Cup final programme that was signed by Shankly and the team on their way back from Wembley. So, if you think what that meant to the fella who owned it, who'd kept it all those twenty-four years ... these were the sorts of things that people were leaving as tributes. All the messages that were left, the things people wrote ... it was just the most beautiful sight I've seen at that ground.

MARTIN THOMPSON

The morning of the funeral, our GP came around to the house to see how I was standing up to everything. I thought I was OK, but she gave me a pill and told me to take half if I started feeling shaky. I thought, 'Half a tablet is no good. If she thinks I need it, I'll take the whole thing.'

Stuart's funeral was in the morning, then Kevin Williams was being buried in the afternoon. They were both laid out in the rest home the night before – Kevin in one room, Stuart in the other. I think they were the first of the Hillsborough funerals – I know Stuart was the first Catholic funeral, anyway. It was at Our Lady's church in Formby – the Archbishop of Liverpool, Derek Worlock, came.

Derek Worlock did a speech, then Alan Hansen got up and read a passage from the Bible. I'm not sure what the tablet was – some kind of sedative, I think – but it was starting to work. I was having to concentrate really hard on just getting through the service. I thought, 'Jesus Christ, you can't fall asleep at your own brother's funeral!' Before the funeral the priest had asked me if I wanted to get up and say a few words: you know, give a little tribute to our Stuart. I just signalled, then, that I wasn't going to be up to it. I couldn't move. If I'd have got up, I would have collapsed.

STEPHEN WRIGHT

We didn't bring Graham back to the house. It was considered a special honour to be placed in the church overnight, the night before his funeral. So that's where he stayed on the Tuesday night, along with his mate James Aspinall. It was a joint funeral. On the Wednesday morning the hearse pulled up. There were crowds like you wouldn't believe. All the way to St Aiden's there was a sea of people. Outside that church there's a grass hill – and that was crowded with people, too. The roads, the pavements, crowds outside. Obviously the church was full, the church hall was full, so they did a video link of the service to the church hall, and they set up a PA system to relay the mass to all the crowds outside. As well as our local parish priest, the Archbishop,

Derek Worlock, was there too. It was a really big thing – I don't think there were many joint funerals.

After the service we went to Anfield Cemetery. We had outriders, a police escort all the way, two hearses, LFC floral tributes; people knew what it was – people were blessing us all along the way. The two of them, James and our Graham – they're not next to each other, but they're virtually next to each other in the cemetery.

BARRY DEVONSIDE

I was getting up at all hours, going out of the house, walking, walking … I couldn't honestly say I had a proper night's sleep in all that time. For three or four weeks after Chris's funeral I would leave the house in the middle of the night and go looking for him in the hope that this was all a nightmare. Even though the funeral had taken place, I possibly thought that Chris would come home. This could not have happened at a football match.

God knows what it must have been like for Jackie – what I must have been like. There was just this hole, this indescribable pain that, as a parent, you can never come to terms with. I just used to walk for hours, turning it over and over in my mind.

SHEILA COLEMAN

I was lecturing at a college of further education at the time. There was still quite a left-wing element to the city council in the late eighties. There was the Independent Labour Party, and my friend Tommy Smith was a part of that. So in the immediate aftermath, Tommy and some of my other friends who were at Hillsborough helped form the

Disaster Working Party at the city council and, right from the start, they were addressing Hillsborough as a cover-up as well as a tragedy.

IAN RUSH

Kenny took the lead in terms of the club's involvement, splitting the players up into groups to go and visit families, survivors and so on. Later, once the bodies had been released, we'd attend the funerals, too. Jan Molby and I lived quite close to each other, and we'd go and visit people who lived around here. I remember Jan and I going to the Traynors' house and their vigil was still being observed. I think Kenny went to six funerals in one day. That was when it really started to hit home to us players, though. You're going to see these poor people, going to their houses, their funerals. You're hoping you can offer some kind of comfort, take their mind off things for a bit, but it was having the opposite effect on us. It was like, this is real, this happened, we were there. This is the real world. But, whatever we were thinking, these people have got to live with it forever.

JOHN BARNES

My view was simply, whatever the bereaved want, whatever the families want, that's what I want, too. What I think doesn't matter. Should we replay the semi-final? Should we play again? Should we cancel the season, as a mark of respect? Whatever they want, we'll do it. We went to the funerals, not to intrude or force ourselves upon anyone, but because they wanted us there; they'd asked us to come. They appreciated it. There wasn't one single funeral where there wasn't a player, and representative from the club.

JOHN ALDRIDGE

The first funeral I went to was tough – really hard. One day I went to three – one in the morning, one at noon, and another later in the afternoon. There was the Hicks girls, the two brothers from Netherley and then ... there was a big coffin came past, then a smaller one came up behind it – a dad and his lad, and it just ... it tears you to bits.

MARTIN THOMPSON

I got a call from Smithdown Lane police station on the Tuesday after Stuart's funeral – my 20th birthday – telling me I could go and pick up his clothes. His other training shoe was never found but, other than that, everything was there. I signed a form to say that one training shoe was missing, but I'd collected the rest. It was another hot, hot day and I remember hauling Stu's clothes around town in this big black bin-bag.

PETER CARNEY

The first six weeks I was a mess. It wasn't so much that I was *suffering* from flashbacks – I had to find them, you know? I had to try to visualise what had happened to me, for my own peace of mind. I couldn't recollect it all immediately, and what I did remember I wasn't sure of when it had happened, in sequence. I couldn't put it into order. But I made myself think about it. I had to. And when those images and recollections went through my mind, I had to try to put them in sequence, really, to try and make sense of it. So I grappled with that. I struggled with it. I had to keep telling myself that this was a real experience that I'd been through – because it was beyond my comprehension.

IAN RUSH

Eventually the decision was taken and we had to start playing again. We'd attended the funerals, we'd been to the services, we'd been there at Anfield, but we hadn't spoken that much about what had happened. This is where Kenny was the best – he had his own way of working out what each player needed, and helping him. Being truthful, some players really just wanted to get back to playing; others didn't. But we stuck together. I think that made us stronger, as a squad. There was nothing of: 'You *have* to play.' We hadn't even trained. But this friendly game was organised, against Celtic.

STEPHEN WRIGHT

I went to Celtic, and it was a definitive occasion for me. For one, I knew our Graham wouldn't have wanted me to stop going to the game. I went everywhere with Liverpool. He wouldn't have wanted that to stop. But, just as important, it showed that I *could* go back. You can never do justice to how magnificent Celtic were. The way the whole ground sang 'You'll Never Walk Alone' – it meant everything to me.

JOHN BARNES

In the time we hadn't played, Arsenal opened up a five-point lead, but we had games in hand. The first game back, we played Everton, at Goodison. It was a bit of a nothing game, 0–0, but the unity in the crowd was the big thing – even the Everton fans were singing 'Walk On'.

DANNY RHODES

Eventually a date was set for the semi-final to be replayed at Old Trafford. Before the game, there was this really moving moment where the Forest fans and the Liverpool fans all sang 'You'll Never Walk Alone' together. Then there's a bit of a lull, then the Liverpool fans do a really loud, 'We hate Nottingham Forest …' And I do know a lot of Forest fans who feel very bitter about that, to this day. It was like – 'We're on a hiding to nothing, here. Nobody wants us to win this game, why are we even bothering? Why are we here?' But we wanted to be there because it was on, you know?

PETER CARNEY

The first time after Hillsborough that I'd been in any kind of a crowd was when we came down to the ground on the Saturday – 22 April – for the memorial service. We went in the Kemlyn Road stand, about twenty rows up. My enduring memory of it is that there were rows and rows of prams on the touchline. And I think it was too much for some people; people started leaving. But we were in no hurry to go at all. We stayed where we were for as long as it was possible to stay. I think we were actually the last out.

But in terms of going back to the match and standing in a crowd, I didn't want to go and watch football again. And yet I forced myself – I thought, 'If I don't go now, I might never go again.' Looking back,

I reacted badly, I think, in a couple of situations. I remember going to the replay at Old Trafford. I can remember to this day, going up the steps to the terracing, and they have this wooden panelling at the top of the stairs. I remember being overcome by this intense anger, and I was banging on the panelling. My mate was looking at me and his face was like, 'What's to do with you?' It was so powerful and so angry, the way I was slapping on the panelling.

I didn't go to Goodison, which was the first league game. Then I think the next game was Forest – again. That would have been the middle of May, by then. It was the first game back at Anfield since the thing. I just thought I *had* to go, you know? I had to make myself go. I was stood in the Kop, over by the big white wall, right by where the boys' pen used to be. I managed the first half OK, but in the second half I had a panic attack. It wasn't long after half-time. I went down under the bottom of the Kop and I paced around by this big set of exit gates; the ones that lead out by the back of the Albert. But I didn't leave. I just stayed there, by the gates. I thought that if I left then, I'd never go back to another match again. It was a tense game, 0–0. We were still in the running for the league and the Double – not that it mattered. I went back up the steps but I didn't go right back in; I just stood and watched from the back of the crowd. I could see little snatches of the game when the action came down that corner – but I couldn't bring myself to dive back in. And then not long from the end, Liverpool got a penalty and I thought to myself, 'What do I do here? I want to see this, but I don't want to be back in the crowd.' So I gets up on this little wall by the exit and I watch Aldo slot the pen, and then I jumped right back down again.

JOHN ALDRIDGE

They extended the season so we could complete our fixtures. We won the replayed semi against Forest, at Old Trafford. Then we won our games in hand; I think we had Norwich and Millwall. We won the eventual final against Everton after extra time, on a baking hot afternoon, then we've got West Ham on the Tuesday night and, of all teams, Arsenal on the Friday night. And I had a World Cup qualifier for Ireland after that, at Landsdowne Road on the Sunday.

JOHN BARNES

Of course it was disappointing, losing to Arsenal like that.* You wouldn't be normal if you said it didn't matter. It still hurts me now. I should have just taken the ball to the corner flag. It mattered *more* because of the circumstances. Whenever I bump into Ronnie Moran, even now, he gives me stick over that: 'Why didn't you just keep the ball in the corner?!'

PETER CARNEY

I got through to the end of the season, and it couldn't have come quick enough for me. I'd have given Everton the FA Cup. Even when Arsenal came to Anfield and won the league with the last kick of the match, I wasn't arsed. I couldn't wait to see the back of the football season. But that was the end of the six-week cycle that began on 15 April. And the significance of that is the Pentecost – the period

---

*   After Liverpool beat West Ham 5–1 on 23 May, Arsenal had to come to Anfield and win by two clear goals to take the league title on goal difference. Michael Thomas scored with the last kick of the season to give Arsenal the win they needed.

around Easter time, when the Holy Spirit is released. It struck me strongly that that was what had gone on – the timeframe and the Pentecost had a relevance to what had happened at Hillsborough. And I struggled for a long time with an idea about the Resurrection, though I'm not that religious. Saying that, I'm more religious now than I've ever been.

STEPHEN WRIGHT

You'd be absolutely gutted, wouldn't you, any other time? Last minute, the league's gone – it'd be a sickener. But it didn't matter to me one bit. It was just a game – that's all it was. Compared to the year before, losing to Wimbledon in the Cup final, the Arsenal game didn't even register with me.

After the match, there was a fundraiser for the Hillsborough Disaster Fund at the supporters club. Already, we were starting to get organised. Little did we know it'd take twenty-seven years …

PART TWO

THE LONG AND WINDING ROAD

SHEILA COLEMAN

I was going down and spending a lot of time with the Hillsborough Disaster Working Party as it all unfolded, helping out and answering the phones, dealing with enquiries. On the basis of what I was hearing first hand, I knew that what had happened at Hillsborough was avoidable. No doubt about it, Hillsborough was an avoidable disaster. I was aware of the cover-up and involved in the fight to challenge that, right from the start.

PETER CARNEY

After that initial period, I think we just concentrated on showing the banner around the city as much as possible. There was the all-dayer Mark Campbell put on that summer, Big Beat – there were sixteen separate concerts across the day and the banner was displayed at each and every one of them. And we had a collection of poems called *Words of Tribute*, which was published by Liverpool University Press, and the banner was on the front cover of the book. So that was my focus at that point, just showing the banner around as much as possible and keeping alive the names and memory of those who had died.

STEPHEN WRIGHT

Apart from the initial grieving, I must have gone into a period of shock. I was leading a surreal life – outwardly fine, but back at home I was starting to become a recluse. I was just staying in the bedroom all the time. Then I went back to work. I was a plumber. I'd be going into people's houses and they'd complain about a dripping tap, and … it was like a thunderstorm opening up on me. I'd feel my head exploding. I'd have to take a breather, go outside and get my head together. A dripping tap!

SHEILA COLEMAN

Initially, the inquests followed the usual procedure for deaths as a result of a large-scale disaster. The inquests were opened by the coroner, then immediately adjourned so that the deceased could be released to their families and loved ones for burial. The coroner's court does not rule on liability – it is primarily a record of who the deceased was and how they came by their death. So it was quite normal when the inquests were opened then postponed shortly after the disaster. What would usually happen next would be that, before the inquests are resumed, the Director of Public Prosecutions will rule whether or not there are to be any prosecutions resulting from the deaths. As we were to find out, though, the inquests were anything but 'usual'.

STEVE KELLY

Social Services set up a resource centre right next to Stanley Park, and every family had access to a social worker, counselling and legal advice and so on. It became known as the Hillsborough Centre. I've got no beef with the social workers, they had a very hard job to do. But once the West Midlands police came on the scene it was them setting the agenda.* West Midlands police were liaising with the Hillsborough Centre for access to clients – using them to communicate with families and survivors and those who wanted to give evidence. It became difficult for the Hillsborough Centre to give impartial advice – and that's being generous.

PETER CARNEY

I started going to the self-help groups that had been set up by social services in what became the Hillsborough Centre. The Family Support Group was set up for the families of the bereaved – survivors were not admitted. So, initially, the only real contact I had with families was through the Hillsborough Centre. But a big focus of my interest was to try to meet people who had been through what I'd been through. I wanted to meet and talk with fellow survivors from the pens – and that did me the world of good. Just by going to the Centre and meeting different people, I got to know a number of survivors, and these people are among my best friends to this day. Over time we came to an agreement with the Centre that there'd be a space that was just for survivors and, if we wanted, the social workers would be on hand after those meetings to offer professional advice about any issues we were experiencing. The main impetus of that was about personal support – helping people to manage their own situation and to help each other through this storm that we were in.

---

* West Midlands Police led the investigation into the role of South Yorkshire police in the disaster. West Midlands police also compiled the evidence that was to go before the coroner's court.

TONY O'KEEFE

I had the visit from West Midlands police to take my statement, and I was very wary. I was worried, for all sorts of reasons – they really got into my head. Their ears pricked up when I mentioned that I'd taken photos. 'Oh, we'll be needing them. Can we have the negatives, please. You'll get them back. It's just routine – the more information we have, the better.' That was the way they spoke to you.

PETER HOOTON

I did a preliminary phone interview with West Midlands police, then two West Midlands officers came round to our house to take my written statement. This took the form of a questionnaire. There were fifty-four questions, and one of the officers asked them while the other wrote my answers into the allocated space. Quite a few of the questions made reference to violence, fighting and drinking – sometimes the same question asked in different language; for example, were you *involved in* any fighting or disturbance? Then, a few questions later, did you *witness* any fighting? The same with drinking: did *you* drink? Were you drunk? Did you see any drunken behaviour? At the end, you could add your own comments and observations about anything relevant. I mentioned what the police officer had said to me about the cordon across the halfway line: 'We can't move until we're given orders.'

STEVE KELLY

I came back after work one day and there's this car parked up outside ours and, as I go to let myself in, these two fellas get out. I knew straight away who they were. They said, 'We're from West Midlands police, based at Smithdown Lane police station. Can we come in and speak to you?' So we go inside and I said, 'What's it about?' They said they were doing a Health and Safety procedure – learning from the mistakes of Hillsborough so they could draw up a list of recommendations to make sure that nothing like that ever happened again. I said to them, 'How can I help?' They beat around the bush for a bit, then they came out with it. Would I be prepared to help them establish exactly where and how my brother had died? I said, 'We've been through all this. We know how he died.' Then they looked at each other and said, 'Well, not really. But we've got the video tapes, now. Would you be prepared to come with us and view the tapes and point out exactly which one your brother is?' I said, 'Let me get this straight. You're asking me to come along and watch my brother dying?' They said, 'Well, no, not exactly.' I said, 'That's exactly how it sounds to me. You're asking me to sit there and watch my brother get crushed to death.' One of them goes, 'I wouldn't quite put it like that.' I said, 'Well I would, and my answer is no. That's beyond the pale.' At that point they stood up and they were very apologetic: 'We're very sorry to have distressed you.' I said, 'That's OK, I'll see you out.' And on the way to the door, one of them stopped and turned to me and said, 'We'll ask your mother.' I said, 'You won't. My mother's got cancer. You're not going anywhere near my mother.' They said, 'Oh yes, sorry, you did mention that. We'll ask your sister.' I said, 'I'm the man of this house and I'm taking care of everything relating to Hillsborough.' They said, 'Well, it's down to you, then. We don't care if it's your mother, your sister or you yourself, Mr Kelly, but one of you will come. One of you *will* come.' So I had no choice in the matter. I had to go.

So I followed the two West Midlands officers down to Smithdown Lane. I went with my social worker, Pat – every family had been allocated a social worker – and me and Pat sat through a few hours of these video tapes. At first it was just like watching any crowd in any high street, just people making their way. But as it got closer to kick-off you'd see more people running – more of a determined jog, you know, like they were running to get the paper or running to get a bet on, something like that. I started seeing people I knew: 'There's so-and-so, there; oh look, there's so-and-so.' But it was like they were softening you up. The next thing, we went into the pens, and … my God. There he was. I found him. I sat there, and I watched him die.

I broke down crying and they were just looking at me and I thought, 'You bastards; this is what you've done to me.' I vowed that I wouldn't let that happen again. I said to myself, 'Never again will I show any emotion in front of them.' So I'd bottle everything up. I'd keep a lid on it, keep it all inside.

MARTIN THOMPSON

I got a letter from West Midlands police inviting me to an interview at Waterloo Town Hall, and another from Sefton Council offering me the services of a social worker to accompany me to the meeting and counsel me, should I need it. I didn't really know what was going to be involved, but I ended up spending the best part of a day there at the town hall. There were four TV screens and a big stack of VHS tapes, each one from CCTV cameras at different locations in and around Hillsborough. So I sat there with these two officers from West Midlands and basically walked them through our day – the route we took, where we parked, how we got down to the ground. I can't remember if they were calling Stuart 'Number 53' or 'Body 53', but there was a stenographer writing everything down.

'We now see Number 53 passing the newsagent's. Where are you at this time?' And I'd point myself out, and we'd move on to the next location. Eventually we get to where Stu is inside the pens and I remembered the photo from *Hello!* I said, there's a photo that will show exactly where he was in the ground. And they pulled it out; they had the photo – Stuart and Kevin Williams, right next to each other. And here's the thing – I've identified Stuart to West Midlands police at different times, still alive. They've got time-coded footage that traces his movements, right up to the point he dies. So if the time code says 3.17 on one of those CCTV clips and the photo in *Hello!* was taken after that point, then what does that say about the supposed 3.15 cut-off?

STEVE KELLY

Having to sit there and watch those videos had the most detrimental effect on my mental health. I became very morose when I thought about what I'd seen, what they forced me to watch. I had very black moods. I began to shut myself off, and when I did go out – I'm not a big drinker, never have been – I'd try to get drunk. Just to blot it out for a little while.

I've never, ever, been the same person since then. I can still picture it all now. Putting me through that – it's the most disgusting act you could visit on a person. I started getting that desperate, I couldn't handle it. There was no one I could tell what I was going through; I wasn't like that with my emotions. I thought it was weakness to admit to anything like that.

And I started … I kept having crashes. Because it hurt so much, it hurt me. I kept seeing this vision of our Michael. I cracked up. It was a horrible time. I was breaking up, collapsing, dying inside, but on the outside I had this façade that I was all right.

PETER CARNEY

Once we started to get together regularly and air our grievances and experiences, well – you can imagine the anger. The social workers used to call it 'the Lion's Den'. But we began to meet regularly and, from it starting out quite a private and personal, low-key thing, the bigger picture started to emerge, and a more determined focus began to grow. The enquiries that were happening, the reports that were being published … we were talking about these things, together; all feeling a common thing.

Among many of the survivors there was a real, hard-line anger; a powerful frustration that not enough was being done. There was one of our regulars who wanted the TUC to go on strike. He wanted the buses to stop running; the City Council to suspend services. He wanted direct, serious action until something was done. He was saying that the working class should come together and stand together until this whole stitch-up was addressed – and he was spot on.

SHEILA COLEMAN

Liverpool City Council then funded the Hillsborough Project at Edge Hill University. I joined the project as a researcher and my brief was to monitor the legal proceedings arising from the disaster and to report on my findings. As a direct consequence of attending legal meetings (especially the original inquests) I got to know a lot of bereaved families and survivors of the disaster.

One of the first things that came to my attention was the existence of the Hillsborough Steering Committee. This was a group of lawyers and it came into being almost immediately after the disaster, when members of Liverpool's Law Society met to decide who was going to represent the bereaved.

STEVE KELLY

Individually we were starting to realise that things weren't adding up. The way West Midlands police were conducting their inquiries, the response in the media, dissatisfaction with the role of the Hillsborough Centre – everything seemed to be swinging against us, and what became obvious was that it was time to get organised. There were adverts in the *Liverpool Echo* and on local radio inviting any members of the bereaved families to a meeting at the Vernon Sangster Centre in Walton Hall Park. The idea was to set up a committee to run a properly organised information centre – that was the main objective, at that stage. Reliable information was severely lacking; everything we were being told, directly or indirectly, was being channelled through West Midlands police.

Up until April or May 1989, you just got up every day and went to work. That was how life worked. But from then on you were challenging the authorities, challenging the police, challenging the government. Things were never going to be the same again.

JOHN ASHTON

I was asked to give evidence at the Taylor Inquiry in Sheffield in May 1989. Little did I realise I was going into the lion's den the moment I set foot in the City Hall. I'd had no pre-briefing as to what to expect. I thought an inquiry was going to be just that – I'd go along and tell Lord Justice Taylor what I'd seen, what I'd done. I went in there and there were fifteen or twenty of the country's leading barristers representing the FA, Sheffield city council, South Yorkshire police – everybody had at least a couple of barristers.

And if I didn't already suspect a cover-up was well underway, my appearance in front of Lord Justice Taylor's inquiry absolutely proved it. I went to give evidence at Sheffield City Hall and what happened next was that I was brutalised in that hearing. Lord Justice Taylor implied that I wasn't a credible medical witness as I was no longer in clinical practice (I was at the university). And he insinuated, also, that I was a publicity seeker. He asked me whether, when I'd got back to Liverpool on the night of the tragedy, I had contacted the media or they'd contacted me. I mean, come on – how would the media have known how to contact me? Of course I went to the media! I was desperate to get the truth out, about the tragedy. But that was portrayed as ego by Taylor, and it hurt. I mean, you only have to look at that Paxman interview and I'm shaking with emotion; I'm passionately angry about what has happened. Anyone can see that.

And, for all that the Taylor Interim Report is rightly damning about the police operation, there's only a brief reference to the emergency response. There's three quarters of a side of paper about the ambulance service, but he says the only complaints came from two Liverpool doctors. One of those doctors made three specific complaints, namely: that there was a late emergency response; the ambulances were inadequately equipped; and that if the emergency response had been better, lives could have been saved. That doctor was wrong on all three counts, Taylor said. That doctor was me.

BARRY DEVONSIDE

The Taylor Interim Report was published in the August, just before the start of the '89–90 football season. This was the first time that public opinion briefly turned in our favour. The report, in no uncertain terms, exonerated the Liverpool supporters. The finger of blame was pointed very clearly at the South Yorkshire police's operational foul-up on the day and, generally, our initial reaction was one of relief. It was case of, at last – someone who understands exactly what went on. There were holes in it, of course. Taylor said he thought the response from the emergency services was adequate, and there is no real criticism of the FA for their choice of venue, or of Sheffield Wednesday, whose ground improvements didn't address the problems they'd experienced many times in Leppings Lane, or of Sheffield city council for failing to inspect the ground. But, in terms of the big issues, I think most of the families were satisfied with the interim report.

MARTIN THOMPSON

The Taylor Report emphatically exonerated Liverpool supporters of any blame, so what did Norman Bettison do? He made his own video tape. He put together his own video, which started with footage of Millwall fans rioting at Luton, and made a special presentation to the Police Federation in October of 1989. The Tory MP Michael Shersby then invited Bettison to come to Westminster to give a private screening to a group of specially invited MPs. He screened the video for the all-party group on 8 November 1989, after which Menzies Campbell told Bettison that he intended to have the Taylor Report overturned! If any one single thing illustrates the way the establishment assumed they could bend anything to their will, it was him, Menzies Campbell, blustering about 'putting the record straight' and having a public inquiry 'reversed!'*

STEPHEN WRIGHT

I remember going into work – it was quite some time after, we were into the next season. And Liverpool were playing Sheffield Wednesday, away. I was in work, and it was all over the papers, in the canteen. All these lads reading the paper: 'Liverpool return to Hillsborough.' I could feel my head starting to explode. Next thing, we're on the way to the job and I just cracked up in the van. I was in floods of tears, bawling my eyes out. The lad who was driving the van said, 'I'm taking you home.' I said, 'I can't go home like this.' So he dropped me off by ours and I just walked the streets. And I think it was then that I realised I needed help. So they got a counsellor for me,

---

* Norman Bettison, a Chief Inspector in the South Yorkshire police force, was seconded to the police's internal review committee after Hillsborough. Part of his role was to ensure that the police point of view on Hillsborough was promoted and understood. As part of this process, he compiled and narrated a video, splicing together scenes of football hooliganism (such as Luton v Millwall from 1985) and highlighting the Heysel Stadium tragedy – along with the role of Liverpool fans in causing it. The existence of Bettison's propaganda video came to light during the Independent Police Complaints Commission – the ongoing inquiry into police conduct before, during and after the Hillsborough disaster. The *Liverpool Echo* published a story on 28 September 2012 confirming the private screening of the video in Westminster.

ruled me off work, finally, slowly, trying to come to terms with what had happened. I needed it.

MARTIN THOMPSON

Sean Boardman's mum had been raising money for a memorial plaque for the lads from Formby who had died. There were four of them, all teenagers – Kevin Williams, Philip Steele, Chris Devonside and our Stuart. The memorial plaque was going to be unveiled in the new shopping centre, and I met a few friends in a bar over the road. We're just sitting there and Kenny Dalglish comes in. He walks over to where we're sitting: 'D'you want a drink?'

I think I just stared at him. Anyway, he brings me a bottle of Becks and sits down. 'How are you getting on? How's the family doing?'

I just didn't know what to say. Do I call him 'Mr Dalglish'? Kenny Dalglish was sitting at our table, asking how I was getting on. Bear in mind that this was towards the end of 1989, so it gives you a measure of how much Kenny took upon himself. I told him we were all doing OK, all things considered. So he got up and shook hands and said that if I needed anything I just had to let him know.

DAMIAN KAVANAGH

I held back for a long time. I felt like the whole world was just one big let-down, and I kept things to myself. I kept thinking, 'Where am I in all this? I got my mate a ticket, and he got killed. But I'm not my mate's widow, I'm not my mate's son, so who I am I to speak ahead of them?'

MARTIN THOMPSON

I went out with my girlfriend on New Year's Eve and I just couldn't face the midnight thing. So when everyone else went outside I said to her, 'I'm going to have to get off. I need to get away. I'm going to go travelling.' The Liverpool Jewish community had sent my mum a certificate to show that they'd planted 95 trees in the Peace Forest in Jerusalem (Tony Bland hadn't died at this point, so it was still 95).* The Peace Forest is the woodlands they planted after the Six-Day War as a symbol of unity, linking East and West Jerusalem. For every child born in Jerusalem, a tree is planted – it's a symbol of hope for future generations; that they don't make the mistakes of their forefathers. It was a thoughtful and fitting gesture from the Jewish community and, even though I'm not at all religious myself, I made it one of my goals to get to the Peace Forest for the first anniversary of Hillsborough.

STEVE KELLY

A year or so after the disaster, the coroner's office in Sheffield sent a team to go through the autopsy reports in person – so myself and our social worker, Pat Dawson, went down to the Hillsborough Centre to hear Mike's. They started reading his report out, about the injuries he'd sustained. They mentioned that he had hardened arteries – they'd

---

* As a result of the injuries he sustained at Hillsborough, Tony Bland remained in a coma until his death on 3 March 1993. Although he could breathe, Tony existed in a persistent vegetative state. His parents, Allan and Barbara, launched a legal appeal to allow their son to die with dignity. They won a historic court battle, allowing Tony's life-sustaining systems to be removed after law lords ruled that his plastic feeding tubes were not, in and of themselves, 'medicine'.

call that high cholesterol now – and they mentioned this, and this, and this – I didn't understand half of the medical terminology. But then they told us that Mike had grazes on his knees, and that cut me to the quick. I thought to myself, 'The poor lad has gone down, there; he's gone to the floor.' And as I started thinking about it, I couldn't shake this thing of … 'I hope no one has stood on him.' I can't explain it, but I just could not stand the thought that anyone would have stood on Michael. And as I sat there I felt a tear forming, and it was like acid. It came down my right cheek and rolled down my face and it was burning – but I wouldn't wipe it away. I thought to myself, 'Do not let these bastards see what they've done to you again. Don't let them see what they've reduced you to.'

It was then, really, that I began to realise what Hillsborough was doing to me. It was slowly destroying me. Pat and I got outside and she said to me, 'Steve, you need to go and see your doctor.' I went to the GP and he told me I was suffering from post-traumatic stress disorder. I'd never heard of post-traumatic stress disorder at the time, but he referred me to a psychiatrist.

I actually went to see a child psychologist from Alder Hey Hospital, Colin Demellweek, and I can honestly say now that Colin saved my life. I was in a dark, lonely place. Loneliness was probably the worst part of it because I wouldn't – I couldn't – talk to anyone about what I was going through. I'd taken on the role of the family protector, but I probably needed protecting myself, too. I was locking myself away in this dark, dark world that I was trapped in – but once a week I'd go and see Colin and I'd erupt. It was such a blessed release. I could let it all out to someone I didn't know, and all my feelings would come pouring out and, like I say, those sessions saved my life.

PETER CARNEY

Looking back, I think we misjudged the mood in the lead-up to the first anniversary. We had a project up and running called the Stanley Park Project, and our idea was to commemorate the first anniversary with a low-key acoustic concert in the park. But there was just no appetite for it, really – certainly not from the bands. There was one or two; John Power offered to do it, but I think we were just out of synch. We were looking to do something that would bring people together – just something small, really, for anyone who might be looking for company and comfort on the day, but it didn't come to anything.

I don't think the club wanted to open up Anfield again to people wanting to pay their respects, so we came up with this alternative in Stanley Park. The idea was that the trees nearest Anfield Road would become the focal point for anyone wanting to leave flowers or whatever. In the end we left 101 footballs in the park. 101 was very deliberate; symbolic. There'd been 95 killed on the terraces at Hillsborough at that point – but we wanted to pay respect to the others killed by Hillsborough too: 101 was our way of saying, 'You can't put a figure on this. It goes on.'

DANNY RHODES

By a weird twist of fate we played Liverpool at Anfield on 14 April 1990. It felt very different from Old Trafford, you felt a real togetherness among the fans. Liverpool, as usual, scored early. I think it was 2–0 at half-time, but we came back into it and came away with a draw; the only point I ever saw us get at Anfield. But it was a good day; a nice day. There was a sense of … if not closure as such, then a bit of healing, to a degree – not that it ever really goes away.

MARTIN THOMPSON

I had all these strange adventures travelling across Europe; it's amazing how many scousers you meet, wherever you go. And I mean, to a degree, it's not completely under your own control, when you're travelling like that. Anything can happen. All sorts of mad things *did* happen. But I was determined I was going to get to Jerusalem for the anniversary.

And, of course, it turned out 15 April that year was Easter Sunday. Arriving in Jerusalem, it was like every freak in the world had descended on the place. There were processions through the streets, people actually physically nailed to the cross, people wailing and self-flagellating … I felt a bit weird going up to passers-by, you know, 'Excuse me, mate, can you tell us where the Peace Forest is, please?'

I went up to this walled, two-thousand-year-old part of the old city and it was just like the *Life of Brian* – little passages leading off, ancient ruins – but I just kept asking people and I kept on walking and I found it. I mean, it was … I don't mean to be disrespectful but it wasn't quite the forest of remembrance I'd been building up in my mind. There was a few shrubs and trees. But it was good. For all my troubles and sins I was there on the anniversary, at six minutes past three.

SHEILA COLEMAN

I attended the original inquests held in the Coroner's Court in Sheffield. They began with the mini-inquests, as they became known, on 18 April 1990. These were to take place at the Medico-Legal Centre in Sheffield, and their primary purpose was to establish the basic circumstances of each of the 95 deaths, as it was then. The idea was, supposedly, that the mini-inquests would quickly establish the basic facts. That part of the inquests would then be adjourned so that the Director of Public Prosecutions could begin investigations into what, if any, criminal proceedings might be brought. The mini-inquests were supposed to be uncomplicated – but they turned out to be just the next stage in the cover-up.

STEPHEN WRIGHT

We were going over in a minibus to the coroner's court every day. We had our lawyer from the steering group, but the West Midlands police had it well boxed off. Part of their brief was to provide the physical evidence that went in front of the coroner, Stefan Popper – but they were hardly impartial, were they? Right from the start it looked like Detective Superintendent Stanley Beechey was acting as the coroner's own personal bodyguard. Wherever Popper went, Beechey seemed to be there, hanging behind his shoulder.

SHEILA COLEMAN

I got a phone call one day, at Edge Hill. It was Stanley Beechey. Beechey had been a head of the discredited and, by that time, disbanded West Midlands Serious Crime Squad. This was an outfit that had been disbanded that summer after repeated allegations of corruption, witness intimidation and evidence-tampering. They were the subject of numerous internal investigations, and several of these became full-scale prosecutions. In light of all that, Beechey was a strange choice to be seconded to work on the Hillsborough case, supposedly in a non-operational capacity.

Anyway, Stanley Beechey rang me and he asked me if I was planning to go to Sheffield the next day. I said, 'Of course.'

And he said, 'Well, this is just a friendly warning telling you not to bother, because you won't be allowed in.'

'What? Are you telling me I won't be allowed into Sheffield?'

'You know exactly what I'm saying.'

So I told him, 'I'll tell you what – I'll come along to the inquests as per usual and you can tell me to my face that I'm not allowed in.'

I thought, 'I'm not going to allow myself to be intimidated like that.' At a later date, my flat was broken into and only my address book was stolen. I, like others, believed that my phone was being tapped – it was not good! I don't know where I found the will, let alone the guts to stand up to these people. It's one of those where you could easily just say to yourself, 'No, I don't need this.' Or you say, 'I'm not giving in to this fear.' But it wasn't easy. Beechey was such a sinister presence. He acted as the coroner's right-hand man and was, in my opinion, a prime mover.

STEPHEN WRIGHT

I have sleepless nights thinking about Popper. That face – he had this sneaky, shifty look about him; he always seemed to be smirking, like he knew something that you didn't. Every individual case he read out, no matter who, he made a reference to blood alcohol. Even if it was a negative reading, even with a 10-year-old boy, he still read out the words 'blood alcohol' and it all went towards giving this impression, building the story – the myth – about drink, disorder, drunken behaviour. It fed the media and fanned the flames, just as Popper knew it would. As he'd been told it would.

SHEILA COLEMAN

I started being followed by these two guys. I guessed that they were West Midlands police as, although they weren't in uniform, I'd seen these men in court. In the end I turned round and said, 'Ok, you want to know who I am. Who are you?' And they made no attempt to dispute that they were following me. They just said, 'You're in court every day, taking notes. We want to know who you are and who you're working for.' So this is what I was up against. This was the prevailing paradigm – the climate in which I was working.

BARRY DEVONSIDE

It was brutal, the coroner's court. Its main purpose was not to judge in legal terms, as such; it was not about right and wrong or who was to blame. It was about the bald facts of establishing who the deceased were, and the circumstances of their death. So what you heard was a basic account of your loved one's last known movements; where they went, who saw them. Sometimes there'd be a map showing the route they took; the last ever photographs of your son, alive. Smiling. Excited about the match that was about to take place. It was very hard to sit through – all the more so because it was taking place in the Medico-Legal Centre, which was, in so many cases, the very place that distraught families had been taken to identify their loved ones on the day of the disaster.

It was in and out, very brusque – that was very much the procedure. The coroner would sum up your case before you were ushered out and the next family ushered in to go through the same thing as you've just been through. And the summing up was very bare; very basic. It was just how and where and when your son died; and the 'when' part became critical to our entire campaign for the real truth about Hillsborough. Ascertaining the actual time of death of our loved ones was fundamental to the process of getting right to the heart of this terrible miscarriage of justice. But, of course, with this being the coroner's court, we weren't allowed to challenge any of the detail of this. We were assured we'd get our chance once the inquests resumed.

ANNE WILLIAMS

They took me to a side room just before we went into the inquest to tell me that Kevin, when he was with Special WPC Debra Martin, had called my name. Well, I just broke down. I asked where she was, and they said she wasn't there [at the inquest] that day. They said when I got into the actual inquest the pathologist would explain Kevin's injuries to us, after which we would come to realise that this [Kevin speaking] could not have happened. They also showed me a photograph of an off-duty policeman trying to resuscitate Kevin on the ground, which I'd never seen before. They asked me if that was Kevin, and I said, 'Yes.'

So then we were led into the inquest court and, by the time I got there, I just lost it. You know, you're all suited up, and I just lost the plot. I couldn't stop crying because of this business at 4 o'clock.* And they started bringing out the different witnesses in Kevin's case. When they brought in Dr Slater, they explained to the jury that Kevin had had this neck injury and that it was so bad, he had so

---

* WPC Debra Martin made a statement to the effect that she'd heard Kevin Williams ask for his mother at 4 p.m. This was disputed by the coroner, who suggested that what WPC Martin actually heard was trapped wind escaping.

many fractures in his neck, there was no way the little boy could have spoken. His was the worst case of traumatic asphyxia out of everyone there, and, in fact, it was so severe that he had no doubt in his mind that Kevin would have been dead and brain dead before he was even lifted out of the enclosure. And that was new to us, because we'd seen Kevin, and when we went to see him he was peaceful. He wasn't bruised and blue like they were saying now.

So, you know, we were hearing this and it's all new to us. And what they were telling me in the side room, about an off-duty policeman, a Special WPC – this was something different again. I really wanted to speak to the police lady. If she was the last person to see Kevin, and hold him at 4 o'clock, then I really needed to speak to her. But they said she was only young, she hadn't been in the force very long. The coroner was sort of saying, 'Well, you know, I don't want to run the poor woman down – it had been a hard day for her, and she'd probably got things mixed up.' And so the jury were listening to this and thinking, 'Oh well, Kevin would have been dead and brain dead by 3.15.'

But then they go on to say about the off-duty policeman who attended Kevin. And I've seen the photograph and it was 3.37 and he said that Kevin was convulsing on that pitch at 3.37. Again, they didn't sort of give us any answer to that, and they didn't give us any answers as to why Kevin had opened his eyes, either.

So I went into a side room and, after I composed myself again, I spoke to a Detective Killoch, the West Midlands police officer who was in charge of our case. Every family had an officer. And I asked Detective Killoch what time did my son die? He said he couldn't tell me. At that point I just asked my husband to take me home because I was so confused, and this was the first time we were hearing all this.

A social worker drove us back, and I didn't even want to stop for a cup of tea, I just wanted to get home. I can remember walking up the path, very, very distraught, very upset. I remember going inside the house – but it was empty, there were no answers. I'd had a hell of a lot of counselling but it felt as if I was just walking into that house after identifying Kevin. All the counselling I'd had seemed to go out of the window.

SHEILA COLEMAN

On the Wednesday of that first, mini-inquest, Kevin Williams's case came before the coroner. This was when the whole thing of Kevin being alive at 4 p.m. came up. I didn't know Anne Williams at the time, but I was at the inquests and I heard and saw everything that unfolded. The Coroner and the police must have been so scared, because there was the off-duty Merseyside policeman Derek Bruder, who'd attempted to resuscitate Kevin; then the Special Constable, Debra Martin, who carried Kevin to the gymnasium and stated that he opened his eyes and said 'mum' – both of them giving evidence to the effect that Kevin Williams was still alive at 4 p.m.

By the Friday there had been this very hasty change of direction from West Midlands police, who were effectively running the inquest. And, of course, it transpired that, on the Thursday, West Midlands police had been to see Derek Bruder and Debra Martin, and they went to see Anne [Williams] and Steve [her husband]. They told them they didn't need to come back for Kevin's hearing. It was all disguised as sympathy – you know, 'Don't put yourself through it again' – but they were massively covering their tracks.

They said to the inquest, 'On reflection, PC Bruder realises he must have been mistaken. He has agreed to undertake more advanced first-aid training. And poor WPC Martin is very young, very inexperienced and she was hugely traumatised by what she saw. She realises now that she must have been mistaken and Kevin Williams must have been dead.' And it was all expressed in that kind of terminology: 'Poor Debra Martin, dismiss the hysterical young woman.' How easy to pathologise the woman! They brought in an expert from Cambridge, Dr Gumpert, and he made this dreadful analogy to the headless chicken, still running around with its wings still flapping after it's dead. They said it would have been the same for Kevin Williams. Even though he was technically dead, there was trapped air escaping, which might have sounded as though he was trying to speak. They just fobbed Anne Williams off by telling her, 'Don't worry, we'll open a special inquest about Kevin – there's no need for you to even be there.' And the lawyers accepted that.

STEPHEN WRIGHT

What was becoming obvious was that, from their side – the authorities, the police, even the ambulance service – they were getting their stories straight. We were just grief stricken. A lot of us, if you ask, mainly remember that period as passing by in a daze. You didn't really know what was going on. But South Yorkshire police, the FA and everyone else had these huge teams of advisors, already dead-set on their version of events.

SHEILA COLEMAN

I think because I wasn't directly involved – I wasn't at Hillsborough, I didn't lose anybody, I wasn't a survivor – I had a level of objectivity, I suppose, that was obviously denied to those people. And what I saw was how their grief and vulnerability was being exploited, and I found it quite obscene. And one of the things I felt strongly about was the families' legal representation. The way the police boxed the Kevin Williams inquest off, telling the family they needn't come back on the Friday – I thought it was appalling, and I said so.

BARRY DEVONSIDE

West Midlands police concluded their inquiries and passed on their findings to the Director of Public Prosecutions. In September of 1990 the Director of Public Prosecutions ruled that there would be no criminal proceedings as a result of the disaster. And, of special relevance to us, he ruled that there would be no further action against South Yorkshire police. He said that there was insufficient evidence to justify any criminal proceedings. This meant that the coroner could now resume and conclude the inquests; and it was at this stage that he imposed his 3.15 cut-off point. He basically ruled that any evidence of any nature relating to any aspect of the emergency and rescue response after 3.15 p.m. on 15 April 1989 was to be deemed inadmissible, as all victims would have been dead by that time.

SHEILA COLEMAN

The inquests resumed in November 1990, at Sheffield City Hall this time. Remember, Popper had decreed that any evidence relating to any time after his 3.15 cut-off point would be deemed inadmissible. His reasoning was that everyone who died had already received their injuries by this point. Well, that is so full of holes it's threadbare. But it was accepted by the families' legal representation. I don't know what they were thinking. Perhaps they thought they were acting in their clients' best interests by speeding up the process. There could have been months and months of to-ing and fro-ing if they had challenged the cut-off point. Who knows why the lawyers accepted it, but they did – and it turned out to be another monumental mistake.

There was one indomitable woman, Joan McBrien, who wasn't having that at all. She'd lost her son, John, and she wasn't happy with the way the steering committee had handled his case at the mini-inquest. Joan decided to represent herself at Sheffield City Hall and she stood up and slugged it out with the heavyweights of the legal establishment. She was brilliant, given what she was up against. However, given the 3.15 cut-off and constraints on evidence, families were never going to get the verdict they wanted.

STEPHEN WRIGHT

Even though we were expecting it by then, it was still a devastating blow when the verdicts were given: accidental death. The police didn't even try to hide their delight. They were drinking champagne outside; they'd got away with it. Some of the mothers started singing 'You'll Never Walk Alone' in the courtroom.

SHEILA COLEMAN

The morning after one of the meetings in the Vernon Sangster Centre, I received a phone call from a woman, Anne Williams. She said, 'I hope you don't mind me ringing you. I went to the family support group meeting last night and John Glover gave me your number; he said you might be able to help me.' So we arranged to meet, and I was able to bring some comfort, I think – simply because I'd been there, at Kevin's inquest, when they'd told Anne she needn't trouble herself being there. Even though it was so bad, so unfair, the fact that I had been there and I was able to tell her what had been said, I'm sure that was of some comfort. So that was the start of my friendship with Anne, and the start of our working together.

ANNE WILLIAMS

That photograph, the kiss of life, that's when it started me thinking, 'There's something wrong; something is very wrong here.' So the scenario then is getting inquest papers, getting police statements from the South Yorkshire police, which was very hard to do. I was ringing the police up, ringing the coroner's, or writing to them, and I finally received a copy of the inquest transcripts.

I was quite horrified because the coroner started off by saying that, 'We are going to deal with this young man again. We already dealt with him a couple of days ago, if you remember, but this boy was convulsing at 3.37, and we're here today to find out what the heck was going on – why he was convulsing at 3.37.' So then they brought in Inspector Sawers from West Midlands police, and he gave evidence to say that he'd been to see Mr Bruder. He had interviewed

Mr Bruder for six hours on his day off, and Mr Bruder thinks now that what he saw was more of a twitch than a convulsion.

Detective Sawers relayed that Mr Bruder saw what was happening to Kevin, and certainly Kevin's head was moving. Sawers then goes on to say that Mr Bruder is mistaken about the pulse in Kevin's neck, he must have been trying the wrong area of the neck, or perhaps he felt the pulse in his own thumb. And Mr Bruder is also mistaken about Kevin being sick, it must have been a bit of spittle or phlegm coming out of his mouth. And Sawers said to the jury that Bruder is adamant that an ambulance passes him at 3.37 while he was tending Kevin. Sawers says, 'I've told him there were no ambulances on the ground, they're not in any of the videos, but Bruder is adamant about the ambulance. He says he screamed for someone to stop it as he wanted to put Kevin in it.'

Then they brought in Dr Slater again, the pathologist; he again explained to the jury how severe Kevin's injuries were. He had no doubt in his mind that Kevin would have been dead and brain dead by 3.15. And what he said then was that Kevin didn't fall into the normal mechanism of death; for some reason Kevin's nerve endings lived on, and this is what Mr Bruder saw at 3.37. Even though Kevin would have been dead and brain dead at 3.15, he was still twitching at 3.37. So the difference between a twitch and a convulsion is: you can twitch when you're dead but you can't convulse, you've got to be alive to convulse. That was the crucial difference as far as they were concerned.

Then Dr Slater explained to the jury – to give them an answer as to why Kevin was twitching at 3.37, when he's dead and brain dead by 3.15 – that this could happen to somebody that hadn't got a head; that they'd still twitch on. And that's when I started thinking,

'There's something funny here.' And I was really upset because I was reading all this in the transcripts. So then the coroner steps in again and he says, 'We don't want to run Mr Bruder down again, but if he was wrong about the ambulance then he must have been wrong about Kevin convulsing. He might have been twitching, but he was not convulsing. Mr Bruder did say he doesn't know the difference between a twitch, a convulsion or an epileptic fit, all he knows is that Kevin was moving, and he went down to help him from the North Stand.'

So I was horrified then, thinking, 'They're saying Kevin had a pulse and now this man's changing his mind; they said that Kevin was sick and he's changing his mind; they said he was convulsing, now it's a twitch.' But, no, that didn't add up because they were just saying what they liked, to fit in; you know – to make sure Kevin was dead by 3.15. To me it was all, 'You're an awkward little boy now, you're not fitting in to the plan.' And I was comparing the statements and thinking, 'There's something wrong. I need forensic.'

SHEILA COLEMAN

The legal fees had been funded by money the families received from the Hillsborough Disaster Fund. After the inquest verdicts, though, that money ran out and, I'm sorry to say, the legal Steering Committee went the same time and the same way the money went.

But there were families who wanted to know what options were still open to them. So I asked Terry Munyard, a QC I knew, if he'd come and speak to the group. Terry offered good advice but for personal reasons would not take on the case. I subsequently contacted Edward Fitzgerald QC and asked him if he would be prepared to listen to six families who were keen to pursue a judicial review of the accidental death verdicts given at the inquests. Ed didn't hold out much hope of a successful application for leave to appeal but agreed to come along, but if he felt there was no case then he wouldn't do it. In the nicest possible way he was telling us we were wasting our time. So I briefed each family individually – Anne Williams was one of them – and told them, 'Look, you've got to tell Ed exactly what you have been through; what you're going through; what this is doing to you.' And when he'd sat there and listened to them Ed said, 'How can I say no?' He wouldn't take any payment either; he said, 'I couldn't possibly take money from these people after the way they've been abused.' He was wonderful. He became our greatest ally.

ANNE WILLIAMS

So, as time went on, I managed to track down Derek Bruder – I think it was in December 1990. All I knew was that he was an off-duty policeman from Liverpool, so I rang up Canning Place, the police headquarters. They told me which station he worked at and then I rang Hope Street and spoke to his superior and told him who I was. He said, 'I can't afford for him to come out to Formby to see you, but if you want to come on Sunday afternoon, you're very welcome.' So myself and Sheila Coleman went down to meet Mr Bruder.

SHEILA COLEMAN

Anne Williams had this tremendous naivety about her, and over the years people used that and manipulated her and took advantage of her innocence, I felt. Sometimes it was terrible to watch. Yet she was also this relentless, indomitable force, and it made you wonder whether she was aware all along. Whether she used that naivety to get the answers she wanted.

ANNE WILLIAMS

I always remember the first thing when we went to see Derek Bruder – because I was nervous again, you're frightened of what they're going to say to you. And this is still the early stages, and I said to him, 'Why did you change your statement?' He said, 'I didn't change my statement.' Then he told me what he'd done for Kevin, and I said, 'Was my son alive?' And he said, 'Well, if you say finding a pulse with the first two fingers …' and he lifted his hand up like that, his right hand ' … if that means he was alive, then he was alive.'

He said, 'They [West Midlands police] came with a medical brief to try to get me to change my statement.' And that's when he told us he didn't know if it was convulsion or a twitch. But Kevin's head was certainly moving, he was alive, and he cleared his airwaves. Mr Bruder said he remembers everything about Kevin, right down to his boxer shorts, because he sort of stripped him, stripped him down. And there was another young lad with Kevin. Mr Bruder said, 'I don't know if he was a friend but he was just saying, "Help me mate."' And he didn't know if the lad was asking for assistance or saying, 'Please help my mate,' but he said he was screaming. And he was the lad that tried to stop the ambulance when it was going past – but it wouldn't stop. So things were getting worse, really, because I thought, 'This man's genuine; he's telling me the truth.' And this was completely different to what was in the inquests. So I thought, 'The next person I need to speak to is that police lady.'

BARRY DEVONSIDE

There was a Police Authority meeting scheduled to take place in Barnsley, South Yorkshire – and some of the main officers from Hillsborough were due to attend. Two Liverpool councillors tipped me off that Norman Bettison was going to be there, as was Peter Wright, the Chief Constable. They'd heard that Hillsborough was going to be top of the agenda, so I said I'd drive over. I was a bit unnerved – there were video cameras recording the proceedings, but I just took my seat and quietly observed, at first. Then I was asking these councillors, I was badgering them to use their privileges and question the committee. Peter Wright became aware of me and he was just staring at me with pure contempt.

After the meeting I was approached by a uniformed police constable. He told me the Chief Constable wanted to speak to me. I asked him what he wanted to see me about but he just said he was only the messenger and would I please come with him. I didn't like the sound of this. The only person I recognised was Sheila Coleman, sitting in the public gallery. I asked Sheila if she'd come along with me.

We were led down two sets of stairs and along this corridor, and there's all these coppers in uniform lined along the way. And there, at the end of the corridor, was Peter Wright, the Chief Constable of South Yorkshire police, in his uniform, with this supercilious smile on his face. I thought to myself, 'Do I shake hands with this bastard?' Then I thought, 'Of course you do. Whatever they might do to you, you do not drop your standards.' So I put my hand out to shake his, and out of nowhere I was assaulted. From behind, an officer hit me in the neck and pushed me against the wall with some force, pinning me there with his forearm across my throat and his other arm across my chest. Peter Wright stood some distance back, like I was a danger to him, with this sneering, disapproving look on his face. He didn't say a single word to me, just stared at me.

I said, 'You bastard!'

He said nothing – just walked off. One of the officers who was restraining me – even though I posed no threat – said, 'Now then, Mr Devonside. Now then …'

Again, it was as though they were trying to be reasonable with an irrational, potentially dangerous man; as though I'd been about to go for him. If Sheila hadn't been there to witness the entire thing, I don't think anyone would have believed it.

ANNE WILLIAMS

So, with regards to finding the police lady, I rang up South Yorkshire police – I had a number for them from the transcripts – and asked if I could speak to Special WPC Martin. I didn't say who I was, and they said that she'd left the force. I asked how could I get in touch with her, and they told me to forward a letter with a stamped addressed envelope. So I did, and it was short and sweet, just saying, 'I believe you were the last person to see my son [and] please would you talk to me?'

She got the letter and she rang me and said she had always intended to come and see me some time, anyway. But she didn't want me to go to Sheffield, she said she would come to Formby to see me, and I asked her if it would be all right if a solicitor sat in. She was quite happy about that, so it was all arranged. Sheila came along and we taped WPC Martin; we've got four hours of tape of what she had to tell us.

And it was horrifying – what they did to her and how they bullied her and browbeat her. In the end, the statement that was put in front of her – she didn't read it. She just signed it to get rid of them. But she did tell us that she didn't change her statement. When you read the copies of her statements – again, they're two different stories. She explained … I mean, she'd been a Special WPC for years, she was actually going into the police force properly that summer. All her records were exemplary and she loved it, she said, especially when there was a match on. When she got called to the ground, she said that she just went on autopilot. She said, 'I was just carrying people in and out, putting the dead on one side, and the injured on the other.'

When she came across Kevin she said she found a pulse and told the police[man] on the door, 'This one's still alive.' And he told her, 'Keep with him, don't go back for more. They're nearly all in. You just carry out the necessary …' So that's what she said she did. She put him in the gymnasium, she carried out heart massage and resuscitation, and Kevin's ribs were actually moving, and that's why she picked him up. She picked him up in her arms and she said that's when he opened his eyes and murmured; she said Kevin actually moved his mouth and went, 'Mum' – and then slumped back and died in her arms.

TONY O'KEEFE

My negatives were sent back to me eventually – some of them. If you remember the old Instamatic-type cameras, your negatives would come in strips, along with the prints – strips of six or eight brown, plastic negatives. You'd hold the negatives up to the light, wouldn't you, and the image was the other way round. Well, when West Midlands police sent mine back to me, they'd cut various negatives off the strip. I've still got the letter, from Detective Chief Superintendent M. J. Foster at West Midlands police:

10 July 1990

Dear Mr O'Keefe

Further to your telephone conversation today with Sergeant Killoch, I return your personal photographs.

I have retained the negatives which show scenes within the Hillsborough ground and which will be required as evidence in possible future proceedings. I will ensure that your negatives are returned at the conclusion of any proceedings.

I'm still waiting.

SHEILA COLEMAN

In October 1993, Ed Fitzgerald successfully applied for leave for us to go for judicial review, which was a big boost for everyone. He didn't think we'd get it, because it went before a judge who was notorious for rejecting a high number of applications. Consequently, we were bracing ourselves for yet another knock-back. So when the news came through that Ed's application had been accepted, we were overjoyed.* It was the first time we'd been successful in any of our attempts – our first 'victory', if you like – and for a short time it felt like a turning point.

So the judicial review went the whole working week at the High Court, Monday to Friday, and even there, there were these lovely little cameos. The second morning I was going in with Anne Williams, and

---

* After the inquest of accidental death, the families' legal representatives advised them to accept the financial settlement on offer – approximately £3,500 for each of the dead. They argued that there was no further course of action open to pursue. Ed Fitzgerald, after looking at the case, applied for the verdicts to be overturned – a judicial review. The case was scheduled for the first week of November, 1993.

there were hundreds of people outside. Anne said to me, 'Oh, Sheila, just look at how many people have turned out for us! Look at the cameras, the press – people are starting to listen to us at last!' I had to put my arm round her and tell her, 'I think they're here for Elton John, Anne.' He has a libel action in the next court! But our hopes were short-lived.

ANNE WILLIAMS

Oh the Judicial Review was terrible, it was awful. I knew by the Wednesday, 'We've lost this. They're not listening to us.' And I think that's when I realised what the system is about, and what I was up against.

SHEILA COLEMAN

So we lost the Judicial Review – I remember it was Bonfire Night and, coming back to Liverpool, it was just horrible, empty. I had this overwhelming sense of failure. Even though I could articulate why it happened, just – at that level – I was starting to feel it was hopeless. I thought, 'There's nowhere else to go now, what do we do?' It was a horrible feeling. I had gotten so used to being around good people and fighting with them and now we were at a loss.

STEPHEN WRIGHT

I'd be out, but I wasn't really there. There was never really a point where you'd switch off. I'd be out in town and all of a sudden it would just hit you, and I'd flag down a cab and go, 'Anfield Cemetery, please.' It didn't matter what time it was, day or night. I'd just sit there. It was still very raw.

ANNE WILLIAMS

Edward Fitzgerald put us in touch with Dr Ian West, who was the top forensic pathologist at the time at Guy's Hospital in London. He'd done Robert Maxwell's autopsy, the Babes in the Wood case – he did all these high-profile cases, and he agreed to do some reports for us.

He sent for autopsy photographs and that is when he said Kevin's report was 'excellent'. Well, excellent in that he could have been saved. I was so upset because I was getting the picture now, and I knew from speaking to these people, speaking with Dr West and knowing that Kevin's injuries weren't what the inquest was saying. He would have been able to call for his mum. So that's when I wrote to all the drama documentaries and that's when Roger Cook came on the scene. *The Cook Report* was the big current affairs investigation series of the day. He'd go undercover, or look at injustices, and he was very interested in Kevin's case.

Roger asked me, 'Can you get a continuity chart from the West Midlands police of the movements of your child?' The continuity chart is basically the route he took, his movements on the day leading right up to his ... you know, his death. And there's a number of photographs on the continuity chart – trying to get them was awful. But in the end I got them, and that's how I got the photographs of the lads who were carrying him. So I appealed through the *Liverpool Echo*. I asked the *Echo* to put the photo out to see who these lads were who carried Kevin on the hoarding. I wanted to speak to them because they would have been among the last to see him, they were carrying my son and I wanted to know what condition my son was in on that hoarding. And I got loads of calls because a lot of people knew Steve Hart. Stevie used to organise a lot of the coaches to the football, so he was well known. And he phoned me himself. Steve was the first of them to get in touch.

STEVE HART

I got a phone call from my niece, and she said, 'You're on the front page of the *Echo*.' They'd published a picture of people carrying Anne's son and she was appealing to find out if anybody knew who these people were. There was a number, so I rang her up and we arranged to meet in town. Apparently, by the time I phoned Anne she'd already had numerous calls identifying myself. So off I goes to meet her and there's a couple of fellas with her – I just assumed they must be family. Anne's got the photograph and she points to this lad and she says, 'Do you remember him?' I says, 'Yes.' She says, 'Do you remember carrying him down on the stretcher?' Remember, the last I've seen of the lad, he's OK. He's getting looked after. So I was expecting her to sort of say, 'Here he is.' I was thinking he was going to walk in any minute. But she tells me, 'Oh, he didn't make it.' It was a bit of a shock. I'd always assumed that he'd been OK, the lad. I never knew he hadn't made it.

Anyway, it turns out that the two fellas with her were from *The Cook Report*. From that point on, any interviews that Anne did, they'd interview me, too – because my story was tied so closely to Kevin's story. Anything that Anne did in relation to getting the inquests quashed and getting what she wanted for Kevin, I'd give evidence, too. But from leaving Kevin on the hoarding in 1989 to meeting Anne for the first time that day in 1994, I'd never known who Kevin was. And I'd thought that he made it.*

---

* The edition of *The Cook Report* entitled *Kevin's Mum* was broadcast on ITV on 2 June 1994.

ANNE WILLIAMS

I realised that in Formby, where I lived, people were wondering why I was persisting. I mean people used to say to me, 'Hang on, you've got two other kids.' Nobody really understood about the 3.15 cut-off point. Everyone thought we'd had the inquiry, Taylor blamed the police, we'd had the inquests, 'Why is this woman rocking the boat?' And after *The Cook Report* I remember people's attitudes changing. They were coming up to me saying, 'Oh we didn't know about that 3.15 cut-off point.' And that was basically the only good thing to come out of Roger's programme. I was so pleased that people were at last beginning to understand the whole thing about that cut-off point.

When I look back it's quite frightening: I find it quite frightening the extremes they've gone to, to cover stuff up. I mean, we were pretty sure that our phones were being bugged. I'd be on the phone to my mum and it would start ringing while I'm already on the phone, talking to my mum. Or you'd be talking to one of the other families, and you'd hear a police radio in the background. We were very close to John Glover.* I'd be on the phone to him and there'd be all this crackling noise and John would say, 'Oh, they're listening in, the

---

* John Glover was a founding member of the Hillsborough Justice Campaign. The Hillsborough Justice Campaign exists to pursue and promote the truth about 15 April 1989, to support its members, the bereaved and the survivors of Hillsborough, and to campaign for the perpetrators of the disaster to be brought to justice.

John Glover's sons Joe and Ian went to Hillsborough together in 1989. Joe gave Ian mouth-to-mouth on the pitch, but spent many years traumatised after watching his brother's life slip away. Joe Glover would go missing for days, sometimes being found asleep on Ian's grave. In 1999 he, too, was killed in tragic circumstances, being crushed by a marble slab at his workplace. John Glover, a modest, generous and insightful man, campaigned for truth and justice from 1989 until his death from cancer on 25 March 2013.

murderers are bugging us.' Then someone from BT came to have a look at our lines, and then another couple came a day later, checking our plugs, but we were naïve, you know? We were just a normal little family, but when you look back, of course, yeah, someone has taken something off, or put something on to our plugs. We had those phones that you could plug into different rooms, and they were round, inspecting them, tampering with them. Even my husband said I was a fool not to question it properly, but you don't think at the time. It's only afterwards that it all fits into place.

STEVE KELLY

I'd been in a very happy marriage with Christine, but my behaviour, over time, put that under tremendous strain. I've always been a worker, but I was listless – I couldn't get up, I didn't go out to work. When I did, I'd just drive. If someone tried to flag me down, I'd just drive past. I wouldn't see them. I'd come home with £4 in my pocket. I was lost, really empty inside. The effect of all this spiralled Christine and me into constant issues and, ultimately, that cost me my marriage. I was all-consumed by Hillsborough and my thought processes went out of the window. All I could think was that there was this enormous wrong that needed correcting, and the injustice of it engulfed me. It took control of me.

I lost my strength as a human being – I lost my power. I conceded control of my life at that time and it was all down to the effect of looking on, helpless, while the authorities ticked their boxes and did a job on us. They buried us. They caused us so much pain and then walked away from it, job done. They didn't give us a crumb of comfort – nothing – because we were worthless bastards, and they could do that to us. And that's how I felt, a lot of the time – worthless. And slowly, slowly, it creeps up on you. It eats away at you. You become this angry, bitter, hostile person, and that wasn't me. I wasn't like that.

ANNE WILLIAMS

I kept at it. He's my son and I had so much evidence – I mean, there's loads of it, there's so much. There's so much that has gone on: the way we were treated by South Yorkshire police. They alone would have been enough to drive you insane! The way they spoke to us on the phone when you were asking for stuff. There was a guy that was in charge of all the Hillsborough documents – if you needed anything, or you wanted anything sending. But he was always, so … 'Oh and my son would have been the same age as yours, Mrs Williams. How do you cope?' All sympathy, you know, when I'm asking for stuff on Kevin. And I used to come downstairs sometimes, crying, 'He's just said this to me.' But Steve, my husband, he's ex-military, and he'd tell me, 'That copper's playing mind games with you!' So Steve taught me, really, he said, 'Take no notice of what he's trying to do to you, he's playing games.' So I got as clever as him, then, with the help of my husband. It became a game, in one respect, with them, and I always seemed to manage to get what I wanted. I was lucky, I suppose – anything I went for, I seemed to find it. And it wasn't always on a downer, there were times I would be laughing to myself. One time they sent me – I got the inquest papers through on the Saturday, 22 February. Then, on the Monday, I got a letter from the Chief Superintendent to inform me that we couldn't have the papers due to disciplinary action! And I'd had them on the Saturday. Things like that, you had to laugh.

JEGSY DODD

There was a period, only six or seven years after the disaster, really, when the whole Hillsborough justice struggle lost its prominence. I used to go to the memorial service at Anfield every year, and the attendances dropped off to about 2,000 or 3,000. No one seemed as interested any more. It dipped, then, obviously in the run-up to the tenth anniversary, there was a lot more focus and a lot more activity, and the interest and the anger began to grow again. But during that period – 1995, 1996 – there wasn't a huge impetus.

STEPHEN WRIGHT

There would be certain things that reminded you that the whole thing wasn't being forgotten. Jimmy McGovern's *Hillsborough* film aired on national television in December 1996, and that sparked fresh debate. Obviously he couldn't dramatise every family's story, but you still identified with it. That moment in Sheffield City Hall, after the coroner's inquest recorded that verdict of accidental death; the mothers all started singing 'You'll Never Walk Alone'. That's in the film. I'm glad that's in.

MARTIN THOMPSON

McGovern's *Hillsborough* is terrific. If anything, it's too real. All that stuff in the boys' club, the gym – all the noise, the wailing, all these people breaking down, crying ... that's exactly what it was like. I've only ever been able to watch it once. I sat down and watched it with a mate, and it was almost too powerful. I got the DVD when it came out, but I haven't sat down and watched it again, yet.

JOHN ASHTON

I think Jimmy McGovern's film was a huge factor, at just the right time. But generally, by then, there wasn't huge public interest in Hillsborough. I think Jimmy McGovern's television drama changed that, though, to a degree. With that empathetic, sympathetic narrative, in colour, on the screen – it was real. It was mothers and sons, real families – mums who refused to let it lie. It was human and desperately sad, right there in your front room, and I think it placed the tragedy and the cover-up back on the national agenda.

JOHN MACKIN

There was a sense that interest in Hillsborough was receding, but Labour coming into power gave us fresh hope. We'd had non-stop Tory government for almost twenty years and, in our heart of hearts, we never expected an Establishment government to give us a fair crack of the whip. But, quite soon after the election, the new Home Secretary Jack Straw promised that Hillsborough would be looked at again.

Sheffield Wednesday FC had still not erected a memorial to the 96, nor indeed made any noises suggesting it was even on their agenda. It was being swept under the carpet. The final straw came just after the eighth anniversary, on 10 May 1997, when there was a fundraising concert held at Anfield, headlined by the Manic Street Preachers, the Beautiful South and the Lightning Seeds. It was hosted by the legendary John Peel, and it was brilliant. Fifty thousand people there, and the message went around the world: Justice for the 96. It placed the campaign right back in the public eye.

Then, the day after the concert, Sunday 11 May, saw the Reds playing Sheffield Wednesday at Hillsborough. It was John Barnes's last game for the club, and many supporters – buoyed by the success of the big gig the night before – travelled over the Pennines in good humour. As usual for games there, many supporters took flowers and tributes to the victims. These would usually be laid at the Leppings Lane turnstiles, though some were taken inside for stewards to place behind the goal at that end. This time, though, things took a nasty turn. Sheffield Wednesday FC and the South Yorkshire police were lying in wait. Flowers and banners were not allowed in, in essence confiscated as 'items not allowed into football grounds'. They also seized flags and banners, fearful they would be critical of Sheffield Wednesday or the police. It was an unnecessary and provocatively heavy-handed operation. The police vans that day bore the motto: JUSTICE WITH COURAGE. Liverpool supporters – many of them Hillsborough survivors and bereaved – were fuming. After the game, many said they'd never go again. I was one of them. And so the seed was sown to actively boycott a Liverpool game at Hillsborough; to let Sheffield Wednesday know that, while they treated us in this manner and continued to ignore the events of 15 April 1989, they wouldn't be getting any more of our money.

SHEILA COLEMAN

Hillsborough was back in the public eye and Peter Kilfoyle, whose constituency included Anfield, called for a new inquiry. The Tories were still in power, and Michael Howard was non-committal. He said that any new inquiry would have to be demonstrably in the public interest.

Jack Straw, who took over as Home Secretary, met with the families and promised a judicial scrutiny into the tragedy. I remember him saying to us, 'I promise you, faithfully – no stone will be left unturned.' And then he goes and appoints possibly the most establishment judge he can find, Lord Justice Stuart-Smith. And it's not going to be a new inquiry, it's a 'scrutiny'. What's a 'scrutiny'? But anyway, Stuart-Smith was appointed to head the process and it was due to start, by government standards at least, quite quickly. So we allowed ourselves, initially anyway, to be quite cautiously optimistic.

That didn't last long – we soon discovered there would be severe limitations to this 'scrutiny'. Under the parameters laid down, Stuart-Smith was only detailed to look at 'new' evidence. In effect this meant he would only consider evidence that had not previously been before the Taylor Inquiry, the Director of Public Prosecutions, the Attorney General or South Yorkshire police. So we immediately smelt a rat. Even though the wider perception was that Labour had instigated a new inquiry, we were already struggling to understand what a 'scrutiny' actually involved – and our conclusion was that it would be whatever Lord Justice Stuart-Smith decided it was going to be! He'd already brought up this thing of 'public interest' again – as though learning the real causes of a major, avoidable disaster that led to large-scale loss of life was not in the public interest – and, if that wasn't bad enough, he set his stall out from the very first sitting in Liverpool.

This was October 1997. He'd convened an initial hearing at the Maritime Museum, where families were invited to present new evidence to him. Looking around the room, he asked, 'Are there more of your people, or are they like the Liverpool fans – turning up at the last minute.'

He apologised for what he described as a 'flippant, off-the-cuff remark', but it was an inauspicious start, and things did not get much better once the hearings began. Stuart-Smith laid out in clear detail that his definition of 'new evidence' would constitute 'evidence which was not available or was not presented to the previous inquiries, courts or authorities'. In reality, this ruled out everything we had intended to raise at the hearings. The only good thing that came of the process was that, for the first time, the families had access to witness statements that had, up until then, been in the possession of South Yorkshire police.

Early in the New Year, Jack Straw summoned us to Westminster. Seemingly, he wanted to give us the news to our faces so, ominously enough, we met him in Room 13 at the House of Commons. It was depressing – the same old story. Straw said he thought the Stuart-Smith scrutiny had been impartial, thorough and rigorous, but that no new evidence had emerged that warranted a re-opening of the case. It was a very, very downcast train journey back to Liverpool. The feeling was, if this evidence doesn't prove that a massive miscarriage of justice has taken place, a massive cover-up and a disgraceful, orchestrated smear campaign, then what is going to convince people? We were heartbroken. After that we referred to it – and still do, to this day – as the 'Stitch Up'. It was just a huge two fingers to the families from New Labour.

PETER CARNEY

The communal feeling and the common ground we shared made it inevitable, I think, that the survivors wanted a voice in the ongoing fight for justice. And the Hillsborough Justice Campaign began, in part, to provide a resource for survivors and *all* the other fans and people directly affected by Hillsborough, as well as the bereaved. The group was originally called The Hillsborough Relatives, Survivors' and Supporters' Association.

What is now the Hillsborough Justice Campaign came into existence directly after the collapse of the nonsense that was the Stuart-Smith scrutiny – or the stitch-up, as we now know it to be. (Lord Justice) Stuart-Smith started off with the infamous line about hoping we didn't turn up late like the fans had. I mean, there and then, people wanted to leave. In retrospect, the families should have insisted that he, Stuart-Smith, was replaced. But they had to go through with it, there was no choice.

If there was one good thing that came out of the scrutiny, it was that, for the first time, families were given access to evidence that had been withheld for all those years by the South Yorkshire police. I think that confirmed what a lot of people knew – or suspected. That evidence had been interfered with. But, of course, Stuart-Smith's recommendation to Jack Straw was that there was no compelling grounds for a fresh inquiry.

Anyway, the fallout from the whole Stuart-Smith thing was a motion from the Family Support Group that they'd be going down the route of a private prosecution against David Duckenfield and Bernard Murray – and that led to problems. For one thing, there was the cost. I think it was going to be two or three grand for each family to throw into a fighting fund, and a lot of people didn't have that. But there also the thing of … a lot of people held the view that it shouldn't be the families taking on a major legal challenge. It should be the authorities doing that. John Glover was very vocal about this – the need for fairness, equality, solidarity – and this is what led to the initial meeting that took place at the Glovers' house. There was John and Theresa Glover, Terry Burkett, Dave Church, Sandra Carlile and myself. I remember writing on this notepad, 'We, the undersigned, formally resolve to initiate an organisation called The Hillsborough

Relatives, Survivors' and Supporters' Association' – or words to that effect. And we all signed it.

STEPHEN WRIGHT

We just kept going, doing what we could. Banners, posters, flyers, marches, fundraisers – anything to keep the campaign in the public eye. We got our first HQ, a little florist's shop – well, used to be a florist's – about ten minutes from the ground, on Oakfield Road. Ricky Tomlinson helped us out with that, he bought the place for us and his brother Albert, who's a joiner, he did the fit-out. The place was in a terrible state when we first moved in there, but we had so much help from so many volunteers. When it was all done it looked great. Even the glaziers next door had their exterior painted red to show their support! It was good – a little bit out of the way compared to the place we've got now – but, still, great to have a Hillsborough Justice Campaign shopfront by the ground.

PETER CARNEY

Ricky Tomlinson played John Glover in the Hillsborough television play. The role had a huge impact on Ricky – him and John Glover became great mates, and Ricky was very involved in the setting up of the Justice Campaign. He found the original shop and he was the site manager, if you like – the project manager in terms of doing the place up. It was great, though – just that thing of having a HQ. It made everything that bit more physical, if you like. It was real.

SHEILA COLEMAN

Getting our first base was a major step – if you could call it a head-quarters! Ricky Tomlinson, the actor, paid our first year's rent, which was very much appreciated. Just having a physical presence near Anfield, so people could come in and pick up our literature, chat with us, spread the message – that was so important. You see, the longer time went on, the less people seemed aware. There was this new generation of fans coming through, and it worried us that they weren't really aware. They knew that Hillsborough had happened, and it was a disaster, but the connection was unravelling. That's where the education side of the campaign was critical.

PETER CARNEY

I couldn't tell you exactly when we changed the name to the Hillsborough Justice Campaign, but what I do know is that in the October of 1989 Dave and Maureen Church went down to Brighton to lobby the Labour Party about Hillsborough. They went to the Labour Party Conference to drum up support, and they introduced themselves as the Campaign for Hillsborough Justice – so maybe the idea came from that.

But we had the shop now, and there was the support mechanism, and a resolve to identify what action could and should be taken. But there was also an objective for solidarity with other causes and struggles. We wanted to reach out to other groups and take a marker, really, on where we were in relation to the struggles and injustices that other people were going through. We were looking at justice on the whole as a struggle. And so one of the first actions the group initiated was a leaflet titled 'Justice Is a Struggle', which I wrote. You could look at that leaflet as a manifesto, highlighting a number of the injustices we were facing, and what we thought should be done. These included calling on the Director of Public Prosecutions to re-open the criminal charges file against certain members of the South Yorkshire police; and calling for a new inquest that would allow evidence after the 3.15 p.m. cut-off point. It called for an independent public inquiry that would scrutinise, among other things, whether evidence and statements had been tampered with – things that now, thankfully, are being looked at. And there was a list of principles, you know, things we were hoping like-minded people would get behind – like shouting for justice at every game, wearing one of our ribbons or T-shirts, continuing with the boycott of the *Sun* newspaper ... things like that.

SHEILA COLEMAN

We were very proactive with our events. Our badges and stickers were widely distributed. We attended social justice marches in London, conferences, meetings, but above all else we listened to the fans, listened to what they wanted to do. It was the fans who wanted to reinforce and increase the boycott of the *Sun*, and we were the focal point for that. We organised big posters, flyers, stickers and so on. To this day circulation of the *Sun* newspaper on Merseyside is massively down on their national average.

ANNE WILLIAMS

Kelvin MacKenzie and the *Sun* – what a disgrace. You know, I'm not a hateful person in any way, and after all we've been through ... but sometimes you'd see him on *Question Time* and you'd get so angry. My children would get angry, they'd want to kick the TV in because he was so adamant about them.

And when I saw the apology about that big – I think it was tucked away on the second page – I was appalled at the size of it, I couldn't believe it, so I rang him. I was so angry and I got through to MacKenzie and said, 'Why didn't you do full coverage? Why not give it a two-page spread and explain how and why you got it so wrong?' And he said, 'Oh, well, it came from the horse's mouth so we never checked it out.'

Well, we always knew it had: it came from the police. We always had an idea that it came from someone, somewhere; someone's passed the information on to the *Sun* but they've never bothered checking it out. But my argument to MacKenzie was: 'Print the truth now. You know what the truth is, let people know …'

But even after that he carried on lying, and on *Question Time* – any programme he went on – he was so hateful. He used to twist his face. He was so hateful against us. It was as if he really hated those Liverpool fans, and that's what made you sort of want to kick the TV in, he was so horrible. Brian Clough was another. The things he wrote in his book, and he was there that day – I can't understand these people.

The Hillsborough Justice Campaign had done a few campaigns against them – well, they've always campaigned against the *Sun*. But MacKenzie was adamant. There was no changing his mind. I wasn't surprised by this time because we were uncovering other stuff.

JEGSY DODD

While the campaign was starting to get a bit of new momentum, the club itself did absolutely nothing – not even merchandise. It seems strange today; it's almost the opposite, there's so much

Hillsborough merchandise that you could argue it loses some of its impact. But in the late nineties you'd never have got anything with '96' or 'Justice' on, not in those days. You couldn't get anything in the club shop at all. If you wanted to show your support, there was only the Hillsborough Justice Campaign producing anything. You could go to the Hillsborough Justice Campaign shop and get a wristband or a badge or a scarf and, certainly among our away support, people identified very strongly with what the HJC was doing. You'd begin to see their stickers, and the HJC scarves were great. It was just a plain red scarf with the logo on; very understated. Apart from it being something we all supported, they produced some really good stuff, just right for the sort of people who went everywhere with Liverpool.

JOHN MACKIN

There was still a lot of anger aimed at Sheffield Wednesday, and this carried on into the following season. We used the fanzines, most notably *Red All Over the Land* and *Through the Wind and Rain*, to initiate the boycott protest. A 'red card' mosaic was organised on the Kop the day we played Sheffield Wednesday at Anfield – the subtext being to publicly 'out' the club's attitude as being completely unacceptable. Liverpool FC paid for the mosaic and the club's Chief Executive Rick Parry expressed the club's concerns to Dave Richards, the chairman of Sheffield Wednesday, after the match. The 'red card' protest was a resounding success, and the focus on trying to get Sheffield Wednesday to engage with us snowballed from there.

SHEILA COLEMAN

The campaign grew. We forged some great alliances and friendships with other supporter groups and also other justice campaigns. We ensured that the Hillsborough Disaster was recognised for what it was – a major miscarriage of justice. Paddy Joe Hill, one of the Birmingham Six, who had suffered at the hands of the notorious West Midlands Serious Crime Squad, became a great ally and friend. On his release from prison, when it had been proved that he was innocent, he formed MOJO (Miscarriages of Justice Organisation) and we were happy to benefit from the advice he could offer. On the football front the Greek team Olympiaos, who had experienced their own tragedy, forged links with us. A Catholic church in Athens holds its own Hillsborough memorial mass every year on 15 April and each year they ask me to send a message from the HJC which is read out at the mass. And also the Scandinavians, especially the Norwegians, were fantastic. Tage Herstad and his friends have done so much in terms of fundraising and spreading the word, right from the start. I remember him walking in and asking if he could take T-shirts to sell back in Norway. He didn't have the money to pay up front but he hoped we'd trust him. Of course we did, and that trust has been repaid in multiples, and was just the start of a solid, lasting bond and friendship; one of the real positives.

JOHN MACKIN

In 1998 we played Sheffield Wednesday on St Valentine's Day, and I stayed at home. It was just as well, as the match was, unbelievably – or deliberately, some say – sponsored by the *Sun*. There was uproar, and many returned home vowing never to set foot inside Hillsborough again. The boycott idea was taking hold on a grand scale. What better time to highlight our grievances than the ten-year anniversary of the disaster? As soon as the fixtures for the 1998–99 season were released, we began planning our boycott of Hillsborough.

It was obviously being taken seriously in Sheffield, too, as Wednesday soon announced that they would be erecting a memorial and called for the boycott to be abandoned. The match was due to take place on 8 May, but as early as February Wednesday announced that they would, at last, be erecting a memorial. The fanzine editors were summoned to a meeting to demand the cancellation of the boycott. We told them that we were not the organisers now, that it had taken hold in the consciousness of supporters generally, and it was, thus, not our boycott to call off. They left disappointed. They felt it would serve no purpose now, but I and many others still believed that Sheffield Wednesday's seeming change of heart was based purely on a fear of losing out financially.

SHEILA COLEMAN

Sheffield Wednesday Football Club themselves were treating Liverpool fans terribly in those days. Whenever they wanted to go over to Hillsborough and leave flowers, the club wouldn't let them, things like that – they were telling our people that flowers were an offensive weapon, it was unbelievable. So we just thought, 'No, we're not being treated like that. We'll boycott the Sheffield Wednesday versus Liverpool game.' People were saying, 'You'll never get Liverpool fans to stop going to the game.' So that was a gamble because, even among our campaign group, there were prominent individuals who went to *every* Liverpool game. But we knew there were key people, and if we got their support for the boycott then that would be a massive help. I remember going to the Colonel* and saying, 'Anthony, are you with us? Are you going to boycott this?' And he said, 'Don't worry, we're with you.' There was no stopping us, then. And – we were known for our stickers by then, the HJC – we had these stickers done. Some of us still have our HJC stickers from the day that proudly state: I STAYED AWAY ON THE 8th MAY.

In the lead-up to the boycott day we also produced T-shirts – each one had a letter, a 'B', an 'O', a 'Y' and so on, spelling out BOYCOTT HILLSBOROUGH. We managed to get enough seats in a row at Liverpool's next game, and there was a big photo of them in the papers spelling out the message. Boycott Hillsborough. Things like that might seem quite small but gave the campaign such a lift – and quite a lot of profile, too.

JOHN MACKIN

The Hillsborough Justice Campaign produced leaflets and stickers, garnering support and promoting the idea of a full-on boycott of Hillsborough. One particularly memorable action came at the Leeds away game when a long line of supporters, each wearing bright yellow T-shirts, stood up throughout the second half, the black letters on their chests spelling out: BOYCOTT HILLSBOROUGH.

In the weeks leading up to the game, Barnes Travel – the locally based coach firm who took thousands of Liverpool and Everton fans to away games – said that, as a gesture of support for the boycott, they wouldn't be running any coaches to Hillsborough. It was a major victory.

---

* Anthony Hogan, a well-known Liverpool fan.

There were fears that there might be friction among fans on the day of the game. Some supporters wanted to travel over and picket the turnstiles, or to protest outside the ground. It would be a recipe for confrontation – and possibly a huge coup for Sheffield Wednesday and South Yorkshire police if trouble were to erupt – and it would be totally counterproductive. It was thus suggested that a rally, a concert in support of the Justice Campaign, be held in Liverpool on the day of the boycott, giving those who wanted to publicly support the boycott a focal point for their protest: a highly visible outlet for their commitment.

In the run-up to the tenth anniversary, though, a group of aggrieved Reds took matters into their own hands when they decided to install their own memorial at Hillsborough. The plan was to replace a paving stone directly outside the Leppings Lane end with a specially commissioned, gold-plated commemorative plaque. 'The Hillsborough Stone' would be cemented into the Leppings Lane pavement with industrial-grade adhesive. So, basically, people would wake up on 15 April 1999 to find the Hillsborough Stone as a Leppings Lane fixture.

However, their daring raid was scuppered in the week leading up to the anniversary, when they discovered that Hillsborough was being heavily guarded by a private security firm. Sheffield Wednesday were obviously expecting some form of protest or incident. The Reds retreated, and the Hillsborough Stone took up residence in the Albert pub, next to Anfield.

MARTIN THOMPSON

On the tenth anniversary, I went to Sheffield. I went to Hillsborough itself. I just didn't want to be in Liverpool, but I had to be somewhere.

I remember getting the train across the Pennines with my mate, and the weather was the complete opposite to how it had been ten years before. It was cold, it was snowing. I went and stood on Leppings Lane. I went to where Stuart died.

SHEILA COLEMAN

So, leading up to the day of the Sheffield Wednesday game, 8 May 1999, we thought, 'It's all very well asking people not to go to the game, but we need an alternative.' St George's Hall is right opposite the station, so we came up with the idea of a festival. We got Pete Wylie, Ian McNabb, Chumbawamba, all sorts, all day, and there was such a feel-good atmosphere. It was a complete success. Ten years on and it was a different type of protest. One of our best days.

JOHN MACKIN

On the day of the game there were only 27,000 in attendance, with Liverpool's support taking up just over 1,000 of their 7,500 ticket allocation. This meant that almost 6,500 Reds snubbed the fixture. The low attendance on a baking hot day in May 1999 was in contrast to a gate of over 35,000 just over a year earlier. The thousands of empty Liverpool seats sent a loud, clear message back to Sheffield Wednesday and their chairman, Dave Richards: that their club's efforts were far too little and way too late.

Meanwhile, the same day, 5,000 attended the event at St George's Hall in Liverpool. It was a resounding success and, we felt, a real red letter day for the campaign.

Wednesday did eventually erect a memorial – if we can call it that – after the tenth anniversary of the disaster. The Sheffield Wednesday memorial is nigh on shameful. It is almost hidden from view, away from the Leppings Lane end, and makes no mention of the fact that 96 Liverpool supporters died there, at that football ground – the words 'Hillsborough' and 'Sheffield Wednesday Football Club' being cynically absent.

The Hillsborough Stone found a lasting and appropriate home, too. In September 2001, in the aftermath of the terrible events of 9/11, *Red All Over the Land* fanzine got in touch with the New York branch of the Liverpool supporters' club. A plan was hatched to raise funds for the relatives of fallen fire-fighters. The big stone plaque was dusted off, and joined a haul of collectables, players' shirts, souvenirs and other goodies that helped raise almost £7,000 for the fund. Phil Hammond of the Hillsborough Family Support Group, who lost his son at Hillsborough, presented a cheque for several thousand pounds as a donation. Regular match-goers can see a framed photo and newspaper article commemorating the fundraiser on the wall of the Albert. And the Hillsborough Stone itself can be found in permanent residence at the LFC supporters' club HQ – the 11th Street Bar on the Lower East Side, New York. It is a far more fitting tribute than Sheffield Wednesday's paltry gesture.

PETER CARNEY

The more that time went on, there was no doubt in our minds that there was one law for us and another one entirely for the police. The trial of the two coppers, Bernard Murray and David Duckenfield – the private prosecution – came up in Leeds in June 2000. Even the fact of it taking place right there in Yorkshire – it was hardly impartial, was it?

There was all sorts of manoeuvring and preconditions being set, even before the case eventually did come to court. The policemen's solicitor suggested that the trial shouldn't go ahead at all because, if these two police officers of such high profile and such long standing went to jail, their lives could be in danger. And the presiding judge – Judge Hooper, it was – was inclined to agree with that. He said that, even they were found guilty during this hearing, they wouldn't go to jail. There's a pre-trial quote from Judge Hooper:

> I can say from my own experience of defending in many criminal cases over the years, that it is the thought of prison that is, for most defendants, the greatest worry. For police officers or ex-police officers the threat of prison has even more significance than for others. These two defendants, if sentenced to prison for the manslaughter of, in effect, 96 people, would necessarily be at considerable risk of serious injury if not death at the hands of those who feel very strongly about Hillsborough. I conclude that the oppression is not such as to prevent the trial from taking place but that I should now reduce to a significant extent the anguish being suffered by these defendants. I do that by making it immediately clear that the two defendants will not lose their liberty should they be convicted. This is, I accept, a highly unusual course of action, but this is a highly unusual case.

For me, that was the first time I'd heard of someone being sentenced before they'd been convicted – but nothing surprised you, by then.

And it was no surprise at all when Murray was acquitted; and, for Duckenfield, it was a hung verdict, with Judge Hooper adding a note that that was it. It wouldn't be possible to stage a fair retrial. So, for a lot of the families, I think that was that. But for us it was game on. We weren't going to be silenced, we wanted to use every opportunity we could to speak up for justice and speak up for the people who weren't here to speak for themselves. There's a quote from Voltaire on the Justice Campaign website, and it says, 'One owes respect to the living – but to the dead one owes only the truth.'

STEVE KELLY

The HJC was totally inclusive – we would accept membership from anybody who needed support or who wanted to offer support, and we embraced the survivors, absolutely. In many ways, at that time, they were the forgotten victims of Hillsborough and they needed help as much as anybody.

SHEILA COLEMAN

One of the things we were able to offer was counselling to those who would benefit most from it, and who might not otherwise have been able to take that course of action. If the option was available to them via their local health authority, then good, but we found that was not always the case; and, in many cases, people couldn't take that first step independently, with an outsider, if you like. They were much more comfortable coming to us.

PETER CARNEY

Another thing that focused our actions was the issue of legal advice. This was a running sore – people were not happy about the way they'd been represented. So many people had just gone with your common-or-garden high street solicitor and they felt badly let down. Across the board, there'd been this token settlement of £3,000, or £3,500, and people were accepting, you know, because they had bills to pay. Because they *had* to accept, and that was the advice they were getting.

And one particular outcome infuriated me. It was heart-breaking. On 1 March 2001 a man called Alf Langley, a survivor from pen 4, died of fibrosis. He was 44 years old. In the aftermath of Hillsborough, Alf had gone on his solicitor's advice and he'd accepted the standard compensation of £3,000 for the trauma he'd experienced as a result of Hillsborough. On the same day that Alf Langley died in Fazakerley Hospital, an ex-South Yorkshire policeman, Martin Long, was awarded £330,000 in compensation for his own suffering after Hillsborough. This policeman had retired from the force on medical grounds after suffering from belated post-traumatic stress disorder related to Hillsborough, finding himself unable to carry on with his job. Now, I don't wish Martin Long any ill-will and I don't deny him his right to seek proper compensation, but ... I don't know what suffering he could possibly have experienced that made his compensation worth a hundred times that of a survivor who was personally, physically crushed in the pens and had to pick up the pieces of his life. Initially, I was in despair – there'd been the farce of the Murray/Duckenfield trial, and now this – but then I was just irate. I wrote 'Justice, My Arse', mainly as a way of getting the anger out and trying to get across the sheer hurt and ... the *wrongness* of what was happening. You can still read the article today on the HJC website.

JEGSY DODD

For me, Hillsborough was like the day the music died. It just took such a long time to get over everything. I never went for counselling and I was very much set against the idea of claiming, you know? I just didn't like that culture, and I didn't put myself forward. But I've got to say, it stuck in your throat a bit when you started to read about traumatised police officers getting these enormous pay-outs when the vast majority of them weren't even directly amongst it.

SHEILA COLEMAN

Moving to the new shop made such a huge difference. It was John McCormick who found the place. We had four John Macs who were all very much involved in the campaign, but this was John Macca from Kirkby. Him finding that shop was, for us, a game-changer. It was literally right opposite the ground. We haggled with the owner over the terms but we got the keys and we were open in time for the start of the 2003–04 season. In fact, we opened on the morning of the pre-season game against Valencia – 9 August 2003; an auspicious day for all Liverpool supporters because, as Valencia manager, it was Rafa Benitez's first visit to Anfield.

So, for the first time we had a real match-day presence, right opposite the ground. We had the meeting room upstairs, we became a real focal point, a kind of drop-in centre before and after the games. Fans started storing their banners there, and we started doing T-shirts and so on with the different fans' groups. We did things like The Untouchables T-shirts, and the plain scarves with the Hillsborough flame, and these became very sought-after items. A lot of our away support would wear these things as a show of solidarity with the campaign, but also a means of distinguishing themselves as Liverpool's core support.

PETER CARNEY

It was huge for the campaign, in so many ways, when we moved to the new shop. I think it was John Mac from Kirkby who found the premises – and there was George Tomkins too, who helped with the financial side. George had become a real close confidant of Anne Williams and Sheila Coleman because, of course, he'd also been stitched up by Stan Beechey. This was when Beechey was still head of the West Midlands Serious Crime Squad, who were notorious for the way they acted. Tomkins had been held in remand for eighteen months, on the basis of Beechey's evidence, for an armed robbery he said he had nothing to do with. He fought the charge, and kept on appealing until it was overturned. Once he was a free man, George made a complaint about Beechey to the Police Complaints Authority (as it was then), so he'd had to go through the same whole legal procedure that Anne was going through, trying to remedy the failings of the justice system – and, like I say, he was a big help when it came to the shop. Moving there placed the campaign right in the heart of Anfield. We were directly opposite the ground, and that was us saying, 'We're here to stay. This is who we are and this is what we stand for – come and join us.'

MARTIN THOMPSON

There was a British hostage in Iraq – Ken Bigley, from Liverpool. His captors executed him in 2004 – he was actually beheaded. Understandably, his murder caused outrage, and Ken Bigley's death was particularly felt in his home town. A short time afterwards, the *Spectator* published an article entitled SELF-PITY CITY about the way Liverpool and Liverpudlians had reacted to Bigley's murder. The gist of the piece was that Ken Bigley knew the risks involved in working in Iraq yet still chose to stay out there and take the money. Bigley's decision should, the *Spectator* argued, be taken into account when complete strangers gushed sympathy and outrage at his execution.

The editorial carried Boris Johnson's byline, though it was actually written by Simon Heffer. One paragraph said that Liverpudlians 'wallow' in their 'victim status'. Heffer continued, 'They cannot accept that they might have made any contribution to their misfortunes, but seek rather to blame someone else for it, thereby deepening their sense of shared tribal grievance about the rest of society.'

The Tory leader of the day, Michael Howard, sent Boris Johnson up to Liverpool to apologise in person. He seemed to treat the whole thing, like everything else, as a bit of a cock-up that he could laugh off. It was another layer of paint on the smear, though. Always the victims. That sort of thing can stick.

SHEILA COLEMAN

Istanbul in 2005 obviously gave the team an even bigger international profile, and we felt the effect, too. There was definitely a surge of interest from abroad. We started doing the wristbands around that time. I think we started with an initial run of two hundred, but they just flew out. Everyone wanted them. We started trying to get professional – we placed a big order with a manufacturer in Shanghai – but you'd have myself, my mother, my brother, Gerry McIver and his wife, Kenny and all the regulars, would be running this cottage industry, stuffing wristbands into envelopes and taking them down to our local post office for dispatch. They were literally getting sent all over the world. I remember going into my post office and asking, 'How much to send a little package to Ho Chi Minh City?' And the postie was saying, 'Do you know, I don't think I have ever sent a parcel to Ho Chi Minh City in my life!'

So we were touching all four corners of the world, and that mattered. In other respects, it was difficult to say where we could take the campaign next – so these tangible aspects really did matter, and not just for morale. We made money from those wristbands, and with that money we were able to put a lot of survivors into therapy, an option that probably would not have been available to them without our support.

DAMIAN KAVANAGH

I have worn my wristband on my right wrist since they came out, in 2005. I'd feel undressed without it now. I always used to wear a small LFC pin badge on whatever shirt I was wearing, but this has replaced it. It's more appropriate; a small way of showing support and raising awareness. I don't know if I'll ever take it off. Maybe if and when Justice is finally done.

JOHN MACKIN

One of the effects of Istanbul was that Liverpool FC woke up on 26 May 2005 with a multitude of new fans. As the 2005–06 season progressed, there was a growing unease among seasoned Liverpool supporters that some of these new fans didn't fully embrace our traditions. A watershed moment came when Liverpool played Bordeaux in the Champions League, late 2006. Before the game there'd been a full-scale fight in a pub near the ground. What happened was, a few of Liverpool's real, go-everywhere, home-and-away fans had walked in to see two fully grown men sitting there, in Liverpool colours, in an Anfield pub, reading the *Sun*. An argument flared up, and the lads I know were surprised how many people either didn't understand or didn't respect the boycott of the *Sun*. The next day, once the dust had settled, a few of us started facing up to the fact that a whole swathe of our support just didn't know about Hillsborough. A lot of them didn't seem to know much about Liverpool at all.

Over the next few days the subject was all over the internet forums, this genuine outpouring of disgust having been fermented by a passionate plea on the Rattle – the RAOTL fan forum – for us to stand up and be counted: to reclaim the support and return to the right ways of doing things. Liverpool fans had a vast catalogue of original songs and a reputation for wit and sarcasm. We lamented what had happened to the support that once had TV documentaries made about it, and was so special that it was 'sampled' on Pink Floyd albums! The Anfield support from the early sixties onwards had virtually created terrace culture, and had always been ahead of the curve, always distinctive and witty. It also had a reputation for biting sarcasm, but only when it was deserved. In short, Liverpool's support had always been witty, never gormless.

So we started Reclaim the Kop, really, to try to ensure that our newer fans understood our history and our culture. And a massive part of that was making sure they knew that Liverpool fans do not buy the *Sun*. We do not read the *Sun*. It's as simple as that.

DAN NICOLSON

Not long after Reclaim the Kop was formed Kelvin MacKenzie reared his head again. In November 2006 he was the guest speaker at a dinner for a law firm in Newcastle. He said, 'All I did wrong there was tell the truth. There was a surge of Liverpool fans who had been drinking and that is what caused the disaster. The only thing different we did was put it under the headline THE TRUTH. I went on *The World at One* the next day and apologised. I only did that because Rupert Murdoch told me to. I wasn't sorry then and I'm not sorry now, because we told the truth.'

There was a wave of revulsion, and that was only compounded when the BBC announced that MacKenzie was going to be a guest on *Question Time* in mid-December. It irked people, as much as the initial comments that re-sparked this furore, that an organisation like the BBC – and a public one at that – would have the gall to employ such a man. It was at this point it was felt something had to be done.

JOHN MAGUIRE

There was outrage about MacKenzie's comments but there was also real anger about the BBC giving him a platform. This is a time just before the social media explosion, and we were big on stickers and flyers to spread the word. There were stickers going round with words like BBC – DON'T HIRE THE LIAR. But there was a growing consensus that we had to do something much bigger – much more powerful.

DAN NICOLSON

Whatever was to be done had to be bold and powerful, and I think what we proposed was. The weekend after MacKenzie appeared on *Question Time*, the draw for the FA Cup was made. Liverpool got Arsenal at home, and the BBC chose it as their live match. It was ideal – the BBC and the FA Cup in front of a live audience of millions; not just here, but around the world. We started with the idea of a mosaic on the Kop. It would say THE TRUTH, and everyone would get the message. Then we decided we'd try to hold the mosaic up for the first six minutes of the match – obviously a reference to the match being halted after six minutes in 1989. And, from that, the idea of six minutes of non-stop 'Justice' chants grew.

JOHN MAGUIRE

I was very nervous. I kept thinking, 'What have we started, here? What if it doesn't work?' None of us was used to public speaking, we were mainly in our twenties, but, between us, we did a whole wave of publicity in the week leading up to the game. All the local radio stations had us on, the *Echo* did a two-page special and Liverpool FC's in-house TV channel gave regular explanations and reminders that 'Truth Day' would be happening.

DAN NICOLSON

Looking back it was a gamble. The idea of chanting non-stop for a set period of the game hadn't really been attempted before, as far as I knew. I remember being apprehensive in the build-up about whether or not it could work. Communication was going to be the key. The revulsion for MacKenzie wasn't in doubt, neither was the message – but this was pre-social media boom so, despite a decent local-press coverage, outside of small-forum communities, that message was going to have to be spread largely on the day by leaflets.

JOHN MACKIN

We were in the ground first thing to finish off laying out the mosaic (some of the volunteers had started on the Friday afternoon). Then it was a case of blitzing Anfield with the flyers. We had to make sure that the whole ground was aware what was happening, and why it was happening – including the Arsenal fans. There were the odd dissenting voices, as you'd expect, but, by and large, everyone seemed receptive.

DAN NICOLSON

We'd put posters up in the toilets of Sam Dodd's – one of the big match-day pubs near Anfield. For whatever reason, I went back in a short while later and someone had scrawled on a poster: 'Let Them Rest in Peace.' It was the first real bit of dissent I'd publicly seen, but it was a thought-provoking moment. I was a lad in my early twenties, helping in a small way to champion a fight that I felt passionate about. But were there others, possibly closer to the cause, who thought differently?

Into the ground, and there was something in the air as kick-off approached. We'd had passionate nights in recent memory at Anfield – the treble season, the European nights of 2004–05 – but there was something a little bit different about this one. There was an edge, something a little more vengeful. I'm not suggesting that we'd never had this before, but I believe it was this game that showed the masses that there is power in public protest.

JOHN MAGUIRE

As kick-off approached, my heart was in my mouth. We were basically asking the Kop to hold these cards up for six minutes and sing 'Justice for the 96' non-stop. If you try holding your arms up straight for six minutes, that's not easy! Try it while you're singing.

DAN NICOLSON

What unfurled over the next few minutes was something never seen before in an English ground. The front of the Kop was a wall of banners and flags – some aimed at MacKenzie, others towards the BBC and many more, of course, calling for Justice.

As 'You'll Never Walk Alone' finished and the players came out, cards were held aloft spelling out THE TRUTH, and a chant of 'Justice for the 96' began. I was at the front. I remember saying to someone, 'This is too early! We'll never keep it up!' A couple of minutes had already passed and I feared the chant and the mosaic would begin to fade. By the time the BBC cameras had panned away from the studio and out on to the pitch, it would all be over.

But I was wrong. If anything, the chanting got louder as the referee prepared for kick-off. The next six minutes were an incredible show of passion, anger, revulsion and belief. All four sides of the ground belted out 'Justice for the 96' in unison, indifferent to what was happening on the pitch.

As the clock ticked on to six minutes, the loudest roar I've ever heard at Anfield – or anywhere, for that matter – erupted. Mosaic sheets that had been held up for approaching ten minutes – no mean feat! – were flung into the air and a shout of 'Liverpool' went up. We'd had our say.

JOHN MAGUIRE

It was unbelievable, really. I remember Thierry Henry standing there, staring up at the Kop. He seemed to be nodding his head in support. And it wasn't just the Kop – the entire ground stood up and sang 'Justice for the 96' with real conviction and passion – and anger, too. It was like everyone had had enough of MacKenzie and his lies.

When the scoreboard went past six minutes, there was this huge eruption of noise and everyone started singing 'Liverpool'. But us lot who'd organised the protest were all hugging each other like we'd scored the winning goal! It really did feel like we'd managed to pull off something very special.

JOHN MACKIN

After the game, even the Arsenal fans were coming up to us to say how special the demonstration had been. They said they'd felt privileged to be a part of it. Some of them had tears in their eyes – they were really emotional about the whole thing. And that's warranted, you know? Truth Day was a massive statement of fan power.

DAN NICOLSON

Later that night, I headed home. I'd recorded the match and fast-forwarded through the studio build-up to the start of the action. Any fears that the BBC might somehow try to swerve the protest were unfounded. John Motson made reference to what was going on – he had to – then went on to say how much the *Sun* newspaper was hated on Merseyside, and why. Truth Day was covered, all right. It was unavoidable. The whole nation, the whole world, couldn't have missed the display of raw power on the Kop.

There is an incredible shot from a camera stationed on the Anfield Road touch line that takes it all in. The noise at the end of the six minutes was captured as well – an incredible roar that meant so much to so many. And then Mark Lawrenson, the BBC's commentator for the day, mouthed something like, 'Now we can get on with the game.' His tone of contempt only served to make me feel that little bit prouder about playing a part in such a monumental show of strength.

MARTIN THOMPSON

There have been journalists like David Conn and Brian Reade who have never let Hillsborough slip completely from the public eye. Hillsborough is a generation away from us now, but there's still this burning sense of injustice among the younger ones. If you look at Truth Day, when we played Arsenal in the Cup in 2007, that was one of the most potent public protests ever about Hillsborough and MacKenzie and the smears and lies; yet it was mainly organised by Liverpool's young lads. None of them would have been at Hillsborough; some of them wouldn't even be old enough to remember it.

PART THREE

THE
TRUTH

ANDY BURNHAM

In January 2008 I was made Culture Secretary, in the year that Liverpool was European Capital of Culture. I see that now as, in some way, an act of fate. And I threw myself into it, straight away. I thought, this is important; we're making a political point here. I'm going to spend all my time in Liverpool this year, we're going to give massive profile to making Liverpool, Capital of Culture, a big success.

While I was back and forth to Liverpool, I got to know Steve Rotheram who, at that time, was the Lord Mayor. We were both helping the Dunne family in their prolonged fight to bring their son's body back from Spain. Ultimately, happily, they prevailed. In the December of that year, the Spanish authorities agreed to release Steven's body.

STEVE ROTHERAM

I was sitting next to Andy Burnham at Steven Dunne's funeral and, while we were waiting for the funeral to start, I mentioned to him that the twentieth anniversary of the Hillsborough tragedy was imminent, and would he come along. At first Andy said he wasn't sure if that was the right thing to do. He was saying, 'The families won't want me there. What am I going to say to them?' And I was saying to him, 'You've got to go. You can't *not* be there. I'm telling the families that you're going.'

ANNE WILLIAMS

In all that time, I had always had Kevin somewhere, submitted legally. There was always an appeal or a new avenue you could take. You might submit to the Attorney General and you'd then have to wait eight months for an answer. And then you'd find somewhere else and there'd be another avenue and I was always happy because I took him down a new route and, win or lose, I knew that I was doing something for Kev. I'd be thinking, 'Oh, I might win it this time, you never know. If not, I'll find another way.' And I always seemed to find another way.

I mean, to this day, there's a death certificate which I will not pick up, which has traumatic asphyxia listed as his cause of death. Traumatic asphyxia was not the cause of Kevin's death. And the only way you can get a death certificate changed is through a new inquest, so that was my aim: to get a new inquest, to get the record put straight, to get the right cause of death on his certificate, the right verdict. Only then would I collect Kevin's death certificate. So that was my aim. I wanted the government to put the record straight.

PETER HOOTON

I got a phone call from Steve Rotheram, who was just starting his stint as Lord Mayor of Liverpool. He told me that this was the first time he'd ever had any political power, and he was determined to use his leverage as Lord Mayor to make sure that Hillsborough was firmly back on the political agenda as we approached the twentieth anniversary of the tragedy. I said to him, 'How are you going to do that, Steve?' He said, 'This is Liverpool: we'll start by making a record.'

STEVE ROTHERAM

I never forgot the coach journey back from Hillsborough. I was a brickie from Kirkby, making my way back, numb from what I'd just seen. There was this feeling of hopelessness, and helplessness – and we all said we'd do whatever we could to help raise funds and raise awareness. Now here was a chance to do it on a much bigger scale. I had plenty of support from the 1989 squad: John Aldridge, Phil Thompson, Bruce Grobbelaar all said they'd do it, then, crucially, Kenny said he'd do it. But do what? I thought we should re-record 'You'll Never Walk Alone'.

PETER HOOTON

I asked John Power and Mick Head to get involved, and things snowballed from there. It all just developed very naturally. We liked the idea of recording 'Fields of Anfield Road'. This was one of the most popular crowd songs at the match, yet there hadn't really been a definitive version recorded. I wrote a new verse, commemorating the 96, and John Power said he wanted to sing it almost *a cappella* – sort of like 'Give Peace a Chance'. We had no idea what demand would be like. Eventually we pressed 20,000 CDs, basically hand-delivered them ourselves to all the record stores in the area – and sold out after two days!

ANDY BURNHAM

I'd pretty much made my mind up that I was going to go, but I kept saying to Steve [Rotheram], 'It's not enough for me to just turn up. It has to mean something. I have to be able to tell them something.' And Steve was going, 'So say something. Tell them something.' A day or two later I picked up the paper and David Conn had written one of his fantastic, forensic pieces where he goes into incredible depth about the police cover-up. What had happened was, after the Stuart-Smith scrutiny, Maria Eagle MP had persuaded the government to put all the documentation Stuart-Smith had looked at into the House of Lords. And there was this pile of evidence, loads of amended statements, boxes and crates of them. And David Conn had been practically the only person to go down there and read through all these hundreds of statements, and he produced this article, which basically said: do people realise that, sitting in dusty boxes in the House of Lords are statement after statement after statement where first-hand accounts by ordinary civilians and police officers have been amended by senior police officers to remove any culpability from the police and make it look as though the fans were to blame? He quoted one statement in particular which, still now, stands out to me, where this officer had been spontaneous and quite emotional about how terrible he felt, how helpless they were just standing there, the lack of any emergency response, the lack of any clear instructions, and how the supporters, in a vacuum, were trying to do their best. And there was a Post-It note attached to the statement, with instructions from a senior officer that read:

Last two pages require amending. These are his own feelings. He also states that PCs were sat down crying when the fans were carrying the dead and injured. This shows they were organised and we were not. Have him rewrite the last two pages excluding points mentioned.

And that thing of 'they were organised, we were not' – them and us, us and them – that brought the very essence of it home to me in a moment of absolute clarity. Them and Us – that was the eighties. That's how football supporters were viewed. And I thought, 'This is it. This is evidence that is there, and yet the country doesn't know. We need to know who and why and where – why were these statements amended?' I'd been trying to think what we could do, how we could re-open Hillsborough, and there it was. That was what we had to go for – full disclosure.

ANNE WILLIAMS

It's been hard, you know, but it's been a big part of my life. But I always got on with my life in-between. When Kev was up before the European Court of Human Rights in 2009 – Oh, I was made up when I got him into the European courts – I thought, '"Williams versus the United Kingdom": that's something.' And so you can get on with your life for a little bit while you're waiting; nothing's going on but you're doing something.

And then it fails, but I'm used to the knock-backs. I was expecting it because I knew why they weren't letting me through, you know? The barristers had told me, and I knew Kev's case could open the floodgates. We always said if Kev gets through [the European Court of Human Rights] that will open the whole thing up, and that's what I wanted him to do. Not just for Kevin, but for all the other families as well. But they threw it out, exactly two weeks before the twentieth anniversary.

STEVE ROTHERAM

I'd been involved in a whole series of meetings with Liverpool Football Club in the lead-up to the twentieth anniversary of Hillsborough – we were all trying to make sure that everything was in place for the memorial service at Anfield, but also to ensure we were fully prepared for the numbers. In years gone by there'd be anything between 5,000 and 10,000 attending, and they'd all be comfortably accommodated on the Kop. But I remember saying to very senior people at Liverpool FC at the time, 'I think this year is going to be much bigger. There could be a massive turn-out.' The club said, 'Not to worry,' they had a plan B, and I said, 'We could well need a plan C, D and E!'

ANDY BURNHAM

I spoke to Maria Eagle and said, 'Why don't you and I go for disclosure?' She was a high-ranking minister of state, I was part of the cabinet but, nevertheless, it was a risky strategy. Technically, it should have been a Home Office call, and you don't usually make a call against another government department. She said, 'OK,' she was ready to support it – but how were we going to do it? So I suggested that we brief David Conn. Tell him that, as local ministers in the lead-up to the twentieth anniversary, we were going to write to the Home Secretary, Jacqui Smith, and call for disclosure. So I started that moving.

STEVE ROTHERAM

I contacted the two cathedrals and asked them if they'd ring their bells 96 times, simultaneously, at six minutes past three. I got hold of Merseytravel, and they agreed to stop all public transport, including the ferries. So, even if a ferry was mid-journey it would have to shut down for those few minutes. We went through Gold Command at police level to implement all the initiatives we had planned. There were the big screens in Williamson Square, so people could watch the service. We had a service, too, behind the Town Hall for all the people in the city centre who wanted to pay their respects, who couldn't get to Anfield. And you could really feel the momentum, heading into 15 April.

PETER HOOTON

Ken Nelson, Coldplay's producer, mixed the single. We were all pretty pleased with it, but demand was such that it was too late to re-stock for the anniversary – but, with all the publicity the record had, it may have been a factor in so many people flocking to Anfield for the memorial service.

ANDY BURNHAM

Even though we'd started this process, Maria Eagle and I, I was still massively conflicted about my presence at the twentieth anniversary itself. On an intuitive level, I just didn't think people would want me there. But on another level I was thinking, 'How's it going to look if the government *isn't* there?' So I told Gordon Brown that I'd be going, representing him, representing the government. The Department of

Culture, Media and Sport tried to talk me out of it, but I said it would be a scandal if the government didn't attend, just as they'd be expected to attend, for example, a service to commemorate the Piper Alpha tragedy, or a military tragedy. The government should be there.

But, still, even the night before, I was agonising over it. And I suppose that conflict was enshrined in me, as an individual. You know, there was me, the person, the lad who'd been in the Cherry Tree before and after the game in '89, and there was me, the government minister – and that was what I was wrestling with, constantly. I often ask my younger brother, John, when it comes to these kinds of things, 'What do you think?' John had been to the memorial down the years, and he was definitely planning to go to that one. He saw the dilemma straight away, but he said to me, 'You've got to go. On balance, you have to be there. Just talk personally. Don't be a minister, don't just go there and give them a speech – just talk as yourself, as a fan. Talk about how the tragedy affected you, on the day, as a person, as a football fan yourself.' Normally the Department of Culture, Media and Sport would try to prep you and give you lines, and I just said them, 'Don't even bother. I'll be writing this one myself.'

MARTIN THOMPSON

The families are sent tickets for the anniversary, but I'd only been to a few. Different people observe the date in different ways. I've always found the service at Anfield a bit public. The players are there, there's all these people there … I don't know how I'd feel going along to a memorial if Stuart hadn't died. I'd imagine it's a different sort of grief – you're grieving for the way the tragedy happened or the way the victims and the city were stereotyped. For us, though, we're right in the middle of it all. On the day, for the bereaved, there's an anxiety, there's a desperation that is very real …

But I decided I'd go to the twentieth anniversary. I had a good mate who'd been in Australia at the time of the disaster – he really wanted to go.

STEVE ROTHERAM

We were there from about midday, and you knew straight away there was going to be a huge crowd. The Kop was full to capacity, so they opened up the Centenary, then the Main Stand. I was getting messages and texts from people, telling me that stewards were directing people to the Anfield Road stands. This was unprecedented – all four stands being open for a memorial service.

ANDY BURNHAM

It was a similar sort of day to the day of the game – bright, bit of a breeze. I remember getting nearer and nearer to Anfield, and it was like a match day. And I remember clearly that my overriding pre-occupation was, 'Can I get through this without crying?' That was where my focus was – could I make my speech without breaking down over the words; and if I did start crying, would it look fake? These are the strange minutiae you focus on. I just wanted to get there and read my speech without looking like a phoney. Then I got a text from my brother, John, 'Don't want to worry you but we're in the Anfield Road end. It's packed!'

I got to Anfield and I was taken into the trophy room. Dalglish was in there, all the big names are there, and that does nothing to calm your nerves as an Evertonian. It ratchets it up another level. And then we went out and I was really beginning to feel the enormity of the occasion, the tension of the occasion. And I was just sitting there, dreading the moment when my name would be called.

MARTIN THOMPSON

The families and guests sit in the front few rows of the Kop so, whoever is speaking, they're right there – within touching distance, almost.

STEVE ROTHERAM

By the time the service got under way, there was 37,000 there. And, for all that it was a memorial service, there was a real atmosphere inside the ground. I was sitting next to Andy Burnham and he was very apprehensive. He said to me, 'I feel sick to my stomach.' But he got up, and he made that speech.

MARTIN THOMPSON

I felt for Andy Burnham. I'd always found him to be sincere – he came across as one of the few who meant what he said. But, as a politician, you're there to be shot at. He'd come to the service as a Labour government minister, and Labour were supposed to be our party. But what Jack Straw did was a crime in itself. You were thinking, 'If this is what we get from the people we support, then what hope have you got?' Labour had let Liverpool down, Jack Straw had let Liverpool down, and you could see it in Burnham's face. He knew. As a politician, he'd set himself up, but you could see in his face he was determined to do something.

ANDY BURNHAM

It was a bit of an out-of-body experience. I'd prepared this speech and I mentioned the government – I mentioned Gordon Brown – and that's what started it. It was just one voice at first, one lone cry of, 'When do we get justice?' Then it built and built, and the entire ground is singing 'Justice for the 96'. The crowd completely drowned me out and, in a strange way, I wanted that; I was expecting it, I was prepared for it. I just knew that something was going to happen and, in a way, it was a bit of a release. So I just stood back, not speaking, quietly nodding, sort of wanting them to carry on, if you like. And the nodding was … it was partly that I knew this was coming. But it was agreement; everything they were feeling, I was feeling. I think there was an element of me hoping the Prime Minister was watching, hoping the cabinet would now understand a bit better. But I was also thinking, 'God, I've really dropped him in it! He's not going to thank me for this …'

The shouting died down and I came back in; I don't think I did it consciously but I put my notes away. I just started talking about the personal stuff, how I was at the other semi-final, the things I'd been talking about with my brother. And I think that unleashed a different range of reactions, such was the emotion of the day. But, equally, I was aware that it was the minister they were shouting at, not the person, the football fan – and quite rightly. The 20-year-old me would have been shouting at the minister. I absolutely understood it.

JEGSY DODD

I really, really like Andy Burnham and I thought he was very brave getting up and saying what he did. I felt for him. There was the moment when he said he'd been sent on behalf of the government and, you know, there was anger. People had felt as though it was us against everyone else for so long, so of course everyone was bristling and looking at each other. It was like, the government has *never* wanted anything to do with Hillsborough, no matter which party was in leadership. It's always been, 'File away, put it in the bottom drawer.' And Andy Burnham says he's there on behalf of the government … people vented their feelings. But it was the way he recovered from that. I don't know whether he just abandoned his notes or whatever, but it seemed spontaneous, what came next. It was obviously from the heart, and I think we all felt that.

STEVE ROTHERAM

For me, Andy Burnham's speech is one of the pivotal moments in what was by then a twenty-year campaign for truth and justice.

BARRY DEVONSIDE

Up to Andy Burnham's speech, we were going nowhere. If it hadn't been for that speech, where would we be now?

SHEILA COLEMAN

Everyone always says Andy Burnham changed it, but I don't really see it that way. He was a politician dispatched to deliver a message on behalf of the then prime minister. One person shouted, 'What about justice! When are we going to get justice?' and from that, the whole ground erupted into demands for justice. For me, that was so powerful – and *that* is the reason that the independent panel was set up. I really do believe, given that the eyes of the media were on Liverpool that day, there was a realisation that we weren't going away. Alan Johnson, then Home Secretary, was smart enough to see that and soon after it was announced that the Hillsborough Independent Panel was to be established.

I don't know what would have happened if Andy Burnham had just made his speech and sat down again and there hadn't been that spontaneous outpouring of anger and emotion from the crowd. Would it have been the same? Or would he have gone home and thought, 'Job done'? I think the government were looking on that day, and they just knew: these people are not going away. They are not going away.

ANDY BURNHAM

I sat back down and I was shaking and collecting myself and thinking, 'Christ, what's just happened?' So I was just trying to get through the rest of the ceremony and keep myself together. The assistant bishop gave me a nudge and sort of said, 'You did OK there.' Then Steve Rotheram got up and gave this fantastic speech, and he really pulled it round and got it back, which was great.

I was still pretty shaky inside and we all made our way back inside to the old Main Stand and I was mainly thinking, 'How quickly can I decently say thanks to everyone and get home?' We had a cabinet awayday in Glasgow the following day, and I was already beginning to think about that. So – and we're talking seconds after the service ended here – I'm walking round the pitch at Anfield and my phone goes and it's the Prime Minister. 'That was brilliant, Andy. Thank you for being there. It was brave, it was honest, I really appreciate what you've done today. Feel proud of yourself.' So, he'd obviously watched it on the telly and got straight on the phone and, from feeling pretty wretched, if I'm honest, I started to feel a bit better about the whole thing. I said to Gordon, 'You know, it was difficult but I still think it was the right thing coming here today.' He agreed, and I said to him, 'I want to do something about this now, Gordon. I'm going to suggest something tomorrow.' And he said, 'Yes, yes, OK, we'll talk about it tomorrow.' So I felt hugely reassured by that.

STEVE ROTHERAM

There was a reception inside the ground straight after the service, and then there was going to be a private function up at the Town Hall, where all the families were getting the Freedom of the City of Liverpool. I was looking for Andy [Burnham] because I hadn't really had a chance to speak to him properly about the reaction he'd had. I'd been expecting something, to be honest – but I don't think anyone could have predicted the whole ground rising up like that. I think that, as a minister, as a representative of government, the response from the crowd was entirely legitimate. But I was churned up for Andy. As my mate, I really felt for him. I wanted to make sure he was OK, but I wanted to make sure he didn't leg it, too!

ANDY BURNHAM

I went up the stairs into the reception and you could feel it already in that function suite, there was this sense building of: 'Yes, at last, our voices will have been heard. Someone will have heard that ...' And of course there were all these banks of media waiting outside, and I had a million and one media requests lined up, and I just thought, 'I'll just go out and do them.' So I do this succession of quite difficult interviews where I was saying, you know, 'I do understand why the crowd reacted the way they did, and perhaps it's time we looked at Hillsborough again.' By that time I was freelancing completely, I had no government cover to say any of the things I was saying.

STEVE ROTHERAM

Andy came back into the reception and he said, 'Listen, I'm going to shoot off now.' I said, 'No you're not.' He says, 'No, I've got to, I've got this thing in Glasgow tomorrow.' I said to him, 'Just come to the Town Hall. You said you would. All the families will be there, you should be there – I'm going to drag you into the car myself and drive you there. You're coming.'

ANDY BURNHAM

Steve just wouldn't let it go. 'Come to the Town Hall, come to the Town Hall,' he was saying. 'Just come and talk to them personally. It'll be more private. It'll mean a lot to them.' I'm saying to him, 'I've got an early start tomorrow ...' But he was adamant. 'I'm not having it. You've got to come.' He must have sent some of the families over, because they're saying, 'Please will you come to the Town Hall? We don't want it to end on a down note.' You know, 'We won't bite,' sort of thing. So I got back to my car, battered, bruised, took a deep breath and headed for the Town Hall.

STEVE ROTHERAM

The Town Hall has this grand central staircase – polished mahogany, beautiful – and it sweeps both left and right as you come in, leading to a first-floor landing. So Andy and I come in and, as we're queuing up on the first few stairs, we look up and there's Alan Hansen, Jamie Carragher, Steven Gerrard and Kenny Dalglish. Kenny looks down, sees Andy Burnham coming up the stairs, and shouts, 'Hey, Burnham! You haven't come to piss the families off again, have you?'

But he was smiling, and it just took all the tension out of the moment.

ANDY BURNHAM

So, as I'm feeling more fragile than I've ever felt in my life, there's my welcoming committee: Kenny Dalglish in this big voice – here's Andy Burnham, come to upset everyone all over again. Everyone started laughing and they were great, to be honest. Him, Carragher, Gerrard – they were half taking the piss, but they kept saying, 'You've done the right thing. Now you've got to make it count.'

So I went into the Freedom of the City function feeling a tiny bit more liberated. It had been traumatic, but it was starting to register that I'd done what I'd come to do – which was to provide a platform, provide a moment that could trigger the process. Reopening Hillsborough. And going into the Town Hall, there was definitely a feeling of – something is starting to happen, here.

STEVE ROTHERAM

We went in, and I gave the introduction speech, then Andy Burnham got up. He gave – I say this without any reservation – one of the best speeches I've ever heard. You know when they say the hairs on the back of your neck stood up? Well, it makes my hairs stand up now, just thinking about it. He could have gone into his shell after what had happened earlier but, without any script, completely from the heart, he stood up in front of the families, thanked them for allowing him to be there, then he went into this passionate address. It was a promise that he would not rest personally until he had taken the message of today to the very heart of government and ensured that we have a fresh look at all the evidence about Hillsborough. 'I will be fighting for you and I assure you I will not give up.' And it was fantastic. He got a standing ovation from everybody. You could feel it in the room – one of those sea-change moments.

ANDY BURNHAM

I spoke much more openly, in that I said to them, 'Look, I didn't talk about it at Anfield, but I'll tell you now: I have made this call for disclosure. I haven't come here to make you any false promises and I don't know what will happen, but I do make this promise to you: I will carry that on.' There was a feeling of, I'm here, I'm looking you in the eye and I'm telling you I will try my utmost for that to happen. I knew I'd kind of crossed a line with that. Emotionally, I'd said, 'I'm in this and I'm committed to it. I'm really going to try to do something for you.'

Anne Williams came up afterwards and she told me, 'Look, I've already got all this evidence! I've got witnesses who will testify that my son was still alive after 3.15. I admire your conviction, but they'll just bury the evidence again. It's too dangerous for them to admit to what really happened.' Then Phil Scraton came up, and the academic in him was asking, 'What do you think disclosure could achieve?' And

I said, 'Well, even if all we achieve is a report that has the Stationery Office's official crest on it and it's basically the facts as laid out in your book, with a government wrapper around it, that alone would make it worth doing. Because those are the facts, we know that those are the facts – but not many other people do. Getting those facts understood by the country as a whole is a massive part of this.'

I went home and I just couldn't stop thinking about it. I had to be up early, but I couldn't sleep – because that was the core of it; we had to get those facts out far and wide.

STEVE ROTHERAM

The contrast in mood, atmosphere, everything – from the justifiable booing and heckling at the service, to him as a person responding magnificently to the concerns of the families – it was fantastic. Andy had to go after a while – but after he'd gone, the buzz in the room was something else.

ANDY BURNHAM

I got up to Glasgow and straight away said to the Prime Minister, 'Gordon, I hope you don't mind but I want to put this on the agenda.' And that is really not the done thing. You can't just put things on the cabinet agenda. In cabinet meetings you'll typically discuss one or two things, and you don't just stick your hand up and say, 'Oh, and another thing …' But Gordon Brown just nodded and said, 'Right, yes, I want you to. I'll bring you in as soon as we've finished the main discussion and I want you to talk about how it was yesterday. You can tell us what you're thinking and we'll have that discussion.'

Just to give this some context: [normally] you'll have civil servants prepping everyone, so it's a meaningful discussion – it's not a complete surprise. With this, the cabinet knew I was going to the twentieth anniversary, they knew how I felt, and some of them might have anticipated that I was going to mention it. But, other than that, it was a complete surprise.

True to his word, the Prime Minister says words to the effect of, 'I'm sure we all saw Andy's address at Anfield yesterday. It was a brave thing, the right thing to do; we're all very proud of you. What thoughts have you taken away with you?' I said, 'Don't just think that because I had a bit of a duffing up yesterday, I'm bringing this up now, just to cover myself. I know this issue inside out. I'm saying to you that something is deeply wrong here and we, Labour, have not put it right. This is the twentieth anniversary of a massive miscarriage of justice. We've got a moment here, and we've absolutely got to do something.'

As ever, the discussion went around the table and there were differences of opinion, some people raised concerns and so on. But Gordon stood up and said, 'Yes, we realise there are going to be issues but we're going to back Andy up on this.' This is less than twenty-four hours after I've spoken at the anniversary and, for me, that was just an unbelievable moment. Can you imagine what that was like? That was the Prime Minister saying, 'Go for it.'

Going home on the train that night, I was texting David Conn, Brian Reade, texting everyone, saying, 'We've reopened it.' It was just … huge. I mean, that was just the start of it, internally – the civil service kicked off straight away with all these objections and obstacles, trying to limit it. But the fact that the Prime Minister said what he said – he backed it – it was huge.

STEVE ROTHERAM

There were three people who were pivotal to the Hillsborough Independent Panel being set up. Obviously Andy Burnham's input was huge and, with him, there was Maria Eagle and Derek Twigg. The idea was to set up, not another public inquiry, but an independent inquiry. Nothing like that had ever been done before, don't forget, so the magnitude of what those three achieved shouldn't be underplayed.

They had some considerable difficulty, initially. Not everybody in the Labour government of the time wanted this to happen. There was a feeling that, where Hillsborough was concerned, there'd been two or three bites at the cherry and nothing new was going to come out; so the three of them had to fight tenaciously to ensure that there was a fresh look at it, even after the Prime Minister had given his support.

ANDY BURNHAM

I rang Jacqui Smith and told her, 'There's loads of pressure building here. The whole of the Home Office are going to be throwing up objections, trying to slow this down, trying to just … do nothing. Don't let them! You've got to push this through.'

On the Sunday I was on my way to our FA Cup semi-final against Manchester United at Wembley. I opened up the *Observer* and Jacqui had briefed them that she'd instructed South Yorkshire police to make all their files to be opened up. And then Everton went and beat Man. United on penalties!

The front cover of the *Mirror* the next morning had a little box photo of the whole of the Everton team at the moment Phil Jagielka's winning penalty went in. And the paper's main headline – in reference to the South Yorkshire police files being ordered up – was

JUSTICE AT LAST. So there was the most momentous week of my life encapsulated on the front page of the *Mirror*. Needless to say I've got that one framed.

PETER CARNEY

When the announcement was first made about the independent panel being formed, I was quite cynical. There was an election on the horizon, and you couldn't help thinking, 'Do they mean this, or is it just more politics?' And it did cross my mind, too: I wondered whether Steve Rotheram had set Andy Burnham up. After Burnham was barracked at the twentieth anniversary, I wondered whether Rotheram manipulated him, so to speak – and I mean that in a positive way. I always felt Rotheram was one step ahead, you know? He was there at Hillsborough himself, he knew what went on and he knew what was *going* on … but he wasn't an MP yet, back in 2009. He was the Lord Mayor. So, there's a limit to what he can do, in reality. There's no doubting Rotheram would have wanted to do something about Hillsborough, but whether he knew *how* to do something about it … it must have been frustrating for him.

What I do know is that Steve Rotheram was brought up at Jack Spriggs's knee. He was a great political hero of mine, Jack Spriggs. He led the 1972 sit-in at Fisher-Bendix in Kirkby and went on to become a very effective councillor and Lord Mayor in his own right. He always seemed slightly ahead of the game, and I see a lot of that in Steve Rotheram – so that's why I wonder whether Rotheram led Andy Burnham by the nose, if you like. Led him to the water. In those circumstances, you can't help wondering whether there's any real political will behind the motion. Anyway, however it came about,

Burnham made his play and the independent panel was formed. And I thought to myself, 'Let's see. What's the worst that can happen?'

STEVE ROTHERAM

Alan Johnson, the Home Secretary, announced the formation of the Hillsborough Independent Panel in December 2009. There were quite a lot of tensions over the make-up of the panel – lots of discussions over individuals that all the families would have confidence in. The game-changer was the appointment of the Right Reverend James Jones, Bishop of Liverpool, as chair. Once the bishop was confirmed, it gave the whole thing a real legitimacy. It was then a case of filling in all the other panel members. It was quite a balancing act: it was important that all these individuals would be perceived as being independent, while still being acceptable to the families. If it had just been a case of the families picking who they wanted, the process might not have had the same validity. So they looked at a very wide spectrum of experience and the sort of objectivity that you'd need, in order to give that panel as broad a perspective as possible. And it was an excellent mix – as well as the bishop we had a world-class group of acknowledged leading experts in the fields of journalism, medicine, legal, academia, national records and archives, and a top former police officer.

PETER CARNEY

The make-up of the panel looked overly academic to me, at first. I take my hat off to them now for the work they did – no hesitation in saying that now – but, when the panel was first announced, where there was maybe cautious optimism among the majority, my reaction was more a qualified cynicism. I hoped it would turn out well, I thought, 'Let them get on with it, you just never know ...' but, myself, I certainly wasn't expecting anything major.

SHEILA COLEMAN

We were invited to what, I think, the panel saw as a kind of meet-and-greet down at the Cunard Building. They seemed to want to keep it quite social, but we had different ideas. We hadn't waited all these years for tea and biscuits and friendly chit-chat. We had previously read and analysed the remit of the panel and were keen to ask questions over what we saw as its limitations. I asked Bishop Jones, 'How long have we got?' He said, 'Is about an hour OK?' So I said, 'Right then, let's get down to it. I've been asked to put a number of questions to you on behalf of the families.' Bishop Jones commented, 'These are very profound questions you're asking. Can you put them in writing?' I replied, 'Yes, of course – I'll send you an email first thing.'

BARRY DEVONSIDE

There had been one or two getting-to-know-you sessions, where the group and the panel laid out their frames of reference and what have you, but I hadn't been able to attend through illness. The first time I met James Jones was when he came along to the Hillsborough Justice Campaign for a proper sit-down meeting. I said to him, 'Bishop – do I call you "Bishop"? You can call me Barry.' He said, 'No, you call me James.'

I said, 'James – I don't wish to offend you, sir, and I don't mean to insult you, but why should I trust you more than any other organisation or body we've encountered in this country in this long struggle for justice?' He said, 'Barry, I'll tell you right now. Any papers I find that I truly believe should be made public, I'll make them public.' Jackie and I stayed behind after the meeting, and there was a lot of doubt, a good deal of suspicion. There was a feeling that the Bishop was too smooth – why should we believe him and so on … We had been let down so many times, it was difficult for us to give our trust. There was a question mark as to whether he'd follow up to the greatest degree of detail. The panel only requested half the papers available from South Yorkshire police, for example – so there was nervousness as to what they would ultimately deliver.

ANDY BURNHAM

The Tories came into government, and Jeremy Hunt, talking about football violence, cited Hillsborough as an example. Then David Cameron made his now infamous remarks about the Hillsborough families being like a 'blind man in a dark room looking for a black cat that isn't there'. Even though he subsequently apologised, we realised that this cabinet just didn't see Hillsborough, or the work of the panel, as a priority.

The News International telephone hacking scandals came to nationwide prominence, and the Leveson Inquiry was set up in the summer of 2011 to forensically investigate standards and ethics in the press. That gave us a bit of impetus. We were, you know, 'This is what we've been saying! This is exactly what we've been telling you.' This was the culture of the day. They thought they could just get away with this sort of thing.

Cameron was also having a bit of a go at me personally. I knew I'd bump into him sooner or later and, sure enough, I spotted him and George Osborne in one of the House of Commons tea rooms. I went over and said to him, 'Look, David, I really didn't appreciate what you said about Hillsborough. I don't think you're fully aware of the facts, and I'd very much like to sit down with you and take you through some of the detail.' He was pretty dismissive and told me to take it up with Jeremy Hunt.

PETER HOOTON

Over the summer of 2011, the Leveson Inquiry into press standards threw the media spotlight back on News International. The inquiry was triggered by outrage over the way the *News of the World*, in particular, had used phone-hacking as tool to get stories. There were private actions by celebrities like Sienna Miller and Hugh Grant, but the tide really turned against Murdoch when it was revealed his journalists had hacked the phone of the murdered schoolgirl Milly Dowler. Tom Watson MP had Murdoch on the back foot, and I thought, 'This is the ideal time to remind people that the same culture, the same journalistic ethics were behind the *Sun*'s reporting of Hillsborough.' And that wasn't against individuals – a whole community was smeared, that time.

Billy Bragg had a song out – 'Scousers Never Buy the *Sun*' – so I started trying to get him to Liverpool for a 'Don't Buy the *Sun*' gig. And that basic idea is what led to us forming The Justice Band. Our friend Davo is the unsung hero, here: he invited Mick Jones to get involved. Pete Wylie came on board, John Power, Ian Prowse – once an idea gathers momentum, there's a lot you can do.

Mick Jones was massively enthusiastic about the social justice message, and he decided he wanted to do Clash songs. I mean, that made the whole thing massive. Every night you'd have the crowd singing along to 'Armagideon Time':

'A lot of people won't get no justice tonight.'

So we became The Justice Tonight Band – and everywhere the band played, there was a special guest. Glasvegas got up with us in Glasgow, James Dean Bradfield in Cardiff, Shane MacGowan in Dublin. We had Paul Simonon in London. I think that was the first time that Mick Jones and Simonon had played live together in something like twenty years. Then we heard this rumour that The Stone Roses might be getting back together and they wanted to get up with us in Manchester. That was a huge, breakthrough moment for me, in terms of the message and the cause being understood and embraced nationwide. You had The Stone Roses, Man United fans, on stage with The Justice Band in front of a Manchester crowd, and every single person in that crowd was united behind the cause. Justice.

SHEILA COLEMAN

Throughout the course of the campaign, there were always events and initiatives that would give us profile or give us a shot in the arm. But the advent of social media moved us on another level. Just having our own website meant we could lay things out in a factual way and send that message all over the world. It was like a one-stop shop and, wherever you were, you could put the words 'Hillsborough tragedy' or 'Hillsborough cover-up' into your search engine and you'd be taken straight to the Hillsborough Justice Campaign website. But Facebook, and then Twitter, took things to another level again.

STEVE ROTHERAM

A big step forward at just the right time was the e-petition in the autumn of 2011. It was a call for all documentation relating to Hillsborough to be made fully available to the public. The system was that, if an e-petition could garner 100,000 signatures during a set time, it would be forwarded to the Backbench Business Committee for Parliamentary debate. They probably didn't believe that 100,000 people could be mobilised in that way.

SHEILA COLEMAN

We succeeded with the first e-petition ever to be debated in the House of Commons mainly on the back of Facebook and Twitter. There's no two ways about it: when key people started tweeting about it – Joe Barton was especially supportive and influential in this respect. The way I see it, the e-petition was a sop to democracy from the coalition government: 'There you go, you can have your say, go on – all you have to do is get 100,000 signatures.' They thought no one could do it. We did it three times.

STEVE ROTHERAM

We got over 140,000 signatures in a little over two weeks. It was phenomenal, and showed the strength of feeling. I opened the Parliamentary debate: 'I beg to move that this House calls for the full disclosure of all government-related documents, including cabinet minutes, relating to the 1989 Hillsborough disaster; requires that such documentation be uncensored and without redaction; and further calls for the families of the 96 and the Hillsborough Independent Panel to have unrestricted access to that information.'

I went on to attack the smear campaign, the establishment cover-up, and I called upon David Cameron to make a full apology in the same way he had done about Bloody Sunday.

The hardest part came when I read out the 96 names. I had genuine mixed feelings about doing that; myself and Andy talked it through, long and hard, asking ourselves, 'Is it appropriate?' He was urging me to do it – what better way to bring home the full enormity of this tragedy to those who don't understand it than to make them listen to every single name? I was worried that I might choke up halfway through. Right up to five minutes before, I still wasn't sure if I'd get through all the names without breaking down. In the event I did it, then Andy got up and gave the most incredibly heartfelt speech.

ANDY BURNHAM

Theresa May stood up, as Home Secretary, to respond to the motion and – it's only right to give credit where it's due – she seemed moved; angry, even. What she said went beyond what we'd been expecting to hear.

Excerpt from Theresa May's response
As Home Secretary, I will do everything in my power to ensure that the families and the public get the truth.

No government papers will be withheld from the Panel, no attempts to suppress publication will be made, no stone will be left unturned.

The principle underlying the process is that of maximum possible disclosure and disclosure to the families first and then to the wider public.

We want to see full disclosure to the panel of all documents relating to Hillsborough, including cabinet minutes. Those documents should be uncensored and unredacted.

The government is not seeking to avoid publication of cabinet minutes or any other papers from Hillsborough. The cabinet papers on Hillsborough can be published, the government will do nothing to prevent the panel publishing them, or indeed publishing whatever they so decide.

MARTIN THOMPSON

I work in a big chemical plant in Speke, and you get all the usual banter in the workplace. I got into a bit of an exchange with this Geordie – he was giving it the usual 'thieving scousers' thing, as though Newcastle is this oasis of law and order. I came back at him with something charming about obesity, and he said, 'At least we don't kill our own.' I just walked out. Obviously the others in the room must have told him about Stuart, because he came to find me and apologise. But this was the thing – it wasn't so much what he'd said, but that he believed it. Just as you're starting to think that the wider public understands what really happened at Hillsborough, you get that slap of reality; most people still think it was our own fault.

STEPHEN WRIGHT

One thing that came about as we prepared our own evidence for the panel was that, for the first time, I saw our Graham's 'body file'.

I'd never ever seen it before, the 'body file' that West Midlands police compiled. It was hard, but it was only through going through those papers that I really found him. There's pictures of Graham dead on the pitch, and I'd never ever seen those pictures – it hit me like a brick. And the actual Polaroid picture of his face that Peter spotted on the wall – that was in there, too. First time I'd seen that Polaroid since the night we went back to find him – so that knocked me for six, too. I couldn't sleep for thinking about it. But in a strange, weird kind of way, looking at that photograph of him lying dead on the pitch – I'd found him. I'd been there on the pitch, looking all over the place for him and, it's difficult to explain but, as hard as it is seeing a photograph of your brother on a football pitch, dead … it helped me, in a weird kind of way. I'd found him at last.

PETER HOOTON

Looking back on it now, it was only fifteen months from the first Justice Tonight gig at the Olympia in September 2011, to the Christmas number 1 with 'He Ain't Heavy …'. But it was a journey. And I think a massive turning point, in terms of public opinion, was the dates we did with The Stone Roses. You had Eric Cantona travelling down to Lyon from Paris to get up on stage with The Justice Tonight Band, because he believed in the cause. I asked him beforehand why he'd come, and he knew all about the *Sun*, the lies, the issues. He was there because he wanted to help spread the message. And the message was getting out. This was a campaign that started with meetings in back rooms and flyers outside the ground, but now it was instant news with Twitter and Instagram. You could feel that, finally, public opinion was turning in our favour. For us, The Justice Tonight Band, the biggest thing was Heaton Park in the summer of 2012. There was 80,000 there, every night – and it wasn't just pockets … you had the whole crowd supporting the cause, understanding the cause; that this was all about justice.

ANDY BURNHAM

The panel had been doing its work and it was coming towards the time when its findings were going to be made public, but still there was a clear sense that the government was nowhere near any kind of a real understanding as to what had actually happened at Hillsborough, and afterwards. It didn't seem as though they wanted to understand.

Steve [Rotheram] and I were really worried. What was needed was a cross-party consensus. If the panel report came out and one party said one thing, and the other said something else, then, whatever the report said, it would have no impact. We needed all-party acceptance. Theresa May, the Home Secretary, was actually very good – but all attempts to engage the Prime Minister fell on deaf ears.

PETER CARNEY

By the time the announcement was due, I'd become slightly more optimistic. That was due in large part to spending so much time with Anne Williams; you couldn't be close to Anne and *not* think that this was all possible. A lot of the time I'd have to sort of tone her down, lower her sights a little. She wanted prosecutions, sentences, every person and every aspect laid bare, and I'd just say to her, 'NEW INQUESTS: that's the headline; that's what we want out of this. New inquests.'

And there were other people, like Damien [Kavanagh], who'd be saying to me, '*Something* has to come of all this. They can't just come back and say the same thing. Why would they have the announcement in the cathedral?' Damien just had this sneaking feeling that things were going to go OK, this confidence that I just didn't have. We were a good balance to each other, I think. I didn't trust anyone over it. I think I just developed a shell, in a way; a kind of defence mechanism, assuming the worst. I'd be saying, 'What is justice? Who guards the guards?' That was my default position, this fundamental philosophical question – what is justice? And my answer was: justice is what we know to have gone on. It's not a judge's decision; it's your own understanding of what has actually occurred. We have our own justice. And we, the people, guard the guards. So yes, justice is getting the right outcome; but it's the whole process too – establishing the platform, giving ourselves a voice so we can validate our own personal histories.

ANDY BURNHAM

The Hillsborough Independent Panel Report was going to be published on 12 September – the Wednesday – and my fear was that the government would be happy to let the moment pass by as a footnote. I just felt we had to do something to get Hillsborough back on the national agenda. I called David Conn at the *Guardian* and told him that we were going to call on the government to make a national apology. On 8 September – the Saturday – he ran the story, but in the same article it had been suggested by a source at Downing Street that an 'expression of regret' might be in order.

STEVE ROTHERAM

When we got wind that the Prime Minister was going to offer an 'expression of regret' I cobbled together a very quick letter to say that this wasn't going to be acceptable and got all the Merseyside MPs to sign it, irrespective of party, and had it sent round to 10 Downing Street urgently. We told David Cameron, in no uncertain terms, that an 'expression of regret' would be meaningless. What does that actually mean, an expression of regret? If you knock into someone at the bar, you don't say, 'Can I offer you an expression of regret?' It's pointless. So we got that off to Number 10, pronto.

ANDY BURNHAM

On the Sunday afternoon I received a phone call from Number 10 asking if I would be available to speak to the Prime Minister that evening. Waiting for the call, wondering if it would come at all, was agonising. But then, to the minute, the phone rings. David Cameron was in his car, on his way to the closing ceremony of the Paralympics. We spoke for nearly an hour, and it was good – it was frank, it was detailed, and I was able to lay things out to him in very clear terms. I said to him that the operational incompetence that had led to the loss of 96 lives was a human tragedy on a huge scale. But I also told him that there had been a second tragedy, which was the way in which the Establishment colluded to cover up the truth and, instead, try to place the blame on the fans themselves.

I'll say this for David Cameron – he's not without empathy. Up until the time when he absolutely had to confront it, he hadn't given Hillsborough the attention it needed. But once the moment came around where he had to start focusing on the panel report and the issues it was bringing to light, you've got to give him his due. He thought about it and he listened and he took it all on board. Perhaps the seeds of his comments about the 'double injustice' were sewn during that conversation, on his way to the Paralympics. After we'd finished our phone call, it was another of those huge moments: massive relief, and a degree of elation.

STEVE ROTHERAM

The bishop had been absolutely scrupulous in his conviction that the families would be the first to hear the report. Even the Prime Minister hadn't seen it. But that's a double-edged sword because, while it's absolutely correct that the families should be the first to know what's in the report, the Prime Minister of the country wasn't actually aware of what the findings were going to be until the morning that he made his speech. So we hadn't had the usual thing where the civil service will let you see a draft speech and you get the chance to say, you know, 'That bit is great, that's acceptable, that part is unacceptable.' That's what usually happens – there's an element of a cross-party understanding.

DAMIAN KAVANAGH

Whenever there's a memorial or an event, a few of the survivors will meet up. It's something we've always done. The night before the panel report at the cathedral, there was myself, Peter Carney and Ade Tempany. Ade had reservations and Carney was not confident at all. I think they just didn't want to build themselves up for yet another let-down. But I was confident. I was supremely confident. It was one of those where you just feel it. I said it was like a penalty shoot-out and you know you've got players who won't miss.

PETER CARNEY

So on the day of the announcement in the cathedral, I went into it with a particularly clear head. I got spruced up, met the others, and I drove us down there in my van. I had a VW transporter back then, it was quite funny, in a way, turning up for this big occasion in a battered old van. We parked up and went in via the West Steps.

MARTIN THOMPSON

I got the invitation to come along to the cathedral to hear what the panel had to say, but I decided not to go. I had no faith in the process. We'd been lied to for all this time – what was going to change? My feeling was that they were going to let us down again. However they dressed it up, they were going to basically tell us it was our own fault.

ANDY BURNHAM

Steve and I had agreed we'd meet first thing, and as soon as we had sight of the speech we'd start highlighting any issues, ready to bring them up with the families. Meanwhile, up in Liverpool, they were already starting to assemble at the cathedral, ready for James Jones to present the panel's findings to them.

STEVE ROTHERAM

We got a draft copy of the Prime Minister's speech about 10 a.m. Both of us were speed-reading it, flicking through, page after page, waiting for the bit about the 'expression of regret'. Remember, this is the same Prime Minister who said to Andy, 'I don't know what more you want. You're like a blind man in a dark room looking for a black cat that isn't there.' But as we read the speech and started to take in what he was proposing to say, it was obvious, finally, that the government was starting to understand. And it's fair to say that Burnham and I were quite emotional.

BARRY DEVONSIDE

It was decided that the findings of the independent panel would be announced to the families and invited guests in the Anglican cathedral. The agenda was going to be that the families would have a private hearing at 9 a.m., then the invited guests – survivors and their families, campaigners, people who had been close to the cause over the duration – they would hear the report next. Then the Prime Minister was expecting to go live at around midday. There was a live link to the Houses of Parliament inside the cathedral.

So we got there first thing. Everybody was waiting for the outcome with bated breath. I was nervously optimistic. We'd been let down, so many times, and I didn't know what to expect. You had to steel yourself, protect yourself, because not only have you lost someone who is very dear and precious to you, but you've gone down every avenue that is humanly available to you and every time you've hit a brick wall. So you had to prepare yourself for yet another disappointment.

DAMIAN KAVANAGH

Looking back it's mad, when you consider how long we'd been campaigning for the truth and how many knock-backs there'd been, how confident I was about the panel. I was so confident that, in the days leading up to it, I was extra careful crossing the road, things like that, because I didn't want to miss this moment for anything. I saw Dave's lad – Dave from by ours who'd been killed. He wasn't overly optimistic. He said there may be things in the report that we won't like hearing. I said to him, 'They've had to lie to do what they did to us. If there was anything they could justifiably pin on us, it would have come out by now.' No way would they have kept anything like that concealed!' I told him, 'The Truth is on our side and it's about to get a national news platform.'

BARRY DEVONSIDE

We were sitting about four rows from the front – myself and our daughter Vicky. Bishop James Jones stood up and his opening address was words to the effect of, 'I wish to tell you all that Liverpool supporters have been exonerated from any blame for the deaths of 96 people.' Well, straight away, there were three people who fainted. It was so very emotional. It was very, very satisfying, and yet you knew that those 96 people shouldn't have been killed. They needn't have died. You knew that if the decisions and the actions and the planning had been correct – if decisions that did need to be taken on the day when something did go awry had been taken, and acted upon, properly – we could have been at home, now, with Chris. We shouldn't have been there in the cathedral in the first place. That was the sort of mixed emotions you were going through. Relief at what we were hearing; anguish at the circumstances of having to hear it.

DAMIAN KAVANAGH

We got these beautiful invitations with the day's order of events. And I went down there with the thought that I was going into the cathedral for everyone, you know, 'I'm there for the whole cause.' People want this to happen, they want the story to come out, they want this moment in time.

So we were in the cathedral, waiting for our turn to hear the report. Obviously the families went in first, we were going to be next. Then Steve Kelly came over – they'd all been given a copy of the report. He just pointed to it, tapped it and grinned and said, 'It's dynamite. Dynamite!' Stevie Wright came over, I'd never seen him like that. He was going, 'This is it! This is it!'

PETER CARNEY

The families were already in the main hall; they were given their briefing first. I remember Stevie Wright from the Justice Campaign coming in to us and saying, 'The bastards. They've blood-tested everyone for alcohol. Even Jon-Paul – they've blood-tested the kids …'

Then John Glover come in, and he's gone, 'They've got them bang to rights, the bastards; they've got them for everything …'

These were seasoned campaigners – and you could feel their … it wasn't joy, it wasn't even relief; it was much angrier than that. But we all knew, then. And after a bit we were called into a room and there was the bishop, there was Phil Scraton, and I think Bill Kirkup was the other one, and they started running through the panel's findings. For myself, it was fading in and out. I just kept thinking, 'At last,' you know. At last.

BARRY DEVONSIDE

After Bishop Jones had given us the run-down on the panel's findings, the main emotion was relief. I think we were all a bit shaky, to be honest – there was shock, euphoria, relief and some anger, too, that it had all taken this long for the truth to become universally known.

The bishop then gave a brief address, then Trevor Hicks got up to say a few words. I caught his eye and indicated that I'd like to say something, too. He passed me the microphone. I stood up and I asked the bishop, 'James, I wonder if you remember our first meeting and what I said to you? I said, "Why should we trust you, any more than anybody else who has looked into Hillsborough?" Well, I want to say a very heartfelt thank you to you, and to all your colleagues on the panel. You've done everything you said you would do.' There was loud applause.

Some of us went outside for a breath of fresh air, and we were all just trying to take it all in. It was enormous, really – one of those huge, huge moments; and when they come around, often it's very hard to take on board. But, above all, there was a feeling of supreme satisfaction.

DAMIAN KAVANAGH

So it was our turn and we went in. There was only three of them – the bishop himself, Phil Scraton and Bill Kirkup, the former Chief

Medical Officer. They'd spent a lot of time with the families and there was going to be a live broadcast from Parliament, so we didn't have long with them. But it was good. I'd been confident, but this was far, far beyond your hopes and expectations.

BARRY DEVONSIDE

We had the live broadcast on from the House of Commons, on this massive big screen in the cathedral. So it went over to David Cameron and I have honestly in all my adult life never heard anything like it.

DAMIAN KAVANAGH

We went back out to the main reception hall in the Anglican cathedral. Our little group made a point of sitting at the back – families at the front, then as you got further back it was the key campaigners, invited guests, social workers and so on. There was this big screen and it cut to this massive image of Cameron, live from the House of Commons. It was like Judgement Day.

Transcript of the Prime Minister's address
Today the Bishop of Liverpool, the Right Reverend James Jones, is publishing the report of the Hillsborough Independent Panel.

The disaster at the Hillsborough football stadium on 15 April 1989 was one of the greatest peacetime tragedies of the last century. Ninety-six people died as a result of a crush in the Leppings Lane terrace at the FA Cup semi-final between Liverpool and Nottingham Forest.

There was a public inquiry at the time by Lord Justice Taylor which found – and I quote – that the main cause of the disaster was 'a failure of police control'.

But the inquiry didn't have access to all the documents that have since become available. It didn't properly examine the response of the emergency services. It was followed by a deeply controversial inquest and by a media version of events that sought to blame the fans.

As a result, the families have not heard the truth and have not found justice. That is why the previous government – and in particular – the Rt Hon. Member for Leigh was right to set up this panel. And it is why this government insisted that no stone should be left unturned and that all papers should be made available to the Bishop of Liverpool and his team.

Mr Speaker, in total over 450,000 pages of evidence have been reviewed. It was right that the families should see the report first. As a result, the government has only had a very limited amount of time to study the evidence so far.

But it is already very clear that many of the report's findings are deeply distressing.

There are three areas in particular. The failure of the authorities to help protect people. The attempt to blame the fans. And the doubt cast on the original coroner's inquest. Let me take each in turn.

First, there is new evidence about how the authorities failed. There is a trail of new documents which show the extent to which the safety of the crowd at Hillsborough was 'compromised at every level'. The ground failed to meet minimum standards and the 'deficiencies were well known'.

The turnstiles were inadequate. The ground capacity had been significantly over-calculated. The crush-barriers failed to meet safety standards. There had been a crush at exactly the same match the year before. And today's report shows clearly that lessons had not been learnt.

The report backs up again the key finding of the Taylor Report on police failure. But it goes further by revealing for the first time the shortcomings of the ambulance and emergency services' response. The major incident plan was not fully implemented. Rescue attempts were held back by failures of leadership and co-ordination. And, significantly, new documents today show there was a delay from the emergency services when people were being crushed and killed.

Second, the families have long believed that some of the authorities attempted to create a completely unjust account of events that sought to blame the fans for what happened. Mr Speaker, the families were right.

The evidence in today's report includes briefings to the media and attempts by the police to change the record of events. On the media: several newspapers reported false allegations that fans were drunk and violent and stole from the dead. The *Sun*'s report sensationalised these allegations under a banner headline, THE TRUTH. This was clearly wrong and caused huge offence, distress and hurt.

News International has co-operated with the panel and, for the first time, today's report reveals that the source for these despicable untruths was a Sheffield news agency reporting conversations with South Yorkshire police and Irvine Patnick, the then MP for Sheffield Hallam.

The report finds that this was part of police efforts – and I quote – 'to develop and publicise a version of events that focused on … allegations of drunkenness, ticketlessness and violence'. In terms of changing the record of events, we already know that police reports were significantly altered but the full extent was not drawn to Lord Justice Taylor's attention.

Today's report finds that 164 statements were significantly amended – and 116 explicitly removed negative comments about the policing operation – including its lack of leadership.

The report also makes important findings about particular actions taken by the police and coroner while investigating the deaths. There is new evidence which shows that police officers carried out police national computer checks on those who had died in an attempt – and I quote from the report – 'to impugn the reputations of the deceased'.

The coroner took blood alcohol levels from all of the deceased including children. The panel finds no rationale whatsoever for what it regards as an 'exceptional' decision. The report states clearly that the attempt of the inquest to draw a link between blood alcohol and late arrival was 'fundamentally flawed'. And that alcohol consumption was 'unremarkable and not exceptional for a social or leisure occasion'.

Mr Speaker, over all these years questions have been raised about the role of the government – including whether it did enough to uncover the truth. It is certainly true that some of the language in the government papers published today was insensitive. But having been through every document – and every government document including cabinet minutes will be published – the panel found no evidence of any government trying to conceal the truth.

At the time of the Taylor Report, the then Prime Minister was briefed by her private secretary that the defensive and – I quote – 'close to deceitful' behaviour of senior South Yorkshire officers was 'depressingly familiar'. And it is clear that the then government thought it right that the chief constable of South Yorkshire should resign. But, as the Rt Hon. Member for Leigh has rightly highlighted, governments then and since have simply not done enough to challenge publicly the unjust and untrue narrative that sought to blame the fans.

Third, and perhaps most significantly of all, the Bishop of Liverpool's report presents new evidence which casts significant doubt over the adequacy of the original inquest. The coroner – on the advice of pathologists – believed that victims suffered traumatic asphyxia leading to unconsciousness within seconds and death within a few minutes. As a result he asserted that beyond 3.15 p.m. there were no actions that could have changed the fate of the victims and he limited the scope of the inquest accordingly.

But by analysing postmortem reports the panel have found that 28 did not have obstruction of blood circulation and 31 had evidence of heart and lungs continuing to function after the crush. This means that individuals in those groups could have had potentially reversible asphyxia beyond 3.15 p.m. in contrast to the findings of the coroner and a subsequent judicial review. And the panel states clearly that 'it is highly likely that what happened to those individuals after 3.15 p.m. was significant' in determining whether they died.

Mr Speaker, the conclusions of this report will be harrowing for many of the families affected. Anyone who has lost a child knows the pain never leaves you. But to read a report years afterwards that says – and I quote – 'a swifter, more appropriate, better focused and properly equipped response had the potential to save more lives' can only add to the pain.

It is for the Attorney-General to decide whether to apply to the High Court to quash the original inquest and seek a new one. In this capacity he acts independently of government. And he will need to examine the evidence himself. But it is clear to me that the new evidence in today's report raises vital questions which must be examined. And the Attorney-General has assured me that he will examine this new evidence immediately and reach a decision as fast as possible. But ultimately it is for the High Court to decide.

It is also right that the House should have an opportunity to debate the issues raised in this report fully. My Rt Hon. friend the Home Secretary will be taking forward a debate in government time. And this will happen when the House returns in October.

Mr Speaker, I want to be very clear about the view the government takes about these findings and why, after twenty-three years, this matters so much, not just for the families but for Liverpool and for our country as a whole. Mr Speaker, what happened that day – and since – was wrong. It was wrong that the responsible authorities knew Hillsborough did not meet minimum safety standards and yet still allowed the match to go ahead. It was wrong that the families have had to wait for so long – and fight so hard – just to get to the truth.

And it was wrong that the police changed the records of what happened and tried to blame the fans.

We ask the police to do difficult and often very dangerous things on our behalf. And South Yorkshire police is a very different organisation today from what it was then. But we do the many, many honourable policemen and women a great disservice if we try to defend the indefensible.

It was also wrong that neither Lord Justice Taylor nor the coroner looked properly at the response of the other emergency services. Again, these are dedicated people who do extraordinary things to serve the public.

But the evidence from today's report makes very difficult reading.

Mr Speaker, with the weight of the new evidence in this report, it is right for me today as prime minister to make a proper apology to the families of the 96 for all they have suffered over the past twenty-three years. Indeed, the new evidence that we are presented with today makes clear that these families have suffered a double injustice. The injustice of the appalling events – the failure of the state to protect their loved ones and the indefensible wait to get to the truth. And the injustice of the denigration of the deceased – that they were somehow at fault for their own deaths.

On behalf of the government – and indeed our country – I am profoundly sorry for this double injustice that has been left uncorrected for so long.

Mr Speaker, because of what I have described as the second injustice – the false version of events – not enough people in this country understand what the people of Merseyside have been through. This appalling death toll of so many loved ones lost was compounded by an attempt to blame the victims. A narrative about hooliganism on that day was created which led many in the country to accept that it was somehow a grey area. Today's report is black and white. The Liverpool fans 'were not the cause of the disaster'.

The panel has quite simply found 'no evidence' in support of allegations of 'exceptional levels of drunkenness, ticketlessness or violence among Liverpool fans', 'no evidence that fans had conspired to arrive late at the stadium' and 'no evidence that they stole from the dead and dying'.

Mr Speaker, I'm sure the whole House will want to thank the Bishop of Liverpool and his panel for all the work they have done. And I am sure that all sides will join with me in paying tribute to the incredible strength and dignity of the Hillsborough families and the community which has backed them in their long search for justice.

While nothing can ever bring back those who have been lost, with all the documents revealed and nothing held back, the families, at last, have access to the truth. And I commend this statement to the House.

DAMIAN KAVANAGH

It echoes in the cathedral – there's a real, sombre, serious atmosphere in there. And there's Cameron's voice, echoing round that room: 'I am profoundly sorry ...' Profoundly sorry. Boom! 'On behalf of the country ... double injustice.' Double injustice. Boom! The acoustics only added to the feeling that you were witnessing history being made.

PETER CARNEY

When Cameron said what he did ... that was massive. I never expected that. Never, ever thought I'd see the day that a Tory Prime Minister comes out and says that, in the words and with the intent that he said it. But, again, that hasn't come out of thin air, has it? That's come from his advisors and ministers who've seen the report and they know what's coming and *they've* said to David Cameron: 'You've got to stand up and say this like you mean it.' But, whatever the circumstances, this was a Conservative Prime Minister speaking with more passion than any Labour leader ever managed ...

STEVE ROTHERAM

We needed him to make that address on behalf of the country. We wanted him to put party politics to one side and be the statesman that you have to be on occasions like this. And, let's be fair, he did exactly what his office required him to do, what was beholden of him, really, as the country's Prime Minister.

When he got up, the House was as quiet as I've ever heard it. There and then, in that moment, I think David Cameron was as moved and as angry as any of us could have been. He was genuinely overwhelmed by the enormity of the evidence. When he read out some of the report's key findings – how many lives could have been saved, how many police statements were altered – there were gasps – genuine gasps – and they came from the Tory benches. And that was when I knew that at long last the tide was beginning to turn in our favour.

ANDY BURNHAM

For me, it was the definition of mixed feelings. There was real elation and satisfaction – but it was mixed with anger, too. Anger that it had taken this long; that it had had to come to this, in the first place. So I was, in the truest sense, completely overwhelmed. I remember looking up and catching Theresa May's eye and I just mouthed the words 'thank you' to her.

SHEILA COLEMAN

Throughout the course of the panel's work, we challenged it on numerous occasions. We were cynical – of course we were. People have said, since, 'You were proved wrong. They delivered the goods.' But I would argue that they delivered the goods because we kept on their case.

BARRY DEVONSIDE

I think that is when it finally began to sink in that the panel's report was really going to make its impact. Hearing Cameron speak like that – the 'double injustice', the sheer vehement power of his condemnation – I thought, 'He'd better not be conning us,' because I could not believe this was coming from a Conservative Prime Minister. I mean, I was absolutely delighted, but he'd better mean what he said …

STEVE ROTHERAM

We were in the House of Commons, waiting to respond to the Prime Minister's speech. Now, obviously, I'm the MP who led on

Hillsborough when we got the Parliamentary debate after the e-petition, I'd led on some of the other Hillsborough initiatives down there, and I'm the MP for the constituency where Liverpool Football Club is located. So I thought I'd be afforded the same privilege as was extended to Mark Durkin when they got the Saville Report on Bloody Sunday in 2010. After the Prime Minister's apology in the House, the MP for that constituency, Mark Durkin, was given additional time to question him. But I was told shortly before he got up to make his speech that this was not going to be offered.

SHEILA COLEMAN

I was not surprised by most of the report, as much of it was what we had known and had been arguing for years. However, I was shocked at the amount of people they said could have survived. That blew my mind. We've always known there were some who could have lived. Anne [Williams] and I got very friendly with Ian West, the pathologist, and through working with him we knew there were others who could have lived. But we had no idea of the sheer numbers of how many could have survived, and that was shocking. The report said 41, but we're hearing now that possibly as many as 58 of the 96 would have lived, if the correct procedures were in place. That appalled me – those facts, these statistics were obscene.

The other thing that shocked and disgusted me was the whole thing with blood alcohol levels, even a 10-year-old boy, that was disgraceful. But then, in instances where they didn't find any alcohol reading whatsoever, they'd then go and access the police's national computer to see if the victims had got criminal records – another shameful attempt at victim-blaming. It's another thing that takes us right back to the political climate of the day – the police thinking they could operate with impunity. They were getting away with murder.

BARRY DEVONSIDE

There was a reception afterwards and a lady came up to me, very well-spoken, and she asked if it was OK if she called me Barry. She said, 'You don't know how much it means to the bishop that you said what you did just then. He's asked me to pass on his personal thanks.' I said, 'It should be us thanking him.' But I was pleased, you know? I'd been very blunt with James Jones and questioned whether he'd follow up to the greatest degree. Well, he did. He did all that could have been expected of him, so I was pleased we'd made that kind of connection.

I've heard some people criticise the independent panel, even after the publication of their report, saying they're just another aspect of the Establishment. I think that's absolute bollocks. Up until Andy Burnham's speech we had nowhere else to go. If it hadn't been for that speech, where would we be?

I was very happy with the report and it turned out to be the greatest thing that happened for the families and the people of Liverpool. Bishop James Jones and his panel were able to delve with such detail into the documents and records and papers, and they were able to show the nation – show the world – that there was a serious conspiracy involved.

STEVE ROTHERAM

Together, the panel did an outstanding piece of work – so much so that that is now the model for independent inquiries. The thinking is now that, with other great injustices, that is the road that they're going to go down, rather than these five-year public inquiries that really go nowhere.

DAMIAN KAVANAGH

What was great was that, after the Cameron speech, there was a kind of reception in the Anglican cathedral and we had silver service scouse. Everyone was starving! You didn't notice at the time, everyone's waiting for the report – 'Their bottle has gone, what if we don't get the result?' and all this – then afterwards you remember you haven't eaten. And that was what we had – silver service scouse! It was great. Everyone was elated. It was a great, great feeling.

MARTIN THOMPSON

I went to work as usual, and I left at 3 p.m. I got in the car, put the radio on and, obviously, Cameron had not long made his speech. It was all over the news. I badly wanted to believe what was being said – that the government was sorry, the nation was sorry, they wanted to put things right – but they're such accomplished liars, aren't they? I turned my phone on and there were texts and messages from my wife, my family, my friends. It took me by surprise how emotional I was. I listened to the Prime Minister's speech and I thought about the Geordie lad in work. I wish everyone could be made to listen to that 'double injustice' admission, because it still goes on. Whatever happens in terms of prosecutions and sentencing, that is the legacy of Hillsborough. Unlawful killings and wholesale character assassination, too.

ANDY BURNHAM

That evening, there was going to be a vigil on the plateau outside St George's Hall, and we were all going – whatever the outcome of the panel report. I shook hands with David Cameron and thanked him, then the Merseyside MPs were off to Euston for the train up to Liverpool.

On the train, I got a text from my mate Steve Turner – a hugely poignant moment, and deeply moving and symbolic for me on a personal level. Obviously as news of the result spread, and more and more people heard the Prime Minister's emphatic apology, the mood in the city has been transformed. By the time we got to Lime Street, there was a party atmosphere.

DAMIAN KAVANAGH

We wandered into town, and I just badly, badly wanted a pint. Myself, Ade Tempany and Jim Sharman walked into the Yankee Bar and I held up my copy of the report like I was lifting the FA Cup. Everyone was cheering, the spirit was unbelievable. This fella came up to me and goes, 'I am buying you a pint!' And that's how it was, that day. It was beautiful.

And, as the day wore on, I could feel this overwhelming sense of relief – this huge burden being lifted off my shoulders. Over the next few days my mum, my sister, my fiancée – the three most important women in my life – all said to me, individually, 'You look younger, you look carefree …'

ANDY BURNHAM

The vigil was incredibly moving – Anne [Williams] and Margaret [Aspinall] gave such powerful speeches. There was the gospel choir and the whole crowd sang 'You'll Never Walk Alone', and it really meant something. We ended up in the Ship and Mitre and it was unbelievable – it was as though everyone who'd been a part of the campaign was in there. There were all the guys from The Justice Band, John Bishop, Mick Jones from The Clash had travelled up … just a wonderful, carnival atmosphere. As ever, I was one of the first to leave and, as I headed for the doors, there's this big loud chorus: 'Blue and white shite, blue and white shite!'

It was brilliant.

PETER HOOTON

I was going on *Newsnight*, live from Anfield. I didn't want Kirsty Wark running rings round me, so I'd prepared a few things that I wanted to say. I was going to say that Hillsborough was the first disaster where the passengers were blamed for crashing the plane. As it turned out, I needn't have worried. Kirsty Wark was sympathetic, she let me speak without interrupting – it seemed like she was, basically, on our side. After twenty-three and a half years of shouting into the wind, that was going to take a bit of getting used to.

BARRY DEVONSIDE

There was understandable euphoria. If nothing else, the unleashing of so many years of pent-up frustration, at being thwarted – being disbelieved. But every interview I did, I kept emphasising one simple fact that continually gets overlooked: no Liverpool supporter was charged with any offence that day. Not one.

PETER HOOTON

The Hillsborough Independent Panel Report is huge – it's enormous. The panel analysed, I think, over 450,000 separate documents, so it's a lot to take on board; but I couldn't find my original statement to West Midlands police online. I had to get a copy of it from the IPCC, and the bit at the end, where the police are lined up across the pitch and I ask why they can't help, and he tells me he can't move without orders – that part of the statement is missing.

MARTIN THOMPSON

It was only after the Hillsborough Independent Panel Report was published that I realised that my statement was missing – the interview from Waterloo Town Hall all those years back. I was there for hours and I gave an in-depth account of basically every step of Stuart's journey. Obviously, as part of that process, I identify Kevin Williams, alive, after the 3.15 shut-off. So you have to ask yourself whether, even then, May 1989, the police were already tutored about the shut-off time? Why else would my evidence go missing?

PETER HOOTON

When you consider how long it took to get us to the Hillsborough Independent Panel Report, things did seem to move quickly in the days and weeks afterwards. There was the application from the Attorney-General to have the initial accidental death verdicts quashed. Then the IPCC came out with their manifesto, so to speak, exactly one month after the panel released its findings.

Statement from Deborah Glass, Deputy Chair of the
Independent Police Complaints Commission (IPCC):

12 October 2012

One month ago the Hillsborough Independent Panel delivered a report that gave the families of those who died, those that were injured and those who were traumatised in the terrible events of 15 April 1989, the details they had sought for twenty-three years.

The report revealed extremely serious and troubling issues for the police. Its contents provoked a demand for those responsible for the actions revealed in the report to be held to account.

We have learned details of the run-up to the disaster, including the unheeded warnings from previous incidents, the disaster itself, and its aftermath, including what appear to be attempts to distort the truth.

These findings are a testament to the tenacity of the Hillsborough families' long campaign for truth and justice. Their dedication to the memory of those they loved – and the support of the people of Merseyside – has been humbling.

But twenty-three years was far too long to wait. It has been a generation of distress and anger. And the picture is not yet complete.

It is now for the Independent Police Complaints Commission and other organisations to try to complete that picture.

Since the report was published, the IPCC has been undertaking a thorough review of it and has also begun to examine the 450,000 pages of supporting evidence to identify what conduct, by named or unnamed police officers, requires investigation.

While the review was ongoing we received referrals from West Yorkshire Police Authority in relation to Sir Norman Bettison, South Yorkshire police in relation to the events before, during and after 15 April 1989, and West Midlands police in relation to their role in the investigation of events.

We have considered all of this and determined there are a number of matters which require investigation by the IPCC.

These are:

- The amendments to statements – who ordered it, who knew about it, who was involved in the process, and was pressure put on individual officers?
- The allegations that misleading information was passed to the media, MPs, Parliament and inquiries in an apparent attempt to deflect blame from the police on to the fans.
- The actions of police officers after the disaster, including the questioning of next of kin about alcohol consumption, the checking of blood alcohol levels and the undertaking of police national computer checks on the dead and injured.
- The role of West Midlands police and those who led that investigation into the disaster.

All of these matters will be subject of an independent investigation by the IPCC. We will be setting up a dedicated Hillsborough team to carry this out.

However, in addition, there are other matters where we believe we will have a role to play.

Ninety-six men, women and children died as a result of Hillsborough. The Attorney-General must decide whether to apply to the High Court to quash the original inquest verdicts and seek new ones. The Director of Public Prosecutions has announced today that he will review the evidence.

The IPCC will work with the Director of Public Prosecutions, and any coroner appointed to hear fresh inquests, to carry out any further investigation that may be required before or after any new inquests are held, and identify the appropriate body to investigate any individual or entity we cannot.

I must stress the scope of our work is not yet clear – and we do not underestimate the size of our task.

We do not yet know how many officers or retired officers fall to be investigated for the various matters we have identified, how many are still serving or still alive. Work will continue to identify individuals and their circumstances, and what potential offences require investigation. We can investigate both criminal and misconduct offences after an officer has retired, though retirement prevents any misconduct sanction. We are continuing to review the underlying documentation in the report and other conduct matters may come to light.

An important part of our work will be liaising with the families and other interested parties. We have made contact with them, and will set out the initial scope and projected timing, and keep them in touch with progress. Justice demands that we do whatever is possible to investigate culpability for any offence that may have been committed, and to do so thoroughly and fairly. The families have already waited for twenty-three years. I want to give them my assurance that we will do everything in our power to investigate these serious and disturbing allegations with the careful and robust scrutiny they deserve.

MARTIN THOMPSON

I put in a formal complaint to the IPCC, saying that my statement had gone missing. They followed this up and discovered that, yes, there was one outstanding matter – the question of Stuart's missing training shoe! Seriously, that's all they could find in my file – that when I'd gone to Smithdown Lane to collect Stuart's clothing I'd noted that one training shoe was still missing. I got a letter from the police to say that, seeing it was now unlikely they would ever find that training shoe, they considered the matter closed. Well, I don't consider it closed at all. Do they honestly, seriously, believe that I'd waste mine and the IPCC's time, going to them about a missing training shoe? What about all the evidence I gave at Waterloo Town Hall? Where has that gone? I find it strange that it's not there.

SHEILA COLEMAN

The Attorney-General, Dominic Grieve, made an application to the High Court for the original inquests to be quashed. We travelled down the day before and, on 19 December 2012, just over three months on from the independent panel report's publication, the case was heard.

ANNE WILLIAMS

I travelled down to London because I didn't want to miss that moment. We were pretty sure we were going to get it, but we'd been knocked back so many times, and I thought, 'I'm going to go, I want to hear it for myself.' Until I hear it for myself, you know, they've never given us anything.

Excerpt from Lord Chief Justice Judge's summing-up
It is desirable and reasonable for a fresh inquest to be heard. However distressing or unpalatable, the truth will be brought to light. In this way, the families of those who died in the disaster will be properly respected. Our earnest wish is that the new inquest will not be delayed for a moment longer than necessary.

ANNE WILLIAMS

It was excellent, the judgment was excellent, and when he quashed that accidental death verdict it was amazing, I was so pleased. Because everyone knows Hillsborough's not an accident, so that sort of got rid of that one. That accidental death verdict used to really, really upset me, because it let them off the hook, didn't it? Let's just hope we get the right verdict in place now, and that the people who are really to blame will get punished.

SHEILA COLEMAN

The irony is that the evidence that we presented to the court for judicial review in November 1993 formed the basis of the evidence that the Attorney-General put before the High Court nearly twenty years later. The Attorney-General was in court to personally present the case as to why the original verdicts should be quashed, which was quite unusual, for him to be there in person. And the judge quashed the accidental death verdicts. On 19 December 2012 he quashed the original verdicts on the basis of evidence we'd presented to that same court in November 1993. And I remember looking across to Anne Williams in her wheelchair and thinking, 'This is what you've done to this woman.'

PART FOUR

JUSTICE?

STEVE ROTHERAM

I don't think there can ever be 'closure' as such, or even any one single result or outcome that people are looking for. We wanted the truth – and we got it. As for justice, one of the enduring miscarriages has been this verdict of unnatural death. Certainly I think most families would be looking for a verdict of unlawful killing from the new inquests. In parallel with that, there's never been one person who has been held accountable for what happened at Hillsborough, and I think you'd expect to see prosecutions resulting from a verdict like that.

Apart from that, you'd want to see action against some of the institutions who have got away scot-free. And this is not vindictive, it's not an eye for an eye – it's a case of the law being seen to be implemented. So the likes of the FA need to be called in, Sheffield Wednesday Football Club, who never had a valid safety certificate, Sheffield city council, who didn't do their job in ensuring that the safety certificate was in place ... In other words, not just the police, who have taken the brunt of criticism – perhaps rightly so – but the architects, the ambulance service, other groups and individuals like the coroner ... I think that, once these groups and individuals have been brought in and subjected to same kind of suspicion and questioning and assumptions as the families have had for twenty-five years, then those families might begin to feel some vindication, and that some sort of justice has been achieved.

MARTIN THOMPSON

Well, it is unlawful killing, isn't it? How is it not? The police are trained first-aiders, but they chose not to help. They let the fans lead the rescue effort while they looked on. They formed a line across the pitch; they pushed fans back into the pens who were trying to escape; they made background checks into the criminal records of the Thompson family; they ordered blood alcohol tests on dead children; but they did not step forward to help. In that way, they deprived victims of the basic human right to live. That's manslaughter.

DANNY RHODES

When you look back at football in those days you realise what happened could have happened anywhere and was going to happen somewhere, and it was just a case of when and where. I can remember so many of those away games – Coventry City, for example, Highfield Road. When you're a young lad, you want to be in that mêlée; you want to be in the middle of it all. That away end, absolutely rammed to capacity and being pushed against the crush barrier and not being able to breathe. And that fear starts to run through you, but then the pressure eases off again. That's how it was. And, in all of this, the cold realisation is that, if the FA *had* agreed to switch ends, if that had gone ahead, I would have been stood at the Leppings Lane end at 2 o'clock on 15 April 1989. I would have gone in early. I would have stood behind the goal. And there's every chance that I would have been one of those people who got shunted forward when the surge happened.

JOHN ASHTON

I mean, my personal beef just doesn't matter in the greater context of the tragedy and the fight for justice. But, yes, I was brutalised and I was vilified, and the stigma endured. It was only really after the findings of the Hillsborough Independent Panel were made public that I was able to say, 'See? This is what I have been saying since the day of the disaster.' So there was, of course, the satisfaction that comes with being vindicated, but it's mixed with real anger over what was allowed to go unchallenged for so many years.

STEPHEN WRIGHT

At 2.56 our Graham is pictured on the terraces, alive. At 3.36 he's dead. I don't know what happened to him in that time. I don't know how he got out there on to the pitch, who got him out, whether he was pulled out alive – or was he dead by then? According to the doctor who did the Hillsborough Independent Panel Report, Graham isn't one of the ones who could have survived. But the marks on his body are pre-death; someone's tried to get him out. Someone knows what happened to him. We need to know the answers.

DAMIAN KAVANAGH

I held back and held back and I think that's why, even now, so many people have yet to come forward. They think they're not worthy. But each of these people has a story to tell, and those individual accounts all go towards telling the overall story of what happened. There are still a lot of people looking for answers.

JEGSY DODD

What is justice? It's not for me to say. Would it serve any purpose if the real perpetrators went to jail? I don't know. My biggest regret in all of this is that so many people – families, relatives, survivors, everyone who was closely affected – are going to die before this is over. It's twenty-seven years and counting. Whatever their justice may be, a lot of them aren't going to be here to see it happen.

JOHN ALDRIDGE

We all know there are still questions that haven't been answered. If it was one of mine, if I was one of those parents, no way would I let it lie. I'd be fighting for the last bit of truth until the day I die. What's for sure is that, in a way, football itself died that day.

BARRY DEVONSIDE

I asked a barrister the other day, 'What are our chances of getting a verdict of unlawful killing?' He said words to the effect of, 'If we thought the fight had been tough already, it was about to get really tough.' I said to him, 'OK, help me understand; tell me if I've got any of this wrong. We've got a man in command on the day who failed to institute a filtering system outside the ground to slow down the crowds on their approach. He failed to respond to a situation of his own making. He froze. He failed to recognise that pens 3 and 4 were over-full. He failed to close off the entrance to the tunnel once pens 3 and 4 were full. He made decisions that cost people their lives. Now, I'm not a vindictive person in any way, shape or form, but there is clear evidence of the most fundamental dereliction of duty. What I'd say to the coroner on the new inquests is that, if he wants that in plain English, that's unlawful killing. It's manslaughter.

ANNE WILLIAMS

When I'm gone, I might as well get a little bit of help up there as well, hey? I'm just hoping now that it'll all get sorted and the families will get what we're looking for. The people who covered everything up, they've got to answer. They should have given us truth, right from the start.

To me it's like Hillsborough has just happened, in one respect. We've had no inquest and there's no verdict yet, it's like you're starting all over again, isn't it?

So, we'll get there. I'm sure we'll get there in the end, the way things are going. But you're still wary; I always am, because you still worry that someone's going to come in and they're going to find something and say, 'Oh no, throw that out!' You know? Because of everything that's gone on in the past.

PETER CARNEY

For myself, what would represent some semblance of justice is for the record to be set straight. This wasn't an accident. People were killed by the ignorance and incompetence of the people in charge on the day; the people responsible for the safety of everyone attending the match that day. That's the simple part of it; let the truth be known and understood.

If you want to follow that on to its logical conclusions, then you're getting into a minefield of potential prosecutions. I've always said there are five culpable bodies: South Yorkshire police, Sheffield Wednesday, Sheffield City Council, the Football Association, and the engineers responsible for Hillsborough. I've got no doubt whatsoever that, inherent in all that, there's been criminal acts. The debate is always: 'Is this manslaughter?' But, if it were left up to me, I'd have them up for State Slaughter, and there'd be so many in the dock you'd fill the penalty box. From the word go, even before people were dead, they were already covering the tracks of those that were responsible – we *know* that now – so the question is: what do we want to do about it?

MARTIN THOMPSON

Someone is culpable. Lots of people – individuals and organisations – have to finally stand up and face the consequences of their actions, or lack of them.

The police were bad, but what about the FA? They have never had to answer for the basic failures that literally led 96 people to their deaths. It took them three days after the independent panel report to come out with an apology. The Prime Minister got the country's apology out within minutes – what took the Football Association so long? I want to see them in the dock – and there are others who have had the luxury of a peaceful retirement on a full pension. There are some who still carry on without shame, as though they are not answerable to the same charges as everyday citizens. These people need to understand, once and for all, there is no 'us' and 'them'. They are not above the law. They have to pay the price for their crimes, as everyone else does.

DAMIAN KAVANAGH

My lad is doing *Of Mice and Men* for GCSE. Great. But I want our story to be taught as well. I want Hillsborough to be a subject on the school syllabus. And history will record that those men were responsible for those deeds. The suffering that has been endured by the bereaved, by the survivors, by those who have been damaged – that has to be recorded in history. This is what those men did.

STEVE KELLY

Without the survivors, there really would not have been any realistic chance of us getting this far; there would have been no way of reclaiming the truth. It's their testimonies and their experiences that have, eventually, exposed the lies; their story is finally being accepted as the real story of Hillsborough. That has to become enshrined in our history, now. Hillsborough has to become the model text about contempt, corruption and deceit at the highest level; as a dire example of something that must never be allowed to happen again. People need to look at Hillsborough and say 'Never again.'

I would like history to show who were the true perpetrators of what we now know was the crime of Hillsborough. I think that would satisfy me. These people – Thatcher and Bettison amongst others – they all want their little place in history; so let history show what they really were, rather than the face they'd have you believe. They were thugs with pens. Let history be their judge.

DANNY RHODES

I want somebody to stand up and say, without any shadow of a doubt, that what happened was not caused by the fans themselves. I want them to say, clearly, that this was mismanagement; incompetence. It was about having the wrong mindset about football fans in general; it was about not being prepared. And I want to hear them admit that. They should have admitted it straight away, then we wouldn't have had to go through all this for twenty-seven years.

BARRY DEVONSIDE

There's no end, there's no such thing as closure. Chris walking through the front door – that would be closure.

This has to be put to bed properly, once and for all. There have to be verdicts against the South Yorkshire police – either manslaughter, or unlawful killing. There has to be arrests of individuals and prosecutions, and court appearances and people being dealt with. Like I've been saying, I'm not vindictive and, after twenty-five years, there's a part of me that thinks, 'What's the point in prosecuting them?' But that *is* the point. It's about principles, it's about the law of the land being seen to be the law of the land – nobody should be above it or beyond it.

SHEILA COLEMAN

The word justice has long been synonymous with the Hillsborough Disaster, precisely because there has been an absence of it. 'Justice for the 96' has been a rallying cry for nearly three decades now. Perhaps the wording on our little HJC flame badge is more inclusive and appropriate because it quite simply says: 'Justice for All'. The fact is, the victims of the Hillsborough Disaster, and therefore those due a measure of justice, far outweighs the ninety-six who were tragically killed. It extends to thousands of survivors, as well as the families of both the deceased and the survivors, who suffered not only trauma but the hurt and injustice of state lies. As someone who has called for justice for twenty-seven years, I have increasingly asked myself what I mean by justice.

Justice will of course mean different things to different people. I think it is important to distinguish between justice and the law. A favourable legal decision does not necessarily mean justice has been served. The law is one thing but justice is something else. The long campaign for truth and 'justice' around Hillsborough rightly focused on having the original inquest verdicts quashed and new inquests ordered. It took twenty-three years to achieve this goal. Was that justice? It was a positive decision which vindicated those of us who had long campaigned against the cover-up of facts, but it wasn't justice. It took us further along the road of truth, but once the legal arena is entered into, in this case fresh inquests, the truth becomes something to be bartered with and negotiated in or out of submissions and evidence. The facts, i.e. 'the truth', operate within a strict legal paradigm and have to compete with the contrary opinions of interested parties. Once you accept this, then, in my opinion, you realise that you will never receive justice in any meaningful sense of the word.

I believe that any notion of justice is subjective. Some people might feel that retribution brings about justice, others are happy with a favourable inquest verdict. Personally, I have always maintained that accountability and responsibility should have been at the forefront in the aftermath of the Hillsborough Disaster. Individual police on the day were part of an organisation. The organisation as an entity should have been held accountable. Maybe then people would have been consoled and felt some justice had been achieved. I would find a measure of satisfaction if systems were put in place to ensure that such a cover-up could never happen again. I think that is unlikely. However, it is fair to say the sustained Hillsborough campaign for justice, by its sheer longevity and persistence, forced the establishment to admit a conspiracy and a cover-up. We should never underestimate that fact. If other people and campaigns are inspired by us then we have achieved change for the better and that has to be a good thing. Our justice slogan served us well but I do not think justice will ever truly be achieved. Too much has happened over the years. Too many sad lives have been lost post Hillsborough that these people have also become victims of that fateful day. The sad fact is that in an increasingly inegalitarian British society we are governed by some who would have difficulty spelling the word justice, let alone understanding the concept of it or placing any value upon it.

MARTIN THOMPSON

The investigations, any prosecutions, any sentencing – that won't finally be over until 2017. That's twenty-eight years after Hillsborough. Stuart would have been 45. That's what you're dealing with, here.

STEPHEN WRIGHT

We don't know what these new inquests are going to reveal. The police statements we've seen so far are not conclusive. We may never get the answers we're looking for – we just don't know. The answers we're looking for – those answers might never be there.

ANNE WILLIAMS

I might not see the end. My daughter will carry on with any legal stuff. But at least I was here to see that – to say that my son did not die from traumatic asphyxia; my son did not die in an accident. We have always known and now everyone knows that he did not die in an accident – Kevin, or the 95 with him.

BARRY DEVONSIDE

Some day I'd like just to be able to play with my two granddaughters with no other thought for anything else. Because Hillsborough never, ever, leaves you alone. When I wake up in the middle of the night, three or four o'clock in the morning, I can't just go back to sleep. It's with you, immediately. I come down and sit here and all I can think about is Chris and what happened to him. There has to be a time, for me and for Jackie, when we can switch off from Hillsborough and have no more of it – nothing. Because there's only so much you can take.

The interviews and accounts in this book were compiled over an eighteen-month period following the publication of the Hillsborough Independent Panel Report on 12 September 2012. Since that time, the momentous verdicts of the new inquests have written a whole new chapter in the history of the Hillsborough Disaster. The voices and stories that make *Hillsborough Voices* a definitive document are a key component of that history. While the verdicts represent a victory of sorts, the quest for justice continues.